THE SOCIAL HISTORY OF ROME

The Social History of
◊ R ◊ O ◊ M ◊ E ◊

Géza Alföldy

Translated by David Braund and Frank Pollock

BARNES & NOBLE BOOKS
Totowa, New Jersey

© 1975, 1979, 1984 G. Alföldy
Translation © 1985 Croom Helm

First published in the USA 1985 by
Barnes & Noble Books,
81 Adams Drive,
Totowa, New Jersey, 07512

ISBN 0-389-20583-4
Library of Congress Cataloging in Publication Data applied for.

Printed in Great Britain

CONTENTS

74838

PREFACE TO THE ENGLISH EDITION

The English edition of this book is not a direct translation either of the original German edition published in 1975 or of the second German edition published in 1979. Whereas the second German edition differs from the original edition only through insignificant changes in the text and a number of bibliographical addenda, the present edition has been appreciably amended, improved and enlarged. Many changes have been made in the text: a few errors have been corrected, many over-broad generalisations have been re-stated more precisely and clearly and some particularly abbreviated passages have been re-written in expanded form. Terminology has been employed more strictly and with greater uniformity. As far as possible the results of new research have been taken into account, short of fundamental structural and conceptual revision. The bibliographical addenda which appeared in the second German edition have been incorporated into the notes, together with the most recent literature, chosen with an eye to its relevance to the purpose of this book.[1]

The purpose of this book remains the same: to inform those studying classics, history and social sciences on the most important problems of Roman social history. The not uncritical, but, on the whole, positive reception accorded to the German editions leads me to hope that this book will also achieve its purpose for an English-speaking readership. All the more so since, as I write these lines, a full and comprehensive account of Roman social history is as much a desideratum as it was a decade ago when this book was written.[2]

In the preparation of the text and notes for the English translation Johannes Hahn, Sigrid Mratschek and Barbara Maurer have rendered invaluable assistance. Moreover, I must also thank numerous reviewers and critics of the German editions who have drawn my attention to errors or led me to think again. From their number I name with particular gratitude M. T. W. Arnheim, H. Botermann, K. Christ, R. Frei, R. Günther, W. V. Harris, H. P. Kohns, F. Kolb, F. Lasserre, L. Perelli, M.-Th. Raepsaet-Charlier, R. J. A. Talbert, F. Vittinghoff and I. Weiler. For the English translation of my certainly complicated German original I am very indebted to David Braund and Frank Pollock.

Notes

1. The text of this edition corresponds to that of the third German edition, published 1984.

2. For further reading I should like to recommend to the reader some comprehensive works, dealing with various problems of Roman social history, which have appeared in the last few years (some very recently). In what follows, their conclusions could be considered only briefly or hardly at all: M. I. Finley, *The Ancient Economy* (2nd edn, London, 1975), translated into German as *Die Antike Wirtschaft* (München, 1977). On which book, cf. especially M. W. Frederiksen, *JRS*, 65 (1975), 164ff. and H. P. Kohns, *Gött.Gel.Anz.*, 230 (1978), 120ff., P. Veyne, *Le pain et le cirque. Sociologie historique d'un pluralisme politique* (Paris, 1976); H. Strasburger *Zum antiken Gesellschaftsideal* Abh.d.Heidelberger Akad, d. Wiss., Phil-hist.Kl., Jg. 1976, 4. Abh., Heidelberg, 1976). Good bibliographies are to be found in the collected essays edited by H. Schneider under the titles *Zur Sozial- und Wirtschaftsgeschichte der späten römischen Republik* (Darmstadt, 1976) and *Sozial- und Wirtschaftsgeschichte der römischen Kaiserzeit* (Darmstadt, 1981). In addition, the respective introductions to these collections, written by H. Schneider, are instructive and informative on the differing approaches to Roman social history.

PREFACE TO THE FIRST GERMAN EDITION (1975)

The principal purpose of the following book is to provide an introduction to the most important problems of Roman social history for those studying classics, history and social sciences. Given this projected audience, the need for a number of generalisations and a degree of repetition is apparent. So too is the need for restriction to particular illustrative examples in the citation of sources and for brief footnotes with references limited to only the more recent literature (not always the best, but providing references to earlier bibliography). In accordance with its intended purpose, this account contains much that is very familiar to the expert – more familiar, often, than it is to the author. Its claim to some value resides above all in its attempt to bring together this material in a monograph and to structure it historically according to a coherent conception of the history of Roman society. Moreover, the chapters on the Empire, in particular, rest upon the results of my own research. It is therefore my hope that the following book will not only serve as an aid to teaching, but will lead to further discussion on the particular nature of Roman society in particular periods and in the whole course of its history.

The degree to which this book achieves its purpose will certainly be open to just question. The 'objective' difficulties encountered in its preparation were not, by and large, generated by a lack of sources for the history of social conditions in antiquity. On the whole, the sources from Graeco-Roman antiquity germane to social history are, despite widespread opinion to the contrary, no more sparse than sources for other central areas of research. The evidence available for Roman society is apparent not only from, for example, M. Rostovtzeff's classic *Social and Economic History of the Roman Empire*, but also from the profusion of excellent monographs which have appeared in the last five years alone.[1] Nevertheless, to date, no comprehensive *Social History of Rome* has been written. Whereas the author of a general, conventional *History of Rome* can look back upon a large number of precursors and can bring to bear the expertise of a richly traditional genre of historiography, the author of a first *Social History of Rome* feels his way along untrodden paths.

The very title of this book raises three fundamental questions;

though an attempt is now made to offer answers, that is not meant to pre-empt either criticism or full theoretical discussion. The first question is: what is the meaning of Roman *social history*? Clearly it is not simply what remains when one has struck out political history from some manual. Nor is it the history of society conceived as the sum total of all positions and relationships deriving from human interaction, community and interpersonal dealings, for that would be to identify its subject matter with that of history as a whole. It is a tenet of this book that the subject matter of social history resides in the social structures of society, thus in those enduring features which determine its particular nature. These figure in the bases and criteria for the division of society into particular parts, in its very system of organisation with particular strata, orders or classes, and, finally, in the interrelationships between particular parts of society, embodied in social bonds, tensions and conflicts, and in mobility within the stratification as well as in a common political framework and system of reference.[2] Of course, this position is assailable from the perspective of the social sciences and from that of classical history alike on the grounds that it may be inadequate or misleading. But it will serve as a heuristic model until it is replaced by a better concept.

The second question which must be asked is this: what is entailed in *Roman* social history? No doubt the simplest and most easily defended answer would be that *Roman* social history is identical to the history of social structures within the political boundaries of the Roman state at any given time. At the very least, within the limits set, it is not possible to go into local conditions – into the social structure of Egypt under Roman rule, for example, or into the kinship organisation of the northern Balkans or into the tribes of north-western Spain. In much the same way as in the field of the history of art in antiquity works bearing the title *Roman Art* cannot devote thorough treatment to, for example, the art of Palmyra. In the forefront of this discussion stand general or at least supra-regional features of social life, wherein the dividing-lines between regional and supra-regional features are often difficult to draw.

Finally, the third question: how is a *Social History of Rome* to be conceived as *history*? Structural analyses furnish snapshots of a society in cross-section and thereby run the risk of presenting a picture that is static. A discussion concerned with more than a thousand years of historical development requires several such snapshots, at the very least one for each particular stage. The stages of Roman social history are: the period of archaic Roman society, the history of the Republic from the fourth century BC down to the Second Punic War, the structural change of the second century BC, the crisis of the Republic, the Early Empire, the crisis of the third century AD and the Late Empire. But to divide social development into periods is fraught with difficulties, for structural features do not suddenly appear and disappear; the case is otherwise with political history. In order to counter the impression that Roman social history simply consists of a series of snapshots, stress has been laid, as far as possible, on the ways in which the social conditions of one stage grew out of those of an earlier period and on the extent to which they also paved the way for further social change. The reason for the relatively full treatment accorded to the Early Empire is not only that it is the particular field of the author, but also that the author is convinced that the study of Roman society in that period is particularly suitable as an introduction to social history both because of the sources and secondary works available and because of its well-defined and relatively stable social hierarchy.

The following book has grown out of lectures and seminars delivered at the Ruhr-Universität Bochum during my time there from 1970 to 1974. It would never have been written without the encouragement and criticism of colleagues, collaborators and, especially, students. This book is dedicated, in gratitude, to them.

Notes

1. Above all, mention must be made of the works of P. Garnsey (note 111), T. P. Wiseman (54), P. A. Brunt (22), E. Badian (58), P. R. C. Weaver (150), J. H. W. G. Liebeschuetz (225), R. Duncan-Jones (99), R. MacMullen (99), R. Teja (204) and also the outstanding work of M. I. Finley (109) which sets out the foundations of the ancient economy.

2. Accordingly, the history of the economy is only the concern of *social history* in so far as economic activity determines the division of society and the nature of its particular strata. There is also a concrete reason for devoting very little space to Roman economic history even within this limited frame of reference: an *Ancient Economic History* is to appear at the same time as this book and in the same series, its author being Th. Pekáry (see Th. Pekáry, *Die Wirtschaft der griechisch-römischen Antike* (1.Aufl., Wiesbaden, 1976 and 2. Aufl., ibid. 1979)).

Translator's Note

The translators have taken no part in the revision of this book and are not responsible for any of the author's interpretations.

1 EARLY ROMAN SOCIETY

Foundations and Beginnings of the Early Roman Social System

As is generally acknowledged, the earliest history of the Roman state in the Regal Period and at the beginning of the Republic is known to us, at best, only in broad outline: the same may be said of the early Roman social system. The beginning of Roman historiography, like those of Roman literature in general, stretch back only as far as the third century BC. The historiography of that time, linked above all with the name of Quintus Fabius Pictor, could only record for earlier periods what was preserved in an oral tradition much coloured by legends. Moreover, this tradition was itself sparse and inadequate for the propagandist aims of the Roman annalists at work during the war against Carthage. In consequence, Fabius Pictor felt himself compelled to flesh out the tradition with his own imagination and to recount the beginnings of Rome in what was therefore an idiosyncratic fashion. Yet we do not have even this version of early Roman history, which at least comes from the third century BC. Our knowledge of it depends largely on Livy and Dionysius of Halicarnassus who used it and embroidered it still further with the concerns of the reign of Augustus.[1] As a result a great deal of our information on events and circumstances in early Rome and therefore on forms of social relationships and their bases at that time is very dubious. Even where we are dealing with accounts which have a kernel of authenticity and are not totally free invention, these sources give us evidence which is at best anachronistic and they seldom permit a chronologically precise organisation of their contents (in particular, most dates down to about 300 BC are not verifiable). Since epigraphic sources are almost completely lacking, it is the archaeological evidence, which permits a degree of control over the literary tradition, that makes possible the clarification of the basic history of the settlement and the establishment of a largely secure chronological framework for the internal development of early Roman society and of the Roman state.[2] If these inadequate sources can be supplemented, it is only through our knowledge of the social, political and religious institutions of later Rome, which preserved many remnants of the archaic social structure.[3]

The story of the foundation of Rome by Romulus is as unhistorical as the foundation date calculated at the end of the Republic by Varro, a date which is, on our reckoning, 753 BC. The beginnings of the settlement on the Palatine, for which the site of the later Forum Romanum served as a cemetery and which may be considered to be the core for the historical development of the city of Rome, stretch back at least to this time and more probably back as far as the tenth century BC. The inhabitants of this settlement were Latins. They belonged to the Latin-Faliscan section of the Indo-European migrants who, under pressure from the great migrations of the peoples of central Europe and of the Balkans from the twelfth century BC, had passed down into Italy where they lived by cattle-raising and, in part, also by agriculture. Nearby, on the Quirinal, were settled Sabines who belonged to the Oscan-Umbrian section of the Indo-European migrants. Their kins were gradually integrated into the Latin-speaking community, as were for example the Fabii and the Aurelii and the Claudii, who seem to have reached Rome somewhat later. The 'urbanisation of Rome', the process by which this community developed into a city state, had come about by the beginning of the sixth century BC at the latest. The city was considerably enlarged by the incorporation of settlements to the south, east and north of the Palatine and was marked off from surrounding territory by a fixed boundary (*pomerium*). It had stable institutions which included magistrates whose competence extended to the civic boundary. At the same time, a stable form of government had been introduced: the monarchy, which was elective. This process is evidently inseparable from an event of crucial historical importance for Rome: the extension of Etruscan rule over Rome.[4] The civic community of Rome was under Etruscan rule and was constructed in accordance with an Etruscan model: the very name of Rome derives from an Etruscan family (Ruma). Rome's institutions and form of government were structured according to an Etruscan pattern and government was exercised by Etruscan kings. Moreover, Rome took from the Etruscans not only a great number of religious and cultural traditions, but also, to a large extent, a social structure. Memories of the time before Etruscan rule, corresponding doubtless to the oldest structures of the Indo-European Latins, survived down into later periods, reinforced, above all, by religious cults.[5] In addition to the Indo-European heritage and the role of the Etruscans, there was a third factor in the early history of Italy which set

Roman development on its course: the influence of the Greeks, particularly important in cultural terms. From the middle of the eighth century BC the Greeks had established themselves on a firm footing in southern Italy and soon after also in Sicily.[6] But it was due to the Etruscans that Rome became a city-state. Therefore, the most important historical foundation of early Roman social history is precisely the rule of the Etruscans over Rome.

From the seventh century BC the history of the Etruscans lies within our grasp. It was from that date that their cities began to grow, largely on the basis of mining and related crafts and trade: the consolidation of their political and cultural identity followed.[7] They did not form a single, unified state: the organ of their shared political activity was a federation of 12 cities which were directed from time to time by a king. Their society was divided into two large groups: the aristocracy and lower strata of men who were in practice slaves.[8] The nobles, from whose number the king was drawn, possessed the fertile lands and probably also the mines. At the same time, they monopolised political activity, since they made up the council of elders of the federation and filled the magistracies. The lower strata consisted of groups dependent upon the aristocracy: retainers of the aristocracy like the servants, athletes and dancers known from our sources, craftsmen and miners and also peasants whom Dionysius of Halicarnassus compares with the Penestae of Thessaly (9.5.4) and who were therefore doubtless agricultural labourers bound to the soil and subject to military service. This model of society was largely transferred to Rome, where the early social system – before the *plebs* became a struggling order in its own right – was made up, on the one hand, of a patrician aristocracy with total power and, on the other, of clients and slaves, very much according to the Etruscan pattern.

The power of the Etruscans reached its acme in the sixth century BC. To the north they pushed as far as the Po valley where they founded new cities. To the south, after Latium, they took Campania. In 535 BC their fleet, in alliance with Carthage, defeated the Phocaeans, the most active Greek colonisers of the western Mediterranean. Their rule over Rome stood unshaken down to the end of the sixth century BC. At most, there may have been political changes, as Rome came, it seems, under the power of different Etruscan cities in turn: among their number were Vulci, Tarquinii and Clusium.[9] The rulers of Rome, whose title (*rex*) was in fact not Etruscan but of Indo-European origin, were Etruscans all the same, as was Tarquinius Superbus, the last of the seven kings of Rome according to legend, and Porsenna too, the king of Clusium, who temporarily held Rome shortly after the expulsion of the last Tarquinius. The latter events marked the end of Etruscan rule over Rome. The story of the expulsion of Tarquinius from the city, traditionally dated about 508 BC, embodied the memory of an historical event: Rome was freed from the rule of the Etruscan kings by an uprising of the aristocracy against the monarchy which seems actually to have taken place around 508BC or some years later.[10] Attempts to restore Etruscan power over Rome, probably repeated, failed and when in 474 BC the Etruscans lost their naval supremacy at the battle of Cumae against Hiero of Syracuse they soon lost their influence over Latium too.

The archaic social system of Rome,[11] developed in the sixth century BC under the rule of the Etruscan kings, remained important even after the Regal Period. The social system, once fixed, remained largely unchanged even after the abolition of the monarchy: the aristocracy only divided amongst themselves the functions of the king as supreme commander, judge and priest. The struggle of the orders in the fifth century BC prepared the way for and ushered in the dissolution of the archaic social structure. But the dissolution was still not complete: many characteristic features survived not only that century but even the whole Republic. The characteristics of this archaic social system, displayed in its structure and in the interrelationships between its strata, were as follows: the structure of this society was distinguished by horizontal division, deriving from the central role of the family and generating the union of various families on the basis of blood-relationship into a complex nexus of kin, *curiae* and 'tribes', comparable to the division of Homeric society into tribes, phratries, kin and families. By comparison the vertical division of society was relatively simple, since, originally at least, it comprised only the aristocracy and the people dependent upon the aristocracy. Yet the extremely close bonds between particular humble individuals and families and particular nobles on the basis of gentile affiliation or even connections deriving from neighbourhood were of the greatest importance (indeed, this may be said not only of archaic society, but, *mutatis mutandis*, of the entire history of Rome). Accordingly, the scope for social tension in the archaic social system was relatively limited. Conflicts could only be generated where the dependent – or, at least, those of them best placed to break their dependency – declared war upon the aristocracy, striving for political parity and for an improvement in their economic position.

The Structure of Archaic Roman Society

In early Rome the family[12] was a discrete economic, social and religious entity. The head of the family (*pater familias*) enjoyed, by virtue of his authority (*auctoritas*), unlimited power over his wife, children, slaves and family property (*res familiaris*). It was for him to administer the family possessions (*bonorum administratio*) and the management of the economic activities of the family, most importantly the farming of the family plot. With a council of adult males he decided legal matters, such as the acceptance of a new member into the family group or the departure of a member from it (by marriage, for example) as well as the punishment of offenders. He also represented the family in external matters. In addition, in the role of a priest, he presided over the cult of the ancestors (*sacra familiae*). His position of almost unrestricted power is best seen in the law as codified in the Twelve Tables, which permitted him to sell his own children into slavery. His position may be seen as a microcosm of the rule of the aristocracy, composed of the most important heads of families, in the political life of the state.

Related families were united by common descent and, often in the beginning, by proximate settlement into a clan (*gens*). As a sacral entity the clan celebrated its own rites (*sacra gentilicia*). The members of the clan bore the clan name besides their personal name. This was the *nomen gentile*, for example Fabius in the case of those belonging to the Fabian clan (*gens Fabia*). Originally, only the patrician aristocracy enjoyed the privilege of forming these clans: plebeian *gentes* were first formed in imitation of their patrician counterparts. Of course, in political struggles and especially in warfare, in which, in early Rome, clans would participate in close alliance, noble *gentes* could call upon armed forces much stronger than the numbers of clan members alone, for they also enlisted their clients. Thus, ancient tradition recounts that when in 479 BC the *gens Fabia* was defeated in the battle at the River Cremera against the Veientines, it sent out against the enemy 306 patrician *gentiles* and several thousand clients. Moreover, that, at about the same time the *gens Claudia*, which had now come to Rome, was made up of 5,000 families.[13]

The clans came together in the *curiae* (a term apparently deriving from *coviria* 'union of men'). Tradition has it that from the foundation of Romulus they numbered 30. While clans themselves had no heads, a *curio* stood at the head of each *curia* and a *curio maximus* at the head of the *curiones*. These unions of clans, above the *gentes*, were very important in public life. Besides their sacral functions, they constituted the organisational structure of the popular assembly and also of the army. The public assembly, structured in *curiae* (the *comitia curiata*), dealt with matters of family law where the head of the family had died without male heirs, decided on public matters of state and had the right to endorse the authority of the highest officers of the community (*lex curiata de imperio*). In warfare, forces took the field in curial order: according to tradition each curia had 10 equestrians (a *decuria*) and 100 infantrymen (a *centuria*). Their total, given as 300 equestrians and 3,000 infantrymen, constituted the original force of the legion.[14]

In the Regal Period the *curiae* came together in three gentile 'tribes' (*tribus*). Each *tribus* consisted of 10 *curiae*. The names of these three tribes (Tities, Ramnes, Luceres) are Etruscan, a clear illustration of the importance of Etruscan influence for the development of the social system of early Rome. Yet these tribes were less important in public life than the *curiae*. The old form of tribal division was relegated still further when a division of the community into tribes formed on a regional basis was carried through. But in the archaic social structure, when still intact, the three tribes comprised the entire Roman people (*populus Romanus*, also known as the *Quirites*, a name which may be connected with the Quirinal or perhaps with *covirites*, 'men of the curiae').

The number of citizens in early Rome can, perhaps, be estimated approximately. The aforementioned figures preserved for particular *gentes* are as exaggerated as the tradition which states that in 508 BC the Roman people numbered 130,000 citizens and in 392 BC 152,573.[15] In the sixth century BC and even as late as 450 BC the territory of the Roman state (on the east bank of the Tiber)[16] was an area with a diameter of roughly only eight kilometres. The total number of those belonging to the community around 500 BC may have amounted to 10,000 or 15,000 at most. Rome's military strength would be of roughly proportional size. As late as about 400 BC, when the territory of the Roman state had already increased considerably, the territory of Veii was still more extensive than that of Rome.

The elite of Roman society during the Regal Period and in the first century of the Republic was the patricians, an aristocracy of birth and landed property which constituted an order with clearly defined privileges. The best explanation of the origin of the patriciate is that an equestrian aristocracy developed under the Etruscan kings of Rome in consequence of the superiority of cavalry in archaic warfare. The members of this aristocracy constituted the mounted guard of the king. So much is indicated in particular by the symbols of the patrician order, which, in part at least, can be traced back to the dress and *insignia* of the cavalry of early Rome. The elite of the old Roman army, the equestrians (*equites*, originally *celeres* which means 'the swift') are evidently to be identified with the patricians. The view that this militarily dominant equestrian aristocracy was also the socially and economically dominant landowning stratum seems more plausible than to suppose that even in early Rome the patrician landowning aristocracy provided the heavy infantry and had only little to do with the cavalry of the royal guard. The 'rule of the cavalry', as we know from early Greece, is entirely appropriate to the conditions of an archaic social system. It is typical that even in the so-called Servian constitution of Rome from the fifth century BC the *equites* are treated as a dominant group set above the ordinary 'classes'. Their position is roughly comparable to that of the cavalry (*hippeis*) in the Athenian constitution before the reforms of Solon.[17]

The patrician aristocracy of early Rome was a closed order, founded upon birth and upon its functions and privileges in the economic, social, political and religious spheres. Members of leading Roman families apart, a few newcomers, at most, from other communities might gain admission to this aristocracy, so long as they belonged to the local aristocracy of their homeland: an example is provided by the story of the Sabine Attius Clausus, the founder of the *gens Claudia* which came to Rome. Very shortly after the beginning of the struggle of the orders the patriciate became still more exclusive: newcomers could only join the *plebs* and marriage between patricians and plebeians was forbidden. In accordance with the aristocratic social ethic, the members of the patriciate considered themselves to be the 'good men' in society ('*viri boni et strenui*', as the elder Marcus Porcius Cato described the Roman aristocracy as late as the second century BC). They even distanced themselves from the ordinary majority by their manner of life. Their consciousness of their position is apparent from the symbols of their order: these were the gold ring (*anulus aureus*), the purple stripe (*clavus*) on their tunics, the short riding cloak (*trabea*), the high, boot-like shoe with thongs (*calceus patricius*) and the caparisons of precious metal (*phalerae*) from the original cavalry equipment.

On the economic front, the patricians owed their pre-eminence to their landed property, which must have constituted a considerable portion of the territory of the Roman state, and to their herds. Tradition has it that, after the acceptance of his clan in Rome, Attius Clausus had 25 iugera of land, while the 5,000 'ordinary' families that followed him had 2 iugera each (Plut. *Publicola*, 21.10). It is typical of the economic power of the patricians in early Rome that they charged the cost of their mounts and the fodder consumed to the community, or, more accurately, to the widows and orphans of the community who were otherwise exempt from taxation. Moreover, the lion's share of war booty, a very important source of wealth in early Rome, fell to them. Until the arrival of the hoplite phalanx the patricians enjoyed clear military dominance: they rode into battle at the head of their client forces, as did the Fabii in 479 BC. They also exercised complete control in the field of politics. The popular assembly in its old form, based on the curial system, which again permitted them to parade with their masses of clients, was entirely under their influence. In the council of elders (*senatus*), which came into being under the Etruscan kings and which after the inauguration of the Republic constituted the highest decision-making body in the Roman state, the patrician members (*patres*) made the decree on which the validity of the decrees of the popular assembly depended. The plebeian senators who gradually came on the scene (*conscripti*, 'the enrolled') were not entitled to vote during The Early Republic. Furthermore, only patricians became magistrates of the community. These magistrates included the two highest officials, whose number was fixed at two as early as the beginning of the Republic and who were known first as *praetores* and later as *consules*, the *dictator* (originally, *magister populi*), who at times of military necessity held office for a maximum of six months with unlimited power, and also the priests.[18] In extraordinary circumstances when there were no leading magistrates (or, in the Regal Period, no king), the patricians chose a regent (*interrex*) from among their own number. Within this homogeneous order social stratification existed at all only in so far as leading groups of men from the most illustrious clans (*patres maiorum gentium*) enjoyed particularly great influence: the president of the Senate (*princeps senatus*) was drawn from this circle.

The other order in early Roman society was the *plebs* ('the multitude', from *plere*, meaning 'to fill'). This was the common people, consisting of free persons: they too were part of the total membership of the state (*populus*).[19] The plebeians enjoyed citizenship, like the patricians, but they did not possess their privileges. The beginnings of the *plebs* stretch back into the Regal Period without doubt, but they first took on a fixed identity after the onset of their organised struggle against the patrician aristocracy shortly after 500 BC, when they came together to form a separate community with their own institutions. That there was a specific order of the *plebs* was therefore not an Etruscan innovation, but a Roman one: the Etruscan social system knew only of masters on one side of society and clients, servants and slaves on the other.

Part of the later ancient tradition suggests that the *plebs* of early Rome constituted an essentially peasant stratum. Peasants able to assert their economic independence in the face of the patriciate always existed in early Rome: their association within the framework of the *plebs* was their only chance of maintaining themselves against the powerful, landowning aristocracy. But, most important, in numbers ever increasing from generation to generation, there were poverty-stricken peasants who possessed virtually nothing as a result of the continual division of family plots among heirs. Their only hope of an improvement in their position lay in a common plebeian struggle. Yet it is probable that in the formation of the *plebs* into an independent order an important part was also played by a rather more urban lower stratum with craftsmen and traders at its heart. Crafts and trade and naturally therefore also the guilds of craftsmen and traders were accorded little esteem in early Roman society, as might be expected in an aristocratic social system based fundamentally on agrarian production. Tradition has it that Romulus forbade the Romans, who were disposed to military service and farming, to follow crafts. Indeed, the concept that it was the farmer, not the craftsman or the trader, who was the morally superior figure in society persisted through the elder Cato and through Cicero into the Empire. According to some later writers, such as Livy (1.56.1) and Pliny (*NH*, 35.154), it was foreigners, in particular migrant Etruscans, who practised the crafts in early Rome and gave the Romans their manufacturing capability. There is no doubt that Rome was very ready to accept foreigners: legend has it that Romulus himself instituted an asylum for foreign refugees. At the time of the rule of the patriciate the social position of these immigrants was certainly unattractive, yet they were personally less dependent upon the powerful noble families than the majority of Roman peasants. The determined stand of the *plebs* against the patrician aristocracy from the beginning of the Republic is only explicable in view of the fact that at least one 'pillar' of the plebeians lived in partial freedom from the economic, social, political and not least moral constraints which bound ordinary members of a clan to its patrician head and thus had a profound affect upon the masses of the peasant population.

It would always be a mistake to equate the *plebs* with just the clients of the patrician aristocracy. The clients constituted a predominantly peasant lower stratum, quite unlike part of the *plebs*. The boundaries between these two social groups were not sharply defined. Clients might win freedom from their bonds to a noble (for example, if he left no heirs upon his death) and might join the *plebs*. Alternatively, it might happen that incoming members of the *plebs* might occasionally find a secure niche in Roman society through a personal connection with a patrician family. Nevertheless, the plebeians had succeeded in forming themselves into a close-knit order, but the clients had not, principally because of their extreme personal dependence upon the aristocracy. This form of connection outlasted the old Roman social system with its clans. The *cliens* (from *cluere*, meaning 'to heed someone') entered into a relationship of loyalty (*fides*) with the powerful and rich noble. The relationship obliged him to various services of an economic and ideological nature (*operae* and *obsequium*). In return the noble as his *patronus* took upon himself a 'fatherly' responsibility, whereby he gave his client personal protection and put a plot of land at his disposal for the client and his family to farm. A similar relationship existed between the master and his freed slave (*libertus*), who, after his liberation (*manumissio*), remained closely bound to his *patronus*, whether as a farmer, a craftsman or a trader.

In the patriarchal social system of the early period, slavery could only develop in so far as it was accorded a function in the family, the framework of social and economic life. Accordingly, this patriarchal form of slavery, which we know from the history of other peoples, as from Greek history through Homeric epic in particular, was very different from the slavery of the Late Republic and Empire. On the one hand, the slave was regarded as the property of his master without personal rights: he was the object of sale and purchase and was accordingly known not only as *servus*, but also as *mancipium*, 'property'. Moreover, he enjoyed less esteem than the free as is very clearly illustrated by a measure in the Twelve Tables: a man who broke the bones of a slave was only liable to half the compensation due if he inflicted the same injury on a free man. But, on the other hand, the position of the slave in the family was not so very different from that of ordinary members of the family. Like them he was a full member of the family unit. He lived with them all day and could enjoy close personal contact with the *pater familias*. He was in the power of the head of the family, but so was the latter's wife or indeed his sons, whom he could punish and even sell into slavery (a maximum of three times according to the law of the Twelve Tables). Moreover, his economic function differed little from that of the free members of the family, for, apart from his duties as a servant in the house, he worked on the family property as a farmer or a herdsman, once again together with 'free' members of the family. The traditionally minded elder Cato is said to have frequently cooked his meals together with his batman when on military service; on his estates he is said to have eaten with his farm-hands, despite his severity towards his slaves, biting the same bread and drinking the same wine, while his own wife nursed the children of slaves side by side with her own (Plut., *Cato*, 1.9.; 3.2; 20.5ff).

The purpose of the institution of slavery in this form was to increase the manpower of the family both in domestic activity (and craft production) and on the land, especially after the effects of Roman expansion from the end of the fifth century BC, which gave rise to an increase in property. At the same time, rich families sought to increase their prestige and power by maintaining as many clients as possible, clients most readily recruited from their manumitted slaves. And there was a need for slaves and various opportunities were taken to meet this need. Down to the fourth century BC two forms of enslavement of free citizens belonging to the *populus Romanus* played a major part. One was the option open to an impoverished family head of selling his own sons into slavery: the law of the Twelve Tables indicates that the father could buy back his son. The other form of enslavement of free citizens was debt-bondage, as found in Athens before Solon. The law on the subject set down in the Twelve Tables forced the debtor to secure his debt with his own body (*nexum*). Should he be unable to meet his debt he must put himself at the disposal of his creditor as a *mancipium*. As late as 385 BC a large number of citizens did just this: they had evidently lost most of their property in the Gallic sack of Rome in 387 BC (Livy, 6.15.8 and 20.6f.). Of course, these sources of slaves were already being supplemented by the enslavement of prisoners of war as well as by the natural reproduction of slaves: the slave born into the family (*verna*) was automatically the property of the *pater familias*.

In view of the patriarchal nature of early Roman slavery the revolts of slaves in the first century of the Republic which are reported by later authors are to be treated with considerable suspicion.[20] They are described in the sources as 'conspiracies'. The first such 'conspiracy' occurred, according to Dionysius of Halicarnassus, in 501 BC, when the Latins sought to restore the banished king Tarquinius. In 500 BC the erstwhile king himself launched a 'conspiracy' of free man and slaves against the young Republic. In 460 BC Rome used external help, according to Livy, against the forces of the Sabine Appius Herdonius, recruited from Roman exiles and slaves. In 409 BC another 'conspiracy' of slaves is held to have taken place. Of course, ancient accounts of early slave movements almost always follow the same pattern: in time of crisis for the Roman community, slaves and some free men conspire with the plan of occupying the hills of the city, liberating the slaves, killing the masters and taking over their property and wives; however, the conspiracy is discovered just in time and dealt with. There can be no doubt that these accounts were written under the influence of the great slave revolts of the Late Republic. They have no more substance than, for instance, the speculations of Livy as to whether King Servius Tullius (not certainly a historical figure) was born as a slave or was only enslaved later in life. Only the action of Appius Herdonius in 460 BC is definitely historical (it is mentioned as early as the elder Cato), but according to Dionysius of Halicarnassus his supporters were not ordinary slaves but clients and 'servants'.[21] Of course, it is possible that slaves occasionally participated in unrest generated by groups marginal to Roman society, as for example by the exiles of 460 BC. But it is symptomatic that they did not participate in the crucial social conflict of the Early Republic, the struggle of the plebeians against the patricians, as a coherent social grouping, for example in alliance with the *plebs*. As long as they were fully integrated within the family they had neither the stimulus nor the opportunity to develop in this way. Characteristically, after the alleged conspiracy of 409 BC Roman tradition records no similar action until 259 BC.

The Struggle of the Orders in Early Rome

The crucial antagonism within the early Roman social system was not the tension between free and slave, but that between groups within the free citizen body. It was this that erupted into severe social and political conflicts and it was this that set in train a process of transformation in the structure of state and society. On one side stood those who belonged to the privileged aristocracy of birth and landed property. On the other, the ordinary citizens, whose political rights were restricted and who, in many cases, were in dire economic straits. This antagonism was played out in the so-called struggle of the orders between the *patres* and the *plebs*. This conflict between patricians and plebeians lasted more than two centuries. It was unique in the history of the peoples and tribes of Italy and was of the greatest consequence for the future of Roman society.[22] The first phase of this struggle, which took place principally in the fifth century and in the first third of the fourth century BC, was characterised by the development of distinct camps: the plebeians defined themselves as an independent order in conscious opposition to the patriciate and brought about a two-order state. In the second phase, which took place between the 360s and the beginning of the third century BC, an accommodation was reached between the leading plebeians and the patricians, an accommodation which gave rise to a new elite. The archaic social system of Rome had already been weakened by the rise of the *plebs* in the fifth century BC. In this second phase, as Roman rule spread through the Italian peninsula, the old system evaporated. The archaic social system was now replaced by a new social structure.

The roots of the conflict between patricians and plebeians lay in the economic, social, political and military development of archaic Rome. They reached back down into the sixth century BC. There were two crucial factors. First, the economic exploitation and political repression of the mass of the population by the patrician aristocracy. Second, from the sixth century BC onwards a stratification had developed within the *plebs* which led to increased tension between the patricians and the ordinary citizens and made it possible for the people to declare war, so to speak, on the aristocracy. There were a few craftsmen and traders who – largely personally independent of the patrician families – were able to exploit the economic growth of the young city as the kings set about building. They managed to accumulate wealth, which consisted above all of military equipment household equipment. But at the same time other groups of the population suffered a disastrous social and economic plight through loss of land and debt, especially many smallholders who had to divide their modest family plots among ever more heirs from generation to generation and who could no longer produce enough from their land to feed themselves. The aims of these two plebeian groups were therefore quite different. The principal desire of the well-to-do plebeians was for political participation – admission to the magistracies and equal rights with the patricians in the Senate – together with social integration through the permission of lawful marriages between noble and ignoble partners. The poor members of the *plebs* sought an improvement in their economic situation and in their social position through the solution of the problem of debt and by a proper share in the holding of public land (*ager publicus*). But of course both had the same enemy, namely the patrician aristocracy. Their only chance was to combine against the patricians, to construct common institutions to organise the struggle and to force through reforms together.

The plebeians were able to seize this chance after the fall of the monarchy in Rome, when the changed position of the community in foreign affairs and the changes in Roman battle tactics offered conditions favourable for the assumption of the decisive political struggle against the rule of the aristocracy. When Rome left the protection of powerful Etruscan cities with the expulsion of the last king, it endured a century of permanent, hostile pressure, both from nearby centres of Etruscan power, especially Veii, and from the mountain tribes of central Italy, such as the Aequi and Volsci. The tactic of the political and military strike (*secessio*), which the people used to exert pressure, according to tradition, as early as the fifth century BC in two very critical situations (494 and 449 BC), or indeed even the simple threat of such a strike forced the aristocracy to give way within the state in view of the pressure from without. The strike was all the more telling because the plebeian infantry was accorded a greater tactical significance from the turn of the sixth into the fifth century BC. Archaic warfare, waged by the mounted aristocracy, proved obsolete in the campaigns against strongly fortified Veii and against the mountain tribes. The emergence of the hoplite, as in Greece in the seventh century BC, brought about an increase in the military strength of the *plebs* and thus in their aspirations: it fired their political activity.[23] In these new battle tactics the crucial role was accorded to heavily armoured formations of infantry. These elite formations were composed of rich plebeians who could afford the necessary equipment or, if craftsmen, could make it themselves. In consequence, the political ambitions of the wealthy members of the *plebs* were most marked and apparent.

The first decisive step and at the same time the first great success of the plebeians was the construction of their own institutions. This was the creation of an organisation for self-protection and for political struggle. It was also integration in the form of a plebeian order to oppose the aristocracy. According to annalistic tradition the latter critical event took place in 494 BC when the first secession of the people was crowned with success and the office of tribune of the people was introduced.[24] The date of foundation of a temple suggests that this traditional date is approximately correct. In 493 BC the temple of the goddess Ceres was built on the Aventine. Her cult there was always the preserve of the plebeians: this foundation of a temple was nothing less than the union of the *plebs* into a sacral community.[25] It is entirely understandable that a separate community formed within the *populus Romanus* should commit itself to the worship of a religious cult, for the *plebs* could only make its union legitimate by invoking divine protection. Yet, at the same time, this act was a conscious imitation of the foundation of the temple of Jupiter on the Capitol, at the religious heart of the patrician state (traditionally, in 507 BC), an imitation designed to express in another way the autonomy of the separate plebeian community. In fact, this community did not confine itself to the worship of a religious cult: it raised the cry that it was a 'state within the state'. Within the framework of their religious community the plebeians held their own meetings (*concilia plebis*) as an alternative to the popular assembly and there they made their own decrees (*plebiscita*). They elected leaders, namely the *aediles* ('temple-wardens', from *aedes*, meaning 'temple') and *tribuni plebis*, of whom there were at first probably two and from the mid fifth century BC, ten. Under sacred statute (*lex sacrata*) they decreed the inviolability (*sacrosanctitas*) of the tribunate of the people, they declared his right to offer assistance (*ius auxilii*) against the wilful actions of patrician magistrates, and they enacted that the tribunes of the people could intervene when the patrician authorities proceeded against a plebeian (*ius intercedendi*). In addition, the tribunes gradually gained a right of veto over the magistrates and Senate. These institutions were not at first recognised by the patriciate as part of the state system, but they became a political reality through the support of the mass of the people.

The second success achieved by the plebeians was the replacement of the tribal division of the population by a method of division more favourable to themselves. The popular assembly thus took on a new structure concordant with plebeian interests. Since the title of the *tribuni plebis* derives from the word *tribus*, it may be that the crucial reforming measures in the gradual reorganisation of the tribal division coincided with the creation of the popular tribunate. The three old gentile associations, the Tities, Ramnes and Luceres, were not abolished, but largely replaced by tribes constituted on a regional basis. Four of these, the *Suburana, Palatina, Esquilina* and *Collina*, corresponded to the four regions of the city of Rome: they were the *tribus urbanae*. In the fifth century BC were added the *tribus rusticae* which lay in a belt around the city. At first, there were 16 of the latter, but their number rose from the end of the fifth century onwards to reach a total of 35 tribes at the end of Roman tribal evolution in 241 BC.[26] Since the tribal division served principally as the basis for the popular assembly, its political importance was considerable, especially in the holding of elections for office. In the popular assembly organised according to tribes constituted on the regional principle (*comitia tributa*) the patricians were no longer able to parade at the head of a close-knit kinship group under their control. Henceforth they could not rule the assembly by the weight of their clients, as they had done in the old form of the assembly (*comitia curiata*). At the same time, the new framework offered good opportunities for plebeian agitation which could no longer simply be silenced. So long as the state magistracies were held only by patricians, the effect of this agitation upon elections was relatively limited, but it could be important, nevertheless, in so far as it was possible for the plebeians to bring about the election to office of congenial patricians who were prepared to compromise.

The plebeians could record a third success in the mid fifth century BC (traditionally, in 451 or 450 BC), namely the codification of law in the so-called law of the Twelve Tables (*leges duodecim tabularum*).[27] This did not involve new legislation favourable to the plebeians. Rather, it was no more than the setting down in writing of the existing law: for the lower strata of the population the terms of this law were by no means generous. These provisions show that the struggle of the *plebs* must have begun some decades earlier from an inconceivably low base. They also show that the position of the common people even after the first great political successes was very far from good. The archaic features of the law are evident: the protection of the absolute power of the *pater familias*, who could sell his children into slavery, the legitimation of debt-bondage in the form of *nexum* and the recognised right of the repayment of physical injury in kind (*talio*). These did not contribute to the easing of the plight of the weak in society. Moreover, legal sanction was given to the sharp division between patricians and plebeians, in particular by the ban on marriage between members of the two respective orders, a ban which even applied to rich plebeians. Yet, the existing law had been written down. This was a political reform of great importance. Henceforth the ordinary citizen could defend himself against the violence and injustice of the powerful by reference to explicit rules of procedure and criminal law, not merely to established custom, which, though generally respected, was also vague. Through the provision that every citizen could be brought to court and that every citizen had the right to a defender (*vindex*), legal protection was secured even for the poor and weak. The course was also set for future social development, for the law of the Twelve Tables no longer envisaged only two groups in society, the aristocracy and the ordinary people: it was already looking to wealth as the criterion of social stratification. It drew a distinction between those with property (*assidui*) – property which was of course fairly limited given the conditions of the archaic city-state – and those without property (*proletarii*), who had nothing but their children (*proles*, meaning 'rising generation').

The concern for property as a social qualification was of particular benefit to the rich plebeians, who might thus no longer be counted simply as part of the mass of ordinary people. Their wealth secured for them prestige and influence. The importance for the leading plebeians of a new Roman social structure based upon wealth is revealed by the fourth great success of the *plebs* in the struggle against the patriciate. It achieved a new division of the citizen body into property classes. This timocratic ordering of the community is ascribed to King Servius Tullius by Roman tradition. Since Servius was, according to tradition, a man of lowly origin, the annalists took him to be the type of the democratic reformer. But in the sixth century BC the economic and social conditions necessary for this reform did not exist: even the Twelve Tables display no knowledge of particular census classes as late as the fifth century BC. This social stratification came about – as the basis for the organisation of the popular assembly, at least – after 450 BC. The institution of the office of *censor* for determining the property qualification of individual citizens may mark its beginning: according to tradition, this took place in 443 BC.[28]

The property qualifications of members of the various property classes were measured, under this so-called Servian reform, according to the military equipment that they could afford. It is quite clear that this reform developed from the new Roman military system, in particular in consequence of the introduction of hoplite tactics. This background is also indicated by the titles of the property classes (*classis* meaning 'military contingent') and their sub-divisions (*centuria*, meaning 'division of 100', part of the oldest military structure). Our earliest knowledge of this constitution in more detailed form comes from the later Republic, when it had been further refined. Above the classes (*supra classem*) stood the *equites*, who were divided into 18 centuries: evidently, these were members of the patrician aristocracy. The first class comprised 80 centuries: these were the heavy-armed infantry, who were equipped with helmet, shield, breastplate, greaves, spear, javelin and sword. These men formed the backbone of the entire Roman army. In this class wealthy plebeians predominated. To the second, third and fourth classes, which comprised 20 centuries respectively, belonged the rest of the propertied: each class had a lower property qualification than its predecessor. The members of the second class bore the same weapons as those of the first, but they wore no breastplate and carried only a small rectilinear shield instead of the round shield. Citizens in the third class had no armour at all – they had only a helmet and offensive weapons. Members of the fourth class were equipped with only a spear and a javelin. The fifth class, comprising 30 centuries, contained the poor: they were merely armed with a sling. In addition, there were also two centuries of *fabri*, who maintained the military machine and were attached to the first class, and two centuries of musicians, ranked with the fifth class. The 'proletarians' who were entirely without property and thus without weapons were formed into a century beneath the class structure (*infra classem*). Their military role was that of a runner or a scout, at most. As with the division of the people into gentile associations and later into regional tribes, so this new structure too became at the same time the basis for the structuring of the popular assembly. In the popular assembly structured by classes and centuries (*comitia centuriata*), each century had a vote, irrespective of the actual number of its members. The composition of the various centuries in a class was not identical: the numerically weaker *seniores*, men over 46 years of age, constituted the same number of centuries in each class as the *iuniores*, so that the votes of the more conservative elders balanced those of their juniors. Of course, the system of voting by centuries meant that the members of the equestrian centuries and of the first class who together had 98 votes could immediately out-vote the remaining 95 centuries, provided that they could direct their interests towards a common goal. As Cicero stresses quite clearly (*De rep*. 2.39), this system ensured the clear superiority of the propertied over the mass of the people when decisions were made.

The political subordination and economic repression of the great majority of the *plebs* were as little affected by this new form of social stratification as they were by the Twelve Tables. The social differences between the aristocracy standing *supra classem* and the ordinary people were established much more firmly, albeit not quite in the same way as before. Thus, the gulf between the camps of the patricians and the plebeians, which had begun with the unification of the people to form a separate community, was made complete. In the following decades, down to the first third of the fourth century BC, this gulf between the two orders lay at the foundation of Roman society. But at the same time the Servian constitution had shaken the archaic social system and had opened the way for the arrival of a new social model. The clan connections of the masses of the population to the families of the aristocracy, which had already been weakened by the new tribal division, now lost still more of their importance. And although the nobles still commanded the heights of this new constitution, they no longer owed their position to superior birth alone: it was their economic credentials that mattered. Still more importantly, a prominent social position had been secured for propertied plebeians: account had been taken of their economic and military significance as well as their political ambitions. At the same time, the leading plebeians had been recognised as potential partners of the aristocracy, since the patricians could no longer control the popular assembly alone: they needed to ally themselves with the *prima classis* of the people. This partnership gained clear expression in the removal of the ban on marriage between noble and commoner. We cannot be sure whether this reform actually occurred in 445 BC under the *lex Canuleia*, as the annalists have it, or whether it was carried through later. Whatever the case it points in the same direction as the timocratic constitution, namely down the road to rapprochement and equilibrium between the patricians and the leading plebeians.

ROMAN SOCIETY FROM THE BEGINNING OF
EXPANSION TO THE SECOND PUNIC WAR

The Dissolution of the Archaic Social System: Equilibrium of the Orders and Expansion

Around the turn of the fifth into the fourth century BC Rome was still an archaic city-state. Its social structure, with the ruling aristocracy on the one side and the politically and economically subordinated-people on the other, rested as before on the simple principle of the order, while its territory was still restricted to a small area in the environs of the city. But changes in the structure of Roman society after the overthrow of the monarchy and the beginning of the struggle of the orders had placed Rome on the threshold of a new period of social development. The plebeians were no longer a silent majority in politics: they had become an integrated, self-confident order which could already point to a string of impressive political achievements. At the same time, beneath the surface of the simple model of aristocracy and people, a more far-reaching division of society had come about with property qualification as its criterion. This new model stretched from the rich landowners, through propertied craftsmen and traders, down to poor peasants and proletarians without property. Moreover, towards 400 BC Rome was no longer the second-rate power it had been a century earlier. Rome had long been kept on the defensive after the expulsion of the Etruscan kings, but from the middle of the fifth century BC it went on to the offensive. With the capture of Fidenae (426 BC) and the defeat of Veii (396 BC) in particular, Rome succeeded in considerably expanding its sphere of dominance. The course was thus set for the future and the dissolution of the archaic system. In the social and political debate within Rome the need of the moment for the plebeians was no longer further separation from the aristocracy; rather, for leading plebeians at least the concern was the attainment of equilibrium with the patriciate. On the outside, the aim of the aristocracy and of all the people too, could only be further expansion which would solve the economic plight of the poor at the expense of third parties and at the same time secure greater wealth for those who already had it. After the apparently uneventful decades from the middle of the fifth century BC, when the weakened archaic structures were ripe for replacement by a new social model, only an acceleration of the historical process was required for the consequences of previous development to come to fruition.

This acceleration of the historical process came about from the first decades of the fourth century BC, with the result that the social stratification of the Roman state was fundamentally changed during the next hundred years or so. Shortly after 400 BC social tensions in Rome were evidently heightened. The numbers of the landless were markedly increased by the natural increase in the population. The expansion of the Roman sphere of dominance after the defeat of Fidenae and Veii had not alleviated the discontent of the poor. It had made it worse. Territory ravaged and annexed by Rome was not parcelled out to those without property. It was occupied by the rich landowners. At the same time, there was an increase in the discontent of the *plebs*, even the rich plebeians, with the political situation. In the victorious wars against Rome's neighbours the plebeian infantry, especially the heavy infantry of the wealthy plebeians, had played the crucial part: they demanded proportional political influence. The situation was further aggravated when in 387 BC a raiding party of Gauls from northern Italy defeated the Roman army, took over Rome as far as the Capitol for a time, sacked the city and laid waste the surrounding territory. Many Roman families had thus lost their possessions and fallen into debt-bondage as a result. But at the same time, the patrician state was also destabilised. The only way out was revolution or fundamental reform. According to the annalistic tradition, the discontented twice attempted to break down the existing structure by force, in 385 and 375 BC (Livy, 6.11.1f.). Their defeat made it clear that the existing social structure could not be changed by force, not least because this ran counter to the interests of the wealthy plebeians. But at the same time, the need for reforms was also made clear. The wing of the patricians that was prepared to compromise pushed them through in alliance with the leaders of the *plebs*.[29]

Tradition has it that the crucial reform was passed in 367 BC under the so-called *leges Liciniae Sextiae*, named after the tribunes Gaius Licinius Stolo and Lucius Sextius Lateranus (Livy, 6.35.3ff.). Through this legislation the economic position of the poor plebeians was greatly improved in one blow. So too was the political position of the *plebs*, which was made more equal by the admission of the leaders of the people to the highest offices. After this reform had been won, the other most-needed reforms were similarly enacted by legislation. Since laws had to be passed by the popular assembly, reforms had to be approved by the majority of the people (or, at least, the majority of the popular assembly). Further, since they also required the consent of the Senate, the latter's support also meant that the reforms were accorded the sanction of the highest body in the state, wherein the interests of the aristocracy bulked most large. At any rate, the legislative progress of the Republic from the Licinian–Sextian laws, which had set things in motion, to the *lex Hortensia* (287 BC) was an unstoppable torrent of social and political reforms to the benefit of the *plebs*. Occasional setbacks caused by the attitude of a few influential and conservative families among the patricians could not halt this development. With the beginning of this policy of reform through the Licinian–Sextian laws, subsequent measures were directed towards two goals. First, there was the need to improve the economic plight of the poor plebeians. Second, complete political equality between plebeians and patricians had still to be attained. The latter required the amalgamation of leading plebeians with the descendants of the old patriciate.

Under the Licinian–Sextian laws of 367 BC strenuous measures had already been taken for the improvement of the situation of those without property and for their welfare. The debts which oppressed the poor and threatened them with the loss of their personal freedom had been cancelled in part (much as Solon did at the beginning of his programme of reforms at Athens in a very similar historical position). At the same time, it had been enacted that no-one should be permitted to hold more than 500 iugera of public land. This last provision of the Licinian–Sextian laws is often regarded as an anachronism, but it can probably be accepted as genuine, not only because the elder Cato mentioned it as an old piece of legislation in 167 BC (Gell.,*NA*, 6.3.37), but also because it is compatible with the size of the Roman state after the annexation of the territories of Fidenae and Veii. Five hundred iugera (about 1.25 square kilometres) was by no means the usual size of a plot of land in this period. The figure evidently indicates the size of the estates of a few leading families, who had carved up amongst themselves areas seized some decades earlier, particularly the territory of the erstwhile state of Veii, which was bigger than the entire original territory of Rome and made it possible for these families to seize estates larger than 500 iugera. The rich landowners who had laid claim to this land had been forced to hand over at least part of it to be distributed among the poor. [30]

Of course, the policy of providing land to ensure the welfare of the poor really only came to fruition after 340 BC with the sudden enlargement of the *ager publicus* in the wake of expansion. A corollary was that debt-bondage, once sanctioned by the Twelve Tables, could now be abolished. For Livy later (8.28.1ff.), the *lex Poetelia Papiria* (326 BC) which introduced this reform was like the beginning of the Republic *(velut aliud initium libertatis)*. Appius Claudius Caecus, who was favourable to the plebeians and to reform, passed during his censorship (312 BC) another measure which pointed the same way as the agrarian reform brought in by the Licinian–Sextian laws. Hitherto, ex-slaves, who were for the most part people without any property at all, usually had no landed property after their manumission and were thus enrolled in the four urban tribes. Claudius divided them among the rural tribes too and thus allowed them a fixed home and a plot of land in the countryside. [31] His measure also meant that freedmen, whose political role had previously been restricted to the urban tribes as citizens of the lowest rank in society, could now also influence the decision making and political activity of the rural population. Although this reform was rescinded in 304 BC (one of the few clear examples of patrician reaction in the second phase of the struggle of the orders), it was only the political scope of the freedmen that was restricted: their economic ambitions could not be stemmed.

At this time reforming efforts were mostly directed towards the attainment of political parity for the plebeians. It was important for the *plebs* to strengthen their defences against the caprice of the state machinery. To this end, in 304 BC, the tribune Gnaeus Flavius set out rules of legal procedure *(ius Flavianum)*, which secured uniform regulations for the treatment of every citizen before a court. The *lex Valeria de provocatione* of 300 BC, accorded the citizen better protection from magistrates. Under this law, a citizen convicted by a magistrate on a capital charge had the right of appeal *(provocatio)* to the popular assembly, which would decide the case in its own proceedings. In criminal cases of a political nature in the city of Rome the popular assembly entirely took over the position of the magistrates. [32] Of course, the principal concern of the leading plebeians was the attainment of parity with the patricians in the government of the state. The only scope for a political role lay in the holding of magistracies, in the debates and decision-making of the Senate and of the popular assembly. The principal aims of the leading plebeians were therefore admission to the highest public offices, parity with the patricians in the Senate and also the attainment of a secure role, vis-à-vis the Senate, for the popular assembly which supported them.

As for their bid for a share in government through the tenure of magistracies, their original tactic was to institute their own offices. This device had made it possible for them to force their way also into those offices which had previously been the sole preserve of the patricians. They achieved a limited degree of success in this direction long before the Licinian-Sextian laws. The military tribunes – an office introduced in 444 BC according to tradition - were from the first part plebeian and part patrician, apparently because the *plebs* would only fight under their own leaders. Due to their military importance the plebeians were quickly able to achieve for their commanders parity with patrician officers. The first plebeian appeared in civil office in 409 BC: significantly in the lowest office, that of *quaestor* (an assistant to the higher magistrates). The achievement of real parity over the magistracies between patricians and plebeians began some decades later in the wake of the political unrest which generated the Licinian–Sextian reforms. The patrician *dictator* of 368 BC, in an extraordinary situation, appointed a plebeian as his deputy *(magister equitum)*. At the same time men drawn from the *plebs* were admitted to the priestly college concerned with oracles. The Licinian–Sextian laws of the following year introduced the critical reform. Henceforth the highest magistrates - concerned with justice as well as with the conduct of war - were the *consuls*, of whom one could be a plebeian. After them came the *praetor*, who also could be either a plebeian or a patrician: his competence was limited to justice. At the same time, the plebeians were also given the right to hold the other high offices *(dictator, censor)*. Furthermore, two patrician *aediles* were appointed (each with the title *aedilis curulis*) in addition to the two *aediles plebis,* so that the functions of the *aediles* might be equally divided between the representatives of the two orders. The first plebeians entered high office immediately after. The first plebeian *consul* was Lucius Sextius Lateranus in 366 according to tradition. The first plebeian *dictator* was Gaius Marcius Rutiius in 356. The first plebeian *censor* was the same senator in 351. The first plebeian *praetor* was Quintus Publilius Philo in 337 BC. This process of integration of the plebeians into the magistracies was brought to a conclusion by the *lex Ogulnia* in 330 BC, when representatives of the *plebs* were also admitted into the highest priesthoods, the *pontifices* and the *augures*.[33]

In the wake of these reforms the leading plebeians also sought to improve their position in the Senate. By the *lex Ovinia* (passed before 312 BC) it was enacted that the censors should make up the numbers of the Senate from time to time. This meant that the Senate could be renewed with wealthy and influential plebeians. At the same time, this law set plebeian senators on a par with patrician senators. Thus the *conscripti* received the full voting rights which had earlier been restricted to the *patres* alone. In the censorship of Appius Claudius Caecus in 312 BC, in particular, many plebeians were accepted into the Senate: among them were the sons of freedmen and thus men who practised the crafts and trade. The Senate was no longer the fortress of an exclusive aristocracy of birth and landed property (Diod.20.36.1ff). At the same time, the rights of the Senate were restricted in favour of the popular assembly which was much under the influence of the wealthy plebeians. Earlier, decrees of the people could be rescinded easily if the Senate subsequently refused to approve them. However, after the *lex Publilia* (339 BC) the arguments of the Senate against a decree of the popular assembly had to be articulated before that assembly. Decrees of the people could therefore no longer simply be declared void by a conservative majority in the Senate. The *lex Hortensia* of 287 BC, which is usually regarded as the conclusion of the struggle of the orders, went still further. The struggle between the plebeians and the patricians seemed to be on the point of flaring-up again in its old form after unrest over personal debts, as the *plebs* were resorting to the desperate measure of secession which they had taken twice before in the fifth century, according to tradition. But, in the words of A. Heuss, 'at that moment the leaders of the *plebs* and of the patriciate must have settled this passing crisis in the spirit of a final, thorough purge of the whole past.' The decrees of the popular assembly (*plebiscita*) were accorded validity without the need for ratification by the Senate. Of course, the very fact that this reform was possible clearly shows the progress that had been made towards the achievement of parity between the orders: the issue could have led to the complete breakdown of the state. Evidently at the root of this reform lay the conviction that by and large the same interests predominated in the Senate and in the popular assembly, since the leaders of the people and of the popular assembly were now also figures and leading members of a newly-formed senatorial aristocracy.

The victory of the plebeians had thus been won. It meant the removal of the boundaries between the patrician and plebeian orders, without opening the way to an egalitarian society. On the contrary, it laid the foundations for further social division. Be that as it may, the victory of the plebeians was due to their resolution in the struggle of the orders and to their consistent policy of alliance between rich and poor plebeians. It was also due to the readiness of the aristocracy (or at least many nobles) to compromise, often under pressure generated by Rome's external situation. Finally, it was due to the common interest shared by all concerned in solving social problems through expansion.

The implications of expansion for Roman social history were of the highest importance. It is not only that the reform of the social system by means of legislation was contemporaneous with the expansion of Roman rule over Italy. Rather, this reform was organically and inseparably connected with the process of expansion. The Roman state was able immediately to overcome the effects of the defeat at the hands of the Gauls in 387 BC. After passing conflicts with neighbours and after Rome's position in Latium and surrounding area had been secured by means of diplomacy, a great offensive began after the mid fourth century BC. It led to the capture of the whole Italian peninsula after a series of successes: difficult wars against the confederacy of Samnite mountain tribes (until 290 BC), crucial victories over the Gauls and Etruscans (285 BC) and the war against Tarentum and Pyrrhus, king of Epirus (282–270 BC).

The reason for these wars of conquest was not some irrational Roman push for expansion. Rather, it was the need to solve the internal problems of Roman society through the expansion of the sphere of Roman domination. There was a similar reason for the push of the Samnites and their allies from the Italian uplands down to the coastal plain between Rome and Naples, parts of which were very fertile (a move which conflicted with Roman interests). For these pastoral tribes the effects of over-population were still more catastrophic than for the agrarian Roman state.[34] Moreover, the remarkable external successes of Rome within a short space of time are only fully understandable in the context of social history. They are to be ascribed not only to the military and diplomatic abilities of Roman generals and politicians, but also to the superiority of Roman society over the social systems of most peoples and tribes of Italy. By contrast with the backward hill tribes of central Italy, the Roman army could rely upon urban centres of supply and equipment: apart from Rome itself, a string of citizen colonies had been established after the foundation of Ostia in the mid fourth century BC – Antium, Tarracina, Minturnae, Sinuessa, Castrum Novum and Sena Gallica, all founded along the Italian coasts between 338 and 283 BC. Etruscan armies, composed of nobles and their armed dependants, faced an army of citizens with a totally different identity. At the same time, by grants of citizenship, Rome gave the various peoples and tribes of Italy the opportunity of taking part in the Roman social system. From the completion of the unification of Italy under Roman rule on the eve of the First Punic War, the Italian peninsula was a network of communities with a variety of rights under Roman supremacy. As well as the 'allies' (*socii*), who had nominal autonomy, there were 'communities of half-citizens' (*civitates sine suffragio*), which had Roman citizenship without the right to participate in the election of Roman magistrates, Latin colonies (*coloniae Latinae*) of the Latin league under the leadership of Rome, communities with a broadly local population, which had Roman citizenship and communal autonomy (*municipia*), and finally the Roman colonies (*coloniae civium Romanorum*). The liberal bestowal of Roman citizenship in its various forms was more than a diplomatic move: it also laid the foundation for an increase in Roman manpower and thus for the unification of the peninsula within the framework of a state.[35]

With legislative reform and the expansion of Roman rule over Italy far-reaching change occurred in the structure of Roman society within the century or so from the Licinian-Sextian laws down to the outbreak of the First Punic War. The reforms entailed a new sort of division in Roman society. Clan bonds, which had been the foundation of the archaic social structure, were perpetuated for centuries by clientage, always vigorous and by private cult: they might exercise a powerful influence on relationships between particular persons and groups. But they were no longer the critical principle in the division of society. Patrician birth, which of course retained its social importance throughout Roman history, was no longer the criterion that determined the possession of the commanding heights in society, as it had once been. Although the special position of the patrician aristocracy of birth was institutionally sanctioned by title, dress and the reservation of some priesthoods for the patricians, the distinction between patricians and non-patricians was no longer the basis of the social structure. The simple system of two orders, *patres* and *plebs*, was replaced by a new model of society. The new elite was an amalgamation of the descendants of the old aristocracy of birth and those of the leading plebeian families, who were brought close together by the establishment of family connections. The members of this elite owed their leading position to the powers which they exercised as magistrates and senators, and to their wealth and property, which gave them the opportunity of holding office. In consequence, they enjoyed high personal prestige. This elite was divided into a leading group, composed of patricians and plebeians who had held high office and their descendants, and a wider group of 'ordinary' senators. Beneath it was no longer a mass of the poorer and totally poor, hardly differentiated. Now there was a variety of strata in the population beneath the upper strata, divided according to the size and nature of their property and according to their legal status. There were rich farmers who held land in the captured areas, minor craftsmen and traders, smallholders and agricultural workers, who were more dependent upon the rich landowners and might be their clients, freedmen, who were generally engaged in occupations in the city, and slaves, who were no longer automatically members of the patriarchal family group as they once had been. The introduction of this model entailed the dissolution of the archaic social structure. It also meant that in the new social system tensions would no longer constitute a simple conflict between the aristocracy and the people. To a large extent the economic causes of conflict had been removed: the political causes still more so. Despite continuing differences between rich and poor, a period of relative peace was now beginning: grave new conflicts came to a head only gradually at first.

The effects of the wars of conquest on Roman society are apparent. The common interest in expansion brought together the groups which were at odds in Roman society. Successful expansion allowed social problems to be solved at the expense of others. Social tensions could be relaxed and the violent change which had threatened the system of government before the Licinian-Sextian laws was now irrelevant. Those who had been without property now had land in the conquered areas, whether in the environs of Rome or in the territory of newly-founded Roman and Latin colonies. At the same time, the sphere of operation of the central model of the Roman social system, which had hitherto been confined to Rome, was liberated from the framework of a city-state through expansion, colonisation and the granting of citizenship. It graduated to become a state system in which there were many urban centres with their own territories. In this process different local social systems were brought within this state – the Greek *poleis* to the south, flourishing agricultural centres in Campania, backward pastoral peoples in the uplands and civic communities with their own particular structures in Etruria.

The Roman Social System of the Third Century BC

The results of the struggle of the orders and the extension of Roman power over the Italian peninsula clearly set the path which the future development of Roman society would follow. Three factors remained after the change that had occurred in the history of Rome in the century from the Licinian-Sextian laws to the First Punic War, factors which were to be important for the division of society and for the relations between its various strata. The combined effect of internal change within the Roman citizen body and successful expansion was that there was now a sharper differentiation in the economic structure of the Roman state and throughout its social stratification. A further result of expansion was that the social system of Rome in the third century BC was no longer supported only by a numerically insignificant body, the inhabitants of a single city, but by a population which amounted to several millions. Henceforth, that system therefore comprised social groups of different kinds. Ultimately, it was inevitable that the different social groups would combine within an aristocratic social order. The political victory of the leading plebeians had not brought about democratisation, as for example at Athens from Cleisthenes. Rather, it had generated a new aristocracy, whose rule was firmly established. This was the context in which an aristocratic social system developed at Rome in the third century BC. Roman victory in the First Punic War (264–241 BC) only served to accelerate this development, while the upheaval of the Second Punic War (218–201 BC) gave it a somewhat new direction.[36]

In the fourth century BC Rome was still a state with a backward, agrarian economic structure: the overwhelming majority of the population lived by agriculture and cattle-breeding and the possession of land was the most important source and, at the same time, the most important index of wealth. The crafts and trade played only a limited role. As for trade, coined money was not in use: the archaic media of exchange remained – cattle, as well as crude copper ingots and plate. Craftsmen and traders can only have constituted a fairly small group within the *plebs*. The primacy of agrarian production remained throughout antiquity down to the industrial revolution of modern times. However, it was of great importance for Roman development that, in tandem with the expansion of the Roman state, the crafts, trade and even a money-based economy played a significant part and led to the strengthening of the groups in society who were engaged in these activities. This differentiation in the economic sphere was markedly accelerated when Rome became a sea power in the wake of her great efforts in the First Punic War. With the conquest of Sicily (241 BC), of Sardinia and Corsica (237 BC) and, especially, with the establishment of these islands as the first Roman provinces in the western Mediterranean (227 BC), Roman sea power promoted economic expansion. The clearest indication of this change in the structure of the Roman economy is the introduction of a regular coinage by 269 BC, the eve of the First Punic War. There were consequences for the nature of the standard by which social position was measured. Membership of the various *census* classes instituted under the so-called Servian constitution could be regulated on the basis of a property qualification which expressed the value of the minimum amount of property prescribed for the various classes in the form of a monetary figure.[37]

Increased differentiation within Roman society was also inevitable in view of the fact that the Roman social system of the third century BC involved the entire population of the Italian peninsula: that population was ethnically, socially and culturally heterogeneous and, by its sheer bulk, made the simple archaic division of society impossible. According to the Roman *census* lists of the third century BC, whose figures may at least indicate the apparent numerical strength of the *cives Romani*, the number of adult male citizens in 276 BC was 271,224. By 265 it had grown to 292,234. After a decline in the population through losses in the First Punic War, there were apparently only 241,712 citizens in 247 BC, but by 234 BC the number had risen again to 270, 713 (Livy, *Epit.*, 14–20). On the basis of the figures given by Polybius (2.24.3ff.) for the fighting strength of Italy in 225 BC, P.A. Brunt estimates that the total population of the peninsula (excluding northern Italy) was in the region of 3,000,000, to whom 2,000,000 slaves are to be added.[38] Even if this is only an imprecise estimate which probably also gives too high a figure for the slaves, at least, it is nevertheless apparent that in the third century BC the further development of Roman society would occur under quite new circumstances. The original simple model of society divided into aristocracy and people was now utterly inconceivable. This population with its internal differentiation was brought together in an aristocratic social system. A new aristocracy and a new social system under its control had emerged in Rome after the struggle of the orders. At the same time, the rule of the archaic aristocracy in Rome had not been replaced by a democratic social system. But this is by no means to be explained as simply the result of the conservative attitude of a Roman citizen body made up for the most part of landowners and farmers. Rather, it was a consequence of the nature of the dispute between the patricians and plebeians. The political victory of the *plebs* was nothing but the political victory of those leading plebeians who had striven since the fifth century BC for integration into the dominant strata of society and for a share in this dominance: they had not striven for an end to the rule of the aristocracy. Their political aims were achieved in the period from the Licinian-Sextian laws to the *lex Hortensia* when they had gained parity with the patricians. The political aim of the leading plebeians had never been a social order in which the lower strata of the free citizen body might gain unlimited power. And, at the same time, the mass of the poor plebeians were concerned with political participation only in so far as it furthered their principal aim – namely, a fair share of public land. When they had been amply provided with land after the Licinian-Sextian laws and the conquest of Italy, their problems seemed largely solved. At the same time, the system of clientage not only remained intact, even after the emergence of new upper strata, but was actually reinforced by connections between the lower groups of the people and rising plebeian families. This social system secured a special influence and at the same time supporters for rich and powerful families on the basis of their personal relationship with their clients. The structure of this system made democratisation on the Athenian model impossible. Thus, in the third century BC and throughout the rest of Roman history, Roman society continued to be ruled by an aristocratic social system.

In the context of all these conditions, Roman society in the third century BC was characterised by a new stratification and, accordingly, by a different kind of relationship between its various strata. The division of society rested upon a complicated network of factors. Privileges of birth were important, but so were personal ability, landed property and money. Political influence, gained through membership of the Senate and, especially, through entry into office, played its part. So too did legal status, dependent on citizenship and personal freedom, participation in agrarian production or in other sectors of the economy and, finally, the political relationships of particular Italian communities to Rome. Under this system of division, there was a spectrum of different social strata from the senatorial aristocracy to the slaves. Nor were the respective strata entirely homogeneous. Although the *plebs* was accorded public recognition as an institution, it was only the newly formed senatorial aristocracy, with its privileges and its evident self-confidence, that enjoyed at least some characteristics of an order, albeit without being exclusive. At the same time, the course was set for the formation of an elite which was interested not only in land-holding but also in profit gained through the crafts, trade and finance. Social tensions between the various strata lay elsewhere. New antagonisms developed to take the place of the conflict between the patricians and plebeians. They lay between the dominant strata and the proletarian groups which were continually formed and re-formed in the city of Rome, between the Romans and their allies who were often repressed and between masters and slaves. But it was exceptional for these antagonisms to lead to serious internal conflicts, for in part they could be relieved by peaceful means and in part they could be controlled by the might and power of those who ruled in Rome. The political power of the dominant strata was definitely the most important factor in holding together the motley groups in society, not least because it found allies in the masses of the smallholders who had been given land. Their support was particularly important in the wars with Carthage.

The clearest indication of the strongly aristocratic character of Roman society, even after the end of the struggle of the orders, is the fact that the ruling senatorial aristocracy constituted only the tiny pinnacle of the whole citizen body. The number of members of the senate and thus also the number of adult male members of the senatorial aristocracy amounted to a total of only about 300. But even within this aristocracy there was a group at the top of society which was still less numerous, namely the nobility, with the greatest prestige, the decisive political influence and a proud awareness of the leading position of its members. These were the *viri nobiles*, though the concept never became a formal one. They were the leading senators; their families and descendants largely provided the men who held the highest public office, the consulship. In the course of the third century BC these men belonged to about 20 noble patrician and plebeian families, in addition to new men who rose in society and added new families to the circle of this nobility. Some of the oldest families long continued to play an important role in Roman history, unlike several patrician clans which died out in the fourth century BC. The old families included the Fabii, from time immemorial the most prestigious family within the Roman aristocracy, the Aemilii and the Cornelii, as well as the Claudii and Valerii, who were of Sabine origin. At the time of the Second Punic War, a typical representative of these families was Quintus Fabius Maximus Verrucosus, the 'Delayer' (*Cunctator*), who was *censor*, five times *consul* and twice *dictator*. He was conscious of the tradition of his family, but at the same time he was not insensitive to new intellectual currents (Plut. *Fabius*, 1.1ff.). As well as patrician families of this sort, there were also plebeian families which occasionally provided consuls after the Licinian–Sextian laws. As early as the second half of the fourth century BC they could become leading men in the Roman state, as, for example, did Quintus Publilius Philo, who was *consul* four times and the spiritual father of the *lex Publilia*. In the third century BC many of them appear in the history of Rome, as, for example, does Marcus Atilius Regulus, who was twice *consul* as well as general in the First Punic War. There was no longer a sharp distinction between patrician and plebeian families. Some leading families – for example, the Veturii – had both a patrician and a plebeian branch, while most families were related to others: the Fabii, for example, were connected with several plebeian families. At the same time, from the last decades of the fourth century BC leading families were also accepted into the senatorial aristocracy from the various Roman and Latin cities of Italy – the Plautii from Tibur, the Mamilii, Fulvii and Coruncanii from Tusculum, the Atilii from Cales, the Otacilii from Beneventum, and the Ogulnii from Etruria. Occasionally, the upper strata of allied communities contracted close connections with the Roman aristocracy: note, for example, the nobles of Capua who were connected with Romans (Livy, 23.4.7).[39]

The senatorial aristocracy with its elite nobility was separated from the other strata of Roman society by its privileges, sphere of activity, wealth and property, prestige and its awareness of its collective identity. It was thus on the way to becoming an order, but it laid no claim to exclusivity. The offspring of non-senatorial families might still be admitted to its circle by virtue of particular ability. Such new men might even attain the consulship, the highest public office. A case in point is that of Gaius Flaminius. Between the First and Second Punic Wars he succeeded in putting through measures to favour the peasantry. His political and religious views often brought him into conflict with his peers. Usually, new men (*novi homines*) absorbed the views of the aristocracy with the greatest speed and to the full. Marcus Porcius Cato (234–139 BC), who was the son of an equestrian from Tusculum, was the best example of the process, according to Cicero: '*quasi exemplum ad industriam virtutemque*' (*De re p.* 1.1).

The aristocracy derived its dominant position in society from its control of policy making. It provided the magistrates,[40] it filled the Senate, and it dominated the popular assembly, largely through its influence over its clients. The creation of a regulated official career structure for public office, rising from the lower offices to the consulship and censorship (*cursus honorum*), meant that entry into the magistracies became in practice a privilege of the aristocracy. It was only the members of the aristocracy who had the wealth required to stand for office and to meet the demands of the electoral process. They had at their disposal large numbers of clients upon whose votes they could depend at elections. They alone enjoyed such economic independence that they could afford to accept unpaid offices which themselves entailed a degree of expenditure. In particular, they alone had grown to manhood steeped in the tradition of the leading families. They alone had been schooled therein and given the proper political education. By virtue of the experience they had gained in office they subsequently formed a body of expert politicians in the Senate: these were the senators most competent to make political decisions. Accordingly, these men enjoyed high status and influence over the views of the mass of the citizens.

The domination exercised by the aristocracy over the *plebs* in general and the popular assembly in particular was institutionally enshrined. Polybius, who was an admirer of the constitution of the Roman Republic, thought that the strength of the Romans lay in the healthy admixture of monarchy, aristocracy and democracy which resided in a system composed, respectively, of magistrates, Senate and popular assembly (6.11.11ff.). The reality was that the aristocracy ruled in Rome. Only the magistrates (that is, members of the aristocracy) could call a meeting of the popular assembly and only they could submit a motion to it. Meetings of the popular assembly were poorly attended in reality, because citizens resident far from Rome rarely came into the city. Many country people came into Rome on market days, but the holding of meetings of the popular assembly on market days was forbidden in the interests of the aristocracy. At the same time, all the previous forms of the popular assembly, with their various functions, were retained side by side: votes were cast by centuries and tribes. The opportunities for manipulation inherent in the division into centuries and tribes continued to be taken to the full, to the disadvantage of the masses, for their numerical strength and the composition of the various tribes and centuries were not accorded due weight in the voting procedure. Moreover, any measure could be blocked in the interests of the aristocracy by the veto of any one of the ten tribunes, who, like all the magistrates, were also members of the aristocracy. It was of the greatest importance that the broad masses of the people were tied to the various noble families by contractual bonds of patronage and clientage. These clients were not only poor relatives, neighbours and freedmen, but now also entire communities in the Italian peninsula.[41] Under this system, it was also important for the aristocracy to control its own members so as to prevent particular noble families, supported by their dependents, from seizing monarchical power, as, for example, the tyrants had done in Greece. Magisterial power was reduced by the principle of annual office-holding and collegiality. But, that aside, particular noble families often pursued different political objectives and were seldom in complete agreement: dominance shifted from family to family, and members of the same family did not necessarily pursue the same political aims.[42]

But the domination of the aristocracy over Roman society did not depend entirely upon its political power and manipulation in its favour. The senatorial aristocracy also stamped the identity of the Roman people with its own traditions: it convinced the free strata of the citizen body of the idea of a state that was the property of the whole of Roman society – the *res publica* that was a *res populi* (Cic. *De re p*. 1.39). The ideological basis of this conception of the state was religion. Polybius clearly stresses the point: 'the greatest advantage of the Roman social structure...lies in my view in their attitude towards the gods. What is in other peoples a reproach is precisely what forms the foundation of the Roman state – an almost superstitious fear of the gods. At Rome religion plays this part in both public and private life: its significance is hardly conceivable' (6.56.6ff.). The aristocracy determined the nature of this *religio*, the correct relationship with the gods. It furnished the state priests, who were called upon to discover divine will and to determine religious regulations. Moreover, the traditions of the families of the aristocracy dictated the religious behaviour proper to the members of society in various situations. The standard for thought and action was the *mos maiorum*, ancestral conduct as expressed in the great deeds of the past. The collective memory of these deeds and their emulation ensured the continuity of state ideology. The poet Ennius wrote, '*moribus antiquis res stat Romana virisque*' (see Cic *De rep.* 5.1). Ennius was an older contemporary of Polybius, who stated, just as explicitly, that 'the memory of public benefactors remains alive in the people and is passed on to children and to children's children. Most important, however, the youth is urged to endure all for the country's sake so as to share in the glory accorded to the deserving' (6.54.2f.). Moreover, the pattern of behaviour enshrined in these deeds was precisely the pattern of thought and action upheld by the senators. The men who had achieved the glorious deeds of the past – politicians, generals and priests – were their ancestors: the glory of the ancestors ensured, in turn, the prestige of the descendants.

The domination of the senatorial aristocracy here described would have been impossible without an economic base. This base remained the ownership of land. Although the emergence of enormous estates was hindered by the Licinian–Sextian laws, the senatorial aristocracy nevertheless constituted the group of the richest landowners in Roman society. The expansion of Roman rule in Italy and, in particular, in the western Mediterranean from the First Punic War gave the senators enticing new opportunities for amassing hitherto unknown profits through trade, entrepreneurial activity and financial dealings. No doubt there were influential senators who were prepared to seize these opportunities. This could have led to a complete change in the structure of the economy and society of Rome. But in 218 BC the *lex Claudia* – supposedly supported by only one senator, the outsider Gaius Flaminius – put a stop to any such change (Livy, 21.63.3f.). Under this law senators and their families were prevented from owning cargo-bearing vessels with a capacity of more than 300 amphorae, the size adjudged sufficient for the transportation of their own agricultural products. The rationale behind this law seems to have been that trade was deemed unworthy of Roman senators (*quaestus omnis patribus indecorus visus*). In fact, it is inconceivable that a Roman assembly could have passed such a measure totally against the will of the ruling aristocracy. On the contrary, influential groupings within the aristocracy must have taken the view that the continuity of the established form of the aristocracy would be guaranteed if the elite remained an aristocracy of landownership. In the latter form the upper strata had far less at risk economically, they maintained unchanged the social ties of the rural population to the aristocracy and were less prone to foreign influences than an elite composed of merchants and entrepreneurs (Cato, *De agr.* praef. 1ff.).

Nevertheless the numbers of traders and craftsmen in Roman society increased in the third century BC together with their social importance. But in terms of social prestige they remained far behind the senatorial aristocracy, as they did throughout Roman history. The wars with Carthage gave a great impetus to the development of broad strata of craftsmen and merchants. According to Polybius, Rome had no warships before the First Punic War and only promoted the crafts needed for shipbuilding from that war on (1.20.10ff.). In 255 BC Rome was able to build 220 ships in three months (1.38.6). The feat was only made possible by the presence at Rome of a large group of specialised craftsmen (some, no doubt, from abroad). It was also in the First Punic War that Italian merchants travelled with the Roman forces to support them in Africa (Polyb. 1.83.7ff.). Shortly after the war Italian traders appeared under Roman protection on the east coast of the Adriatic (Polyb. 2.8.1ff.). In the Second Punic War Roman traders accompanied the army not only to provision it but also to buy up the booty it seized (Polyb.14.7.2ff.). They thereby realised large profits. There were now already in Rome rich entrepreneurs who could assist the state by making it large loans for armaments and building (Livy, 23.49.1ff.; 24.18.10). Thus began the process which led in the second century BC to the emergence of a very important social stratum of wealthy entrepreneurs, traders and bankers, and thus contributed to the rise of the equestrian order.[43]

Peasants constituted the great majority in Roman society. They ranged from well-to-do landowners in the environs of new Roman and Latin colonies to the farm labourers and clients, who were very much personally dependent upon the aristocracy. As a result of continuing Roman colonisation through the period of the Punic wars, the poorer and the ever-increasing proletarian masses of Rome were, for the most part, adequately provided with land. The upper and middle strata of the peasantry gained from this process in particular: earlier colonisation had had the same effect. These strata were the most important supporters of the aristocracy which presided over the social and political system. These strata guaranteed Roman rule in the conquered territories and played the decisive part in the Roman army. The aristocracy therefore made them a number of economic concessions so as to ensure their uniformity of interest. The creation of the last Roman tribe in 241 BC[44] led to the numerical reinforcement and the greater economic security of these strata of the peasantry. It also led to the foundation of new colonies, in particular, to the colonisation of the so-called *ager Gallicus* near Sena Gallica in 232 BC by Gaius Flaminius, in the face of opposition from conservative nobles[45] (Polyb. 2.21.7ff., according to whom this measure was the first rift in the structure of a Roman social system which he considered to be perfectly balanced). The reform of the popular assembly at Rome in 241 BC or shortly after was a political consequence of this economic and social strengthening of these strata of the peasantry. The tribal structure was interrelated with the centuriate structure to form a complex system. The voting system was arranged in such a way that the votes of the wealthier peasants now had more weight than before. Rome owed her victories in the First and Second Punic Wars to these peasants in particular. Their catastrophic losses, especially in the second war, had serious consequences for the future development of Roman society.

At the time of the Punic wars the freedmen, whose numbers and importance had increased in Rome and the other cities in particular, but also in the countryside, had a legal status in Roman society lower than that of the free peasantry. Many slaves had been emancipated by leading Romans who would parade in the popular assembly at the head of their loyal claques so as to achieve their political ends. These freed slaves received Roman citizenship upon their emancipation: they supported the political aims of their patrons in the assembly and at the same time they put their useful economic and personal services at their patrons' disposal. As early as 357 BC, according to Livy (7.16.7), a tax was set on manumission at 5 per cent of the value of the slave concerned. Yet the number of slaves manumitted rose markedly in the course of the third century BC. A high rate of manumission may be inferred from the fact that, down to 209 BC, the income of the Roman state from the tax on manumission rose to almost 4.000 lb of gold (Livy, 27.10.11f.).[46]

From the end of the archaic social system to the Early Empire the lowest position in Roman society was that of the slaves. In the context of the social and economic development of Rome from the fourth century BC the importance of slavery increased. Slaves could be used as a work-force on the estates of the landowners in particular, but also on the lands of wealthier peasants. It was also much easier now to obtain slaves. The cumbersome archaic means by which the Roman community had obtained slaves were obsolete. The enslavement of the children of free citizens lost its purpose after the poor plebeians had been furnished with plots of land. And slavery for debt had been legally prohibited from 326 BC. The importance of trading in slaves with other states and peoples rose in consequence. As early as 348 BC the slave trade had been taken into account in a treaty between Rome and Carthage which prohibited the selling into slavery of the allies of the contracting parties within their spheres of influence (Polyb. 3.24.6ff.). However, constant wars played the largest part by allowing the Romans to increase their slaveholdings through the enslavement of prisoners of war – wars fought first against the peoples of Italy and then against Carthage and her allies. In 307 BC, it is said 7,000 allies of the Samnites were sold into slavery in a body (Livy, 9.42.8). In 262 BC, more than 25,000 inhabitants of Agrigentum came on to the slave market, as did 13,000 prisoners at Panormus in 254 BC (Diod. 23.9.11 and 18.5). In the Second Punic War mass enslavements were quite usual: they introduced the period in which slavery reached the height of its importance. However, before the Second Punic War a Roman society whose economic production was largely based on slave labour was still far off. At that time, patriarchal forms of slavery still survived in part. At this stage prisoners of war were often ransomed, not enslaved: this was done, for example, in the case of most of the inhabitants of Panormus in 254 BC. Even rich Romans did not yet always have masses of slaves: for example, Marcus Atilius Regulus, the general, who is said to have had only one slave and one paid labourer at his disposal (Val. Max. 4.4.6). Our sources first speak of the large-scale use of slaves in the economy, for example in the crafts (Polyb. 10.17.9f.), for the period of the Second Punic War.

In accordance with the relatively minor importance of slavery in the third century BC, there were no significant slave revolts in that century. It is said that in 259 BC 3,000 slaves conspired with 4,000 allied sailors (*navales socii*) against the Roman state. The action of these slaves, who were probably recently enslaved prisoners of war from the mountains of central Italy, may be described as a revolt atypical of the defeated enemies enslaved within the Roman social structure at that time. A similar view is probably to be taken of a conspiracy of 25 slaves at Rome in 217 BC, which was apparently incited by a Carthaginian agent. The small number of those involved in this conspiracy betrays its insignificance.[47] In Rome's ally, Volsinii, the

Etruscan nobles freed their slaves in 280 BC and handed over power to them. The aristocracy then considered itself ill-treated by its new masters and turned to Rome for help: it was only with this help that the nobles regained their former position in 264 BC after a bloody conflict.[48] Such an episode was quite inconceivable at Rome. The strength of the Roman system of government and the relatively slight impact of slavery as yet combined to make it impossible.

In the third century BC Rome was threatened neither by slave revolts nor by unrest among the lower strata in city and countryside alike. Threats from abroad apart, the central issue was whether the communities of Italy, which were both very numerous and heterogeneous in their structures, were prepared to accept Roman domination in perpetuity, whether they would combine with Rome within a more or less coherent social system. The defection of some Roman allies during the Second Punic War illustrates the difficulty of achieving the unification of Italy: the defectors had even included Capua, despite its close links with leading families at Rome. Even when this war was over the problem would only be solved after a long evolutionary process and an Italian uprising against Rome. However, long before the Second Punic War it had been apparent that Rome could secure its dominance over Italy through the creation, by various methods, of a more or less unified Italian social system. The means to this end were the admission of leading Italian families into the senatorial order, the nurture of social and political relationships between the Roman aristocracy and the upper strata of the various communities and, moreover, the creation of strata of peasants up and down Italy who regarded themselves as Roman, strata expanded by colonisation. Furthermore, the episode at Volsinii made it quite clear that Roman might could suit the interests of the upper strata of the various Etruscan or Italian communities.

In any case the Roman aristocracy was strong enough in the third century BC to hold together under its system of government the different strata in Roman society and Italy with its political, social and cultural diversity. Under this aristocracy the Roman state emerged after the two great wars against Carthage as a victorious world power. With the Second Punic War and energetic Roman expansion, which was also proceeding apace in the east, a new epoch dawned for Roman society: a new social structure swiftly developed and new social tensions with it. But even during the third century BC the direction that this change must take had become clear. Most processes of change in the later Republic had their roots in the course of earlier Roman history, partly before the Second Punic War and partly after it: the change of the nobility into an oligarchy, the formation of a rich stratum of traders, entrepreneurs and bankers, the decline of the Italian peasantry, the use of gangs of slaves in production and the integration of the population of Italy into the Roman social system.

3 THE STRUCTURAL CHANGE OF THE SECOND CENTURY BC

Conditions and General Characteristics

The Second Punic War marked the beginning of a period of transformation in Roman history which saw swift and far-reaching changes in the structure of the Roman state and of Roman society. Rome had become a world power. Her economic structure and social system thus came under new conditions, wherein they displayed a greater diversity than ever before. At the same time, this swift change generated a social and political crisis at Rome which brought about grave and previously unimagined conflicts, only two generations after the victory over Hannibal.

To an extent, these new conditions were created by the immediate consequences of the Second Punic War: the decline and proletarianisation of the Italian peasantry, the development of large estates and the shift to the use of slaves in production on a large scale. Even in antiquity writers such as Plutarch (*Ti. Gracchus*, 8.1ff.) and Appian (*B. Civ.* 1. 32ff.) chronicled this change clearly, while A.J. Toynbee saw in the wounds inflicted on the economy and society of Rome by the Second Punic War the belated revenge of Hannibal for the success of Roman expansion.[49] But the consequences of expansion itself were of the greatest importance for the social and economic development of the later Republic. In rather less than a century, from the outbreak of the Second Punic War to the ignition of social conflicts in the 130s, Rome became the dominant power over the entire Mediterranean area and thus at the same time an empire. [50] Her forces destroyed two powers of long standing, Macedon (in the Third Macedonian War, 171–168 BC) and Carthage (in the Third Punic War, 149–146 BC), they weakened and humiliated the Seleucid Empire, subjugated the greater part of the Iberian peninsula and occupied Greece (146 BC). The lands conquered were incorporated into the Roman state in the form of provinces – Hispania Citerior and Ulterior (197 BC), Macedonia (148 BC), Africa (146 BC) and Asia (133 BC). The consequences were immeasurable. The young empire had enormous lands with a highly developed form of agrarian production. This made it possible for her to import agrarian products into Italy and it rendered largely superfluous the cultivation in Italy of, for example, cereals. Rome possessed almost inexhaustible resources of raw materials which were exploited in her own interest, as were, for example, the silver mines of Spain. She had an unlimited supply of cheap labour at her disposal – millions of prisoners of war who had been enslaved and provincials who had no rights. She had extensive markets for the products she manufactured without fear of competition. She provided unlimited opportunities for investment, entrepreneurial activity and financial dealings. A restructuring of society was the inevitable result of all these new factors.

Thus a new social system quickly emerged in the Roman state after the Second Punic War, particularly from the beginning of an active period of expansion in the eastern Mediterranean. The principal characteristics of this new system were clearly defined by the mid second century BC.[51] This new model was fundamentally distinct from that of archaic Roman society by virtue of its marked social differentiation. It was also quite unlike the social model of the third century BC which had still been relatively simple. Now the social status of an individual depended upon the interplay of a variety of factors – birth, political training and experience, ownership of land, money, ambition, ability to exploit the economic boom, role in production whether urban or rural, legal status and affiliation to an ethnic or at least regional grouping. The stratification of society was now really complex. The senatorial aristocracy constituted a social elite with the privileges of political leadership based on birth, the appropriate political background and experience, together with the economic independence afforded by the ownership of large estates and commercial profits. A second elite was formed by the equestrians. They were for the most part rich landowners, like the senators. Some were entrepreneurs, merchants and bankers, often of lowly origin, but even they preferred to invest their substance in real estate. There were also local upper strata in the many Italian communities and in the provinces: they consisted for the most part of landowners, but they differed in form from region to region or even from city to city with respect to legal status, property owned and culture. In Italy there were many peasants who enjoyed Roman citizenship, but they were under pressure and a large number of them flooded into the cities, especially Rome. There they contributed to the formation of a large proletarian mass. The large numbers of freedmen also made their own contribution. Severe pressure was also experienced by the vast majority of the Italian *socii* and the provincials: they did not even have Roman citizenship and were exploited by their own masters as well as by the Roman state. But at the bottom of society were the multitude of slaves who had no personal rights and who suffered brutal exploitation, particularly on rural estates and in the mines.

This deep and very sudden differentiation in society generated a series of grave conflicts. The various disadvantaged groups and the dominant group formed two camps, but there were also conflicts between various groupings within the elite. At the same time, the Roman political system had become an anachronism: the equally outdated Roman social tradition proved unable to contain the opposing social strata and groupings in a balanced whole. Most of these conflicts were not open to peaceful solution. The few attempts that were made to arrest the process or to lead reforms in a new direction were failures. The inevitable consequence for Roman society was crisis – the civil wars and revolts which undermined the Republic.

Upper Strata

The aristocracy was able to consolidate its dominance still further after the Second Punic War. Rome's successes against Hannibal and in the east were taken to be confirmation of its policy. Moreover, these successes brought benefits particularly to the aristocracy. It enjoyed massive prestige not only among citizens, but even outside the Roman state. In a famous incident in Egypt in 168 BC an arrogant senator forced the Seleucid king, Antiochus IV, into humiliating submission before his own army (Livy, 45.12.1ff.). Again, in the following year, Prusias II of Bithynia prostrated himself on the threshold of the Senate House at Rome, kissed the ground and addressed the senators as 'saviour gods' (Polyb., 30.18.1ff.). The aristocracy became much more sure of its identity. It could be proud of the glory of its families which it had increased by its own great achievements – '*virtutes generis mieis (sic) moribus accumulavi*', runs the elogium of a member of the Scipionic family, around 140 BC (*ILS*,6). The aristocracy set itself still further apart from the ordinary mass of citizens. It began to approximate to an order, as, for example, the use of the term *ordo senatorius* makes clear. The gulf was made very obvious shortly after the Second Punic War when special seats were allotted to senators at public games. Senators seem to have been particularly concerned to establish the distinction between themselves and the *nouveaux riches*, who began to form themselves into a separate social group, the equestrian order. In the popular assembly senators left the centuries of the *equites*: these centuries, once filled by the mounted aristocracy and subsequently by the senators, comprised, from the second century BC, members of the gradually-emerging equestrian order as well. But now, when *equites* were admitted to public office they had to surrender the symbol of their erstwhile status, the public horse.[52]

Equites of substance were often able to win entry to the lower magistracies. Thus men of lower social rank might regularly enter the aristocracy. The constant supplementation of the elite was a necessity, for a number of senatorial families died out through their failure to produce male issue. An indication of the low rate of reproduction within old noble families is the fact that families as important as the Fabii and Cornelii could only ensure their survival by the adoption of young men from the family of the Aemilii. Publicus Cornelius Scipio Aemilianus, the destroyer of Carthage and Numantia, and Quintus Fabius Maximus Aemilianus, one of the most important Fabii of the second century BC, were the natural sons of Lucius Aemilius Paullus, the victor of Pydna. But the highest state offices were anything but open to those rising in society and to the general mass of senators. The career structure of magistrates was regularised under the *lex Villia Annalis* (180 BC). Having proceeded through earlier office, one could enter the praetorship only from the age of 38 and the consulship only from 43.[53] The number of high offices was very small: while there were ten tribunes there were only two consuls each year. Holders of high office thus constituted a small elite in the senatorial aristocracy. This elite was the nobility, made up of men who had held high office and their descendants, a nobility which had been formed before the Second Punic War. But it was after the war with Hannibal that it finally closed ranks. Entry to the consulship was the privilege of the members of some 25 families of the nobility. These men stubbornly defended their dominance for several generations and excluded other senators from the consulship. Between Manius Acilius Glabrio (*consul*, 191 BC) and Gaius Marius (first *consul* in 107 BC) only two *novi homines* fought their way to the consulship: namely Quintus Pompeius (*consul* 141 BC), the first *consul* from the family of the Pompeii, and Publius Rupilius (*consul*, 132 BC), a leading entrepreneur. Moreover, of the

222 consulships available from the outbreak of the Second Punic War to the first consulship of Gaius Marius (218–107 BC) 24 were held by the Cornelii, 15 by the Claudii, 10 by the Fulvii, 9 by the Aemilii and Postumii respectively, and 8 each by the Fabii and Sempronii.[54] Later, Sallust (*Bell. Jug.* 63.6f.) bitterly observed that the nobility of this period considered the consulship to be its own private property (*'consulatum nobilitas inter se per manus tradebat'*). By contrast, the *homo novus*, however illustrious and remarkable, was regarded as unworthy of the office and almost impure through his lowly birth (*quasi pollutus*).

This oligarchy within the senatorial aristocracy owed its position, in the first instance, to its political experience and success. An upbringing in a noble family, steeped in tradition, was almost the only qualification which a statesman required in the new conditions of the second century BC. This was the qualification for conducting campaigns in foreign lands and diplomacy with Hellenistic kings. Every victory gained by generals and politicians, whether military or diplomatic, reinforced the prestige of the families of the oligarchy still further. The successful scions of these families could rely upon the widest political support and thus great influence: they were popular with the Roman people and with the army and they had clients not only in Italy but also in the provinces. There was thus now a consolidated oligarchical system. Again according to Sallust, 'affairs of state, in war and peace, were conducted through the arbitrary decisions of a few persons. State finances, the provinces, offices, honours and triumphs lay in their hands. The people, however, were oppressed by poverty and military service. While the generals and their cliques seized the spoils of war, their soldiers' parents and children were driven from house and home if they had stronger neighbours' (Sall. *Bell. Jug.* 41.7f.).

Sallust's words indicate the growth of the economic power of the aristocracy and, again, in particular, of the leading families. Victorious generals returned to Rome with vast amounts of booty and up to their necks in the money they had extorted, particularly in the form of ransom money. Gnaeus Manlius Vulso's notorious campaign of robbery in Asia Minor in 189 BC (Polyb. 21.34.3ff.; Livy, 38.12.1ff.) caused Augustine, some six centuries later, to regard states without justice as no more than *magna latrocinia* (*De Civ. Dei*, 4.4). The elder Scipio left his daughters a fortune of 300,000 denarii apiece (Polyb. 31.27.1ff.). The fortune of Lucius Aemilius Paullus stood at 370,000 denarii at the time of his death (Plut. *Aem.*

39.10). The size of these sums can be measured against the property qualifications required for membership of the leading *ordines*: even in the first century BC this stood at only 100,000 denarii (400,000 sesterces) for both senators and knights. This wealth was mainly invested in land in Italy and in slaves. The richest families bought up the land of the peasants or took it by threats and force (App. *BC*, 1.26ff.). The Licinian–Sextian law that no one should hold more than 500 iugera of public land was useless. Large amounts of land were acquired – particularly by members of the nobility. For example, the Scipiones had lands and villas in various parts of Italy: at the time of the attempted reforms of the Gracchi, they held many times more than 500 iugera of land. Publius Licinius Crassus Dives Mucianus, *consul* in 131 BC, had some 100,000 iugera at least, including estates on both *ager publicus* and *ager privatus*. However, this tendency did not develop uniformly throughout Italy: the estates of the second century BC are for the most part not comparable in size with the *latifundia* of the Empire. Even so the change in the agrarian structure is clear enough.[55]

From estates and from other property the greatest possible profit was extracted. A definite ideology of profit reared its head. The best example of a leading senator after the Second Punic War in respect of his economic ambitions and opportunities is Marcus Porcius Cato, who was a great traditionalist in other respects. [56]His ideal was the senator who considered service to the Roman state to be a divine duty (Plut., *Cato*, 24.11), who embodied the religious and moral traditions of the state and who regarded intellectual innovations as dangerous. But the dominant concern of his private life was to increase the wealth he had inherited (ibid., 21.8). Similarly, the principal concern of Cato's work on agriculture is the attainment of maximum profit from the land by minimum investment. He recommended that production on large estates should be centred around products that can be sold at a profit (*'patrem familias vendacem, non emacem esse oportet: Agr.*, 2.7). Accordingly he held that the production of cereals should be replaced by the production of wine and olive-oil and that the labour force should be driven to maximum efficiency. He invested his profits – so as to increase them still further – in woodlands, pastures, fish-ponds, in manufacturing activity and even in long-distance trade and banking. He circumvented the *lex Claudia*, which prohibited senators from mercantile activity, by organising a 'public liability company' for maritime trade and large business enterprises, wherein he was represented by men of straw

(Plut.,*Cato*,21.5ff.).

It was the prestige of the nobility that safe guarded its oligarchial interests and its growing wealth. But that prestige could not prevent the evolution of conflicts behind the splendour of the senatorial aristocracy which were bound to have grave consequences in the future. The nobility of the second century BC, which distanced itself ever further from other senators and aspiring *novi homines* in the Senate, was able to maintain the unrestricted rule of its few leading families. Yet its strongly oligarchic nature shut out able, gifted men who would provide new blood. And this despite the fact that at all periods of Roman history there were social climbers ready and willing to adopt the views and interests of the elite of their day and to champion them with particular fervour. The gulf between the nobility and other senators, widened by the former's extraordinary pride and arrogance, led to discontent among many aspiring families, who were economically powerful yet politically disadvantaged. Marius' attitude was typical of such men. He was the typical example of the *novus homo* with his inferiority complex and his pride in his own achievements. He boasted that he had fought for his office and had taken it from the degenerate aristocracy like the spoils of war, that he could display wounds on his own body as marks of his glory, not the tombstones of his ancestors (Plut.,*Marius*,9.1ff.). Conflicts lay not only between the oligarchy and the broader senatorial groupings, but also between members of the oligarchy itself. The very factors that had increased the collective power of the nobility after the Second Punic War also generated tensions within the ruling oligarchy. There had always been rivalries and conflicts of interest between the various families, but, before the Second Punic War, they had not put the very system of aristocratic government in danger. But after that war there were new opportunities for particular families – even particular *nobiles* – to achieve supremacy. The equilibrium of the leading families, which was the foundation of the oligarchic system was now under potential threat. Particularly able generals and politicians held repeated consulships. They could boast extraordinary military successes; their campaigns were inevitably extended beyond the single year of the past. And they enjoyed close personal relationships with the troops as well as with the provincial population through the extension of the system of clientage. All this increased the power of particular prominent personalities.

This tendency is most clearly visible in the Scipiones.[57] The elder Scipio Africanus received a command at the age of only 25 and without passing through a regular senatorial career. After his defeat of Hannibal he was pre-eminent at Rome. This, together with his unconventional views and actions, brought him into conflict with his peers. His rivals managed his downfall through a lawsuit. The *lex Villia Annalis*, passed soon afterwards in 180 BC, was designed to prohibit the meteoric rise of such young men by statute: it permitted entry to the highest offices only at a mature age and after a regulated career. But when the younger Scipio was voted *consul* in 147 BC, this law was simply set aside. Scipio gained the consulship without having held the previous office of *praetor* and at an unlawful age. He even obtained a second consulship in 134 BC, despite the fact that from 152 BC repeated consulships had been prohibited, not least to prevent the emergence of extraordinary power. It is also symptomatic that during the century or so after the Second Punic War the Cornelii alone furnished 10 per cent of all Roman consuls. Nor was it a matter of chance that the family of Hannibal's conqueror and of the destroyer of Carthage and Numantia was one of the wealthiest senatorial families of the second century BC. At the same time, it is remarkable that, in their enlightened attitude to the Greek intellectual world, the Scipiones stood square against their leading contemporaries, the likes of Cato. Thus from the end of the Second Punic War a process began within the oligarchy which allowed outstanding personalities to emerge above the aristocracy. There was also an indication that such personalities did not automatically identify with the views and interests of their order.

But the wealth of the new world power was not entirely concentrated in the hands of the aristocracy. There were now new opportunities for Roman long-distance trade in the Mediterranean. The raw materials and the massive labour force in the conquered lands were ripe for exploitation. Rome's financial resources were constantly increasing as a result of the vast sums of money and treasures that were captured and extorted. There followed in consequence an increase in trade, business and financial activity on a scale previously inconceivable. Its corollary was the emergence of a powerful and important stratum of businessmen. Gradually these men began to form themselves into a separate equestrian *ordo*, though it was only from the time of the Gracchi that it became an actual *ordo equester*. The decisive step in the consolidation of the order was the institution of the regulation by which senators left the equestrian centuries and *equites* who entered the Senate through holding a magistracy had to give up their status symbol, the public horse (*lex reddendorum equorum*, 129 BC). The public horse thereby became the symbol of an organised order separate from the senators. Moreover, additional new status symbols were soon introduced which made their own contribution to the consolidation and the identity of the *ordo equester*: these were the gold ring, the narrow purple stripe *(angustus clavus)* distinct from the wide purple stripe of the senators *(latus clavus)*, and special seats of honour in public shows, definitively regulated by the *lex Roscia* of 67 BC. [58]

The importance of this social stratum was recognised as early as the Second Punic War. Wealthy persons had formed companies which assisted the state by taking upon themselves public functions (Livy, 23.49.1ff. and 24.18.10). These companies *(societates publicanorum)* held public contracts: they provisioned the army, carried out public works such as the construction or reconstruction of buildings, roads and bridges, leased the state mines and collected customs dues and taxes. They became essential in these areas of the economy (cf.Livy, 45.18.3). They came from the broad mass of the people, according to Polybius who describes them particularly clearly (6.17.2ff.). Polybius was no doubt right to an extent: many businessmen were of low birth. The same social stratum produced the moneylenders, bankers, wealthy merchants and middle men whom Plautus (died 184 BC) vividly describes in his comedies. An indication of their increased importance after the Second Punic War is the fact that the enormous fortune which the elder Scipio left to his daughters upon his death in 183 BC was deposited with a banker (Polyb.,31.27.15). Nevertheless, great landowners also figured among the *equites*. In Cicero's terms the *equites* included *publicani* (businessmen active in large public contracts), *faeneratores* (moneylenders, also called *argentarii*), *negotiatores* (traders) and above all *agricolae* (farmers), many of whom came from the colonies and *municipia* of Italy. Therefore, this order was, in its social composition not so very different from the senatorial order.

New tensions in Roman society were also created by the growth and strengthening of this social stratum. Parvenus who strove after profit without the moderation traditionally demanded by norms which the aristocracy had not quite forgotten were often unscrupulous, reckless and exploitative. These men aroused popular hatred in the provinces especially, and they did not shrink from cheating the state. Their practices were well known at Rome from the time of the Hannibalic War (Livy, 25.1.4 and 25.3.9ff.): the illegal behaviour of the *publicani* became almost proverbial – '*ubi publicanus esset, ibi aut ius publicum vanum aut libertatem sociis nullam esse'* (Livy, 45.18.3). The Roman authorities had repeatedly to intervene against the excesses of the *publicani*, as did Cato as *censor* in 184 BC (Livy, 39.44.7f.; Plut.,*Cato*, 19.2). Such incidents could foment conflicts between senators and *equites* (cf.Livy,43.16.1ff.). Yet the *publicani* were very efficient: their excesses were only possible because the oligarchic regime exercised no systematic control over the economy.

Lower Strata, Italians, Provincials

Of course the majority of traders at Rome and in the other cities – the small-scale traders – did not belong to the wealthy stratum of businessmen, the holders of public contracts. Rather, they formed, together with the craftsmen, particular groups of some size in society. In urban society they ranked with the lower strata: they were not a 'middle order'. In the second century BC there also emerged at Rome and in many Italian cities groups of craftsmen with an importance greater than before. The change was caused by the transition to the profitable system of large estates in the agrarian sector and, at the same time, by the greater importance of long-distance trade, business and financial dealings. The comedies of Plautus and, in particular, the monograph of Cato on agriculture reveal the increasing importance of a variety of specialised craftsmen. Cato lists at length the Italian cities which produced the best versions of the manufactured goods used by an estate owner (*Agr*, 135.1ff.). His list reveals that there were in Rome, amongst others, many weavers, cobblers, potters, smiths, locksmiths and wheelwrights.

Several craftsmen belonged to the broad group of freedmen, who, like the slaves, had greatly increased in number in Rome and the other cities after the Second Punic War. It is said that in 131 BC Scipio Aemilianus affirmed that the urban *plebs* of Rome consisted mostly of one-time slaves whom he had brought to the city as prisoners of war (Val. Max., 6.2.3). Even shortly after the victory over Hannibal there were so many freedmen in Rome that precise regulations on manumission were required. In 177 BC a prohibition was set upon manumission for the sole purpose of obtaining Roman citizenship (Livy, 41.9.11). From 168 BC *liberti* could only be enrolled in one tribe (so that a restriction was placed upon the importance of the broad stratum of freedmen in the popular assembly (Livy,

45.15.5)). Many ex-slaves were able to exploit the economic opportunities available in the cities and even to achieve prosperity. But
many of them were not able to obtain a steady living as craftsmen or
traders in Rome: they formed a proletarian mob. This 'lumpenproletariat' lived under poor conditions – not helped by the increase
in rents from the mid second century BC. High food prices were also
a problem: many of them depended upon hand-outs. There is evidence for such hand-outs (*congiaria*), bestowed by the mighty, from
213 BC: they assured the popularity of their donors among the poor
(cf. Livy, 37.57.11 (189 BC)). But the bulk of this proletariat was
made up not only of freedmen but of the Roman peasantry: these
peasants had lost the lands upon which they depended for a liveli-
hood and had streamed into Rome and the other cities to become
the largest part of the proletariat which grew markedly in Rome
after the Second Punic War.[59]

The impoverishment and proletarianisation of many peasants was
one of the most severe consequences of the Second Punic War and
of the expansion that followed it. The Roman peasantry suffered terrible losses in the war with Hannibal. It suffered doubly from the
burden of that war. The Roman forces were recruited from the mass
of the peasantry: whole armies were destroyed in the battles lost to
Hannibal – 70,000 men at Cannae alone (Polyb., 3.117.4). But at the
same time, it was also the rural population of Italy that bore the
brunt of the long war fought out by Hannibal and Rome, a war in
which, acording to Appian (*Lib.* 134), 400 larger settlements were
destroyed and hundreds of thousands of Italians were killed. The
peasantry made further sacrifices in the wars of expansion that followed, particularly in the very bloody fighting in Spain in the mid
second century BC. The difficulties experienced in recruiting
Roman armies for these wars were early yet quite clear indications
of the decline of the peasantry. In addition to this serious weakening
of the rural population, the peasants who survived the Hannibalic
War were no longer in a position to reconstitute the economic base
which had previously supported the higher and middle peasantry.
The fertility of the soil of Italy had not changed, despite the devastation suffered in the war with Hannibal. But settlements and
hardware had been destroyed and livestock had been slaughtered.
Reconstruction required capital investment and not every peasant
had the requisite means. Moreover, even after the Second Punic
War the sturdiest members of the labour force served in the armies:
peasant families were therefore often short of labour. At the same

time, the landowners did everything in their power to expropriate the land held by peasants. As soon as Hannibal had been expelled from Italy they had occupied deserted lands on the *ager publicus*. With their capital resources they could buy up plots of land and finance the necessary investment. They also had a labour force at their disposal: the masses of cheap slaves produced by the wars themselves who could be exploited even more easily than hired labour. The greater the economic power of the large landowners, the fewer were the restrictions upon the steps they might take against obstinate peasants. Since the *ager publicus* could be occupied by anyone who could cultivate it, it was an easy matter for the strong and wealthy landowners simply to drive off the peasants (cf. Sall., *Bell. Jug.*, 41.8).

Only two generations after the victory over Hannibal Tiberius Sempronius Gracchus could describe the plight of the once prosperous and sturdy peasantry in the following terms: 'The beasts of Italy have a house and home: they know where they can find shelter. But the men who risked their lives in fighting for Italy are granted only air and light: house and home are denied them and they are left to wander with their wives and children in the open air ... They have neither ancestral altar nor tombstone. They die for foreign luxury and riches, in name the masters of the world, in fact not even masters of their own plots of land' (Plut., *Ti. Gracchus*, 9.4). Yet the most recent research, centred upon archaeological observations on rural settlement in the last two centuries of the Republic, underlines the fact that uniform development throughout Italy should not be supposed. In many parts of the peninsula, even in southern Etruria, smallholders persisted well into the Empire. But the trend was clear;[60] southern Italy felt its fullest effects.

The old recipe for the solution of agrarian problems was the settlement of the landless in colonies. But this was no cure for the ills of the impoverished peasants and after the mid second century BC few colonies were founded. Many peasants survived by taking on seasonal work as day-labourers (*mercenarii, operarii*) on the estates of the rich (see, for example, Cato, *Agr.* 145.1). Their fate was often little better than that of the slaves. Peasants flooded into the cities, especially Rome, in order to live on the hand-outs and casual work available there. They would support absolutely any politician prepared to help them. The urban proletariat of Rome thus became a mass of significant size. But its importance resided not simply in its size but also in its political potential. The congregation of 'have-nots' at Rome was the concentration of a highly explosive social and political force. This was a body of people who were fully aware of their plight and who definitely wanted to improve it. Their concentration in the city made communication easy: they were thus capable of swift action. At the same time their Roman citizenship allowed them to attend the popular assembly where they might form a constitutional political force. They only needed leaders to articulate their demands. Such leaders could draw upon their support to break the opposition of the nobility and fulfil these demands. And these leaders had sufficient wealth to cushion the most severe effects of deprivation by bestowing hand-outs until their ends had been achieved: their wealth thus ensured their position at the head of the masses. The inevitable consequence was that these leaders could not come from the proletariat itself: they were members of the aristocracy – either *novi homines* struggling against the power of the oligarchy or leading *nobiles* who had risen above the aristocracy and thus come into conflict with their own group in society.

After the Second Punic War conflicts were brewing between the Italian *socii* and the power-brokers in Rome, conflicts which had a good deal in common with those between the Roman peasants and the rich. The non-Roman population of Italy – especially in the south of the peninsula – had also suffered from the devastations of the war with Hannibal. On top of this came the revenge exacted by the victorious Romans from communities that had deserted the city, as, particularly, in the case of Capua. The *socii* were also required to give Rome military support: just like the Roman peasantry, they too fought in the debilitating wars of the second century BC. At the same time, the power-brokers in Rome still discriminated against them because they were non-Romans. Gaius Gracchus could recall almost incredible examples of the arrogance and caprice with which Roman officials treated the local upper strata of the various Italian communities (Gell., *Noct. Att.*,10.3.1ff.). The *socii* did not enjoy the political rights of the Roman citizen: thus, they could not look to the protection which the popular assembly afforded to the Roman proletariat. In war they lost out in the distribution of booty and the punishments to which they were subject while on military service were particularly harsh and humiliating. Italians in the cities were in a better position economically: many could find a living as craftsmen and traders. But Italians in the countryside often shared the plight of Roman peasants. The impoverished Italian peasants also flooded into Rome where they hoped to seize the opportunities available in a capital city. But they were forcibly removed from the city by the Roman authorities, for non-citizens were required to report for service in the Roman army in their own communities. The tension thus generated did not simply drive a wedge between rich and poor, for the upper strata of the *socii* were also discriminated against in this way. But the bulk of the discontented consisted of the poor rural population which was of substantial size. They strove for both political parity and the solution of their social problems.[61]

As fundamental as the tensions between the Italian allies and Roman leadership were the conflicts which arose in the provinces between the Romans and the local populations. In Rome's wars of conquest the populations of Spain, Africa, Macedonia, Greece and Asia Minor had been subjected to tremendous suffering, particularly towards the middle of the second century BC when the Romans acted with extraordinary brutality – a phase which may be considered a crisis of Roman imperialism. Cities like Carthage and Corinth were razed to the ground. Vast numbers of prisoners were massacred or sold into slavery: those who escaped through the payment of ransom could consider themselves fortunate. But the position of the provincials was often appalling even in peacetime. The governors, members of the senatorial aristocracy, and the *nouveaux riches publicani* usually regarded the provinces simply as a source of wealth to be exploited for private purposes: they behaved almost as cruelly in peace as in wartime. The consequence was resistance, which flared up repeatedly in Spain and Greece in particular. But this resistance was not the revolt of a homogeneous stratum. The provincial upper strata joined in the resistance, striving for political independence or at least for an end to unrestricted political repression. In the provinces, too, the burden of Roman rule fell mainly upon the poorer strata of the population. For them resistance seemed the only solution: they were thus its principal standard-bearers. It is significant that Viriathus, the leader of the struggle for freedom from Rome in Spain, had previously been a shepherd (Livy, *Epit.*,52). In Greece the social origins of revolts and uprisings against Rome are most clearly visible. After Rome had declared the freedom of Greece in 196 BC the upper strata were swiftly and deeply disappointed: it was they who fanned the fires of resistance. But after the Third Macedonian War the initiative passed to the lower social strata, as the upper strata became resigned to Roman rule.[62]

But there was no social group in so terrible a position in the second century BC as the slaves – in the countryside at least. Slavery became much more important in Roman society immediately after the Second Punic War. At the same time there was a sharp increase in the demand for and the supply of slaves, who constituted a profitable labour force.[63] The owners of large estates wanted large quantities of cheap labour. Peasants were not available, for they had suffered huge losses. Moreover, peasants were conscripted into the army for the best years of their lives (Plut.,*Ti.Gracchus*,8.1ff.;App., *BC*,1.29ff.). Slaves were on hand to fill the gap. Since they had no rights they could be exploited even more harshly than the peasants. Moreover, slaves did not have to be released for military service and, particularly in the decades after the Second Punic War, they were very cheap as a result of the vast numbers of prisoners of war who were enslaved. Hordes of foreign slaves flooded into Italy after each Roman campaign. A survey of the most important data provided by the sources on the numbers of prisoners enslaved in various campaigns indicates the quantity of slaves which the Roman economy had to absorb: 30,000 at Tarentum in 209 BC (Livy, 27.16.7), 8,000 in Africa in 204 BC (Livy, 29.29.3), 5,632 in Histria in 177 BC (Livy, 41.11.8), about 40,000 in Sardinia in 174 BC (Livy, 41.28.8: of 80,000 some were killed, others enslaved),150,000 in Epirus in 167 BC (Polyb., 30.15 and Livy, 45.34.5f.), and at least 50,000 at Carthage in 146 BC (App., *Lib.*, 130).[64] Slave families produced more slaves by their reproduction. But the most important source of large quantities of slaves seems to have been the slave trade in the east. These slaves were the products of wars between the Hellenistic states or of abduction. They were sent to the great slave markets, such as Delos, where, according to Strabo later (14.5.2), as many as 10,000 slaves could be sold in one day, mostly to Italy. In the second century BC the average price of a slave was perhaps about 300-500 denarii (1,200-2,000 sesterces).[65]

Thus the importance of slavery increased quickly from the turn of the third into the second century BC. As early as the comedies of Plautus and his younger contemporary Terence (who was himself a former slave from Africa), slaves appear as figures with a normal place in the social milieu at Rome, performing their various tasks. The Roman economy made great use of them in a variety of fields, though slaves did not entirely replace free labour in this or in any other period of Roman history. On the large estates of rich landowners in Italy, slaves played a great part in production. Cato recommended the use of 13 slaves to 240 iugera (60 hectares) on a normal olive plantation and 16 slaves to 100 iugera (25 hectares) on a vineyard of normal size (*Agr.*,10.1ff.). Gaius Sempronius Gracchus wrote that his brother Tiberius was encouraged to attempt reform on a journey through Etruria in 137 BC, when he saw that the peasants had totally disappeared and that the agricultural workers and herdsmen were slaves of foreign origin (Plut.,*Ti.Gracchus*, 8.4). Many slaves were employed in the mines: 40,000 worked in the Spanish silver mines near New Carthage in Polybius' day (34.9.8f.). On Cato's estate slaves were also employed in the crafts. The evidence of Plautus and of pottery stamps from the city of Cales and brick stamps from Etruria shows that there were also slaves in the urban centres among the specialist craftsmen, working beside the free and freedmen. Slaves were also to be found in the cities and in the villas of large landowners who performed intellectual functions, as for example pedagogues: there was such a pedagogue in Cato's establishment (Plut., *Cato*, 20.5). They also served as servants and in luxury areas.[66]

In a system of this sort the patriarchal characteristics of earlier Roman slavery could only disappear by and large. Slaves were not now usually part of the family unit: they had become a distinct social stratum separate from the other strata in society through their lack of rights, the harshness with which they were exploited and the contempt they suffered. A significant indication of Cato's attitude towards slaves is the fact that he counted them with the farm equipment, as if they were livestock or implements. This was an attitude articulated a century later by Varro who defined slaves as '*instrumenti genus vocale*' *(De re rustica*,1.17.1). But the slaves were by no means a homogeneous mass. On the whole, urban slaves had a happier lot than slaves on the estates and in the mines, first of all because they could not be stimulated to higher efficiency in their often specialised occupations by brutal treatment. It was precisely to encourage them to higher efficiency that they were often promised manumission. Most of the manumitted in Rome and in the other cities were former urban slaves. But there was hardly a sign of humane treatment for slaves on large estates and in the mines. Cato held his slaves under strict discipline: he had them whipped even for minor misdemeanours (Plut., *Cato*, 21.2ff.). He never left them idle, not even on feast days or in bad weather. They worked in the vineyards chained together in gangs. Sick slaves were not given a full ration of food. When slaves became unfit for work through illness or old age Cato sold them off (*Agr.*, 2.1ff., 56 and 57). He would not discuss manumission. And the sufferings of slaves were increased still further by other brutalities, even torture and crucifixion (Plaut., *Amphit.*, 280; *Mil. Glor.*, 372f.). Yet all slaves were not equally ill-treated even on the estates. Within the slave population there was a certain hierarchy ranging from the estate manager *(vilicus)* through overseer and specialised labour to the simple agricultural chain gangs. But by and large the treatment of slaves in the later Republic was worse than ever it was either earlier or later in Roman history.

The unrestricted exploitation of hordes of slaves, who could be replaced time and again through trade and new prisoners of war, led, under these particularly brutal conditions, to conflicts in which the most powerful and strongest in society were ranged against the most severely repressed. The hatred felt by slaves who had in many cases been free, independent citizens before their capture could not remain hidden from their masters. Cato took great trouble to sow seeds of division among his slaves, for he feared their unanimity (Plut., *Cato*, 21.4). Of course, given the might of the Roman state, slaves had very little scope for resistance against their masters. Disobedience was punished promptly and very harshly. It was difficult to escape from an estate and escapes were rarely successful in the end. The fact that Plautus and Cato (*Agr.*, 2.2) mention slave escapes is only evidence of the hopeless fate of those who made the attempt. Still more difficult was open revolt against their masters. Quite apart from the fact that slaves on many estates were closely supervised and chained there were scant opportunities for the communication necessary for the preparation of revolt. Such opportunities were available in the cities, but the position of urban slaves was better and they had little cause to revolt. There was only one group of slaves in a position to launch armed uprising, apart from special groups of slaves such as the gladiators who later followed Spartacus. That group was the shepherds. They were not kept under such strict control as estate labourers, nor could their freedom of movement be closely restricted. At the same time, they were discontented with their lot through ill-treatment and harsh working conditions to the same extent as the slaves of the olive plantations and vineyards. There is no explicit evidence as to whether a *coniuratio servorum* in Etruria in 198 BC was precipitated by shepherds, but an entire Roman legion had to be sent against it (Livy, 33.36.1ff.). But in 185/4 BC there was a *magnus motus servilis* which generated guerrilla warfare in Apulia and ended with the condemnation of 7,000 participants. According to Livy this was a *pastorum coniuratio* (39.29.8f. and 39.41.6f.). The road that led to the great Sicilian slave revolts was thus marked out.

The Road to the Crisis

Our survey of the various strata of Roman society from the Second Punic War to the Gracchan period makes it clear that the swift change in social and economic structures that occurred in this short period brought about more than a restructuring whereby particular social strata were markedly strengthened, while others were weakened and yet others created. The change in the history of each particular social stratum gave rise to or heightened social tensions and conflicts. Conflicts between leading families of the nobility were no longer simply harmless rivalries between particular families within an aristocratic system of government. Antagonism between the nobility and social climbers in the Senate and between the oligarchy and the *nouveaux riches* of the equestrian order generated further conflicts within the leading strata. The impoverishment of the Roman peasantry and the formation of proletarian masses in Rome added more very dangerous material for conflict and at the same time a massive base for attempts at revolt. The situation was further complicated by tensions between the rulers in Rome and their Italian allies and between the beneficiaries of Roman rule and the downtrodden provincials, tensions which were often not only politically but socially motivated. Finally, the hatred felt by the hordes of slaves for their masters constituted a threat to the whole Roman system of government. Rome became an Empire within a very short time, but the change was too quick for Roman society. The splendid victories of the Roman armies in east and west could not obscure the fact that a crisis was brewing at the very heart of Roman society which threatened to subvert all her successes. Yet the first danger signs did not reveal the wide-ranging nature of the crisis to come – the conflict between the Scipiones and the rest of the nobility, the weakness of Rome in the Spanish wars of the mid second century BC, the ever-simmering resistance to Rome among the masses in Greece and the revolt of the shepherds in Apulia. But they did show that a series of new problems had come into being and that the situation was now completely different from the decisive phase of confrontation between patricians and plebeians in the mid fourth century BC.

The situation was further aggravated by the fact that the social structure was only slightly flexible in part. Members of a few social strata had opportunities for social mobility. Urban slaves were often manumitted; freedmen could advance into the strata of craftsmen and traders. Merchants and entrepreneurs could accumulate large fortunes and advance into the *equites*, the second order in Roman society. Wealthy *equites* could obtain senatorial appointments and thus enter the senatorial aristocracy as *homines novi*. This did not mean that these strata were untouched by social conflict, though it is significant that they remained most at peace when serious outbreaks flared up in the 130s. Urban slaves did not usually join in the revolts of the countryside; traders and craftsmen did not usually form revolutionary conspiracies and the politicisation of the *equites* was still limited. But social mobility was confined to urban society and, even in the cities, to strata able to benefit from craft production, trade and financial dealings. The situation in the countryside was quite different, as was that of the proletarian masses at Rome who had no part in economic production. For slaves on estates and in the mines there was hardly any prospect of manumission. For the impoverished Roman peasantry and proletariat there was hardly any prospect of a better standard of living. For the Italian masses and the provincials there was hardly any prospect of equality with Romans through the attainment of citizenship. At the same time, the nobility was unwilling to admit ordinary senators and *novi homines* to high office and real power. In this respect too the situation on the eve of the great changes that came with the Gracchi was very different from that obtaining in the mid fourth century BC. In the latter period the gates to power lay wide open to 'new men' in Roman society. They were not at all so in the second century BC. The great masses were denied social elevation, a better economic position and political parity.

The final major change was that from the second century BC Roman society no longer had the unbreakable bonds that might have held together the opposed social strata. In the past these bonds had been created by the stable political system – the senatorial magistracies, the Senate and the popular assembly, which could guarantee the unrestricted rule of the aristocracy, whose position was further buttressed by its alliance with the peasantry, in foreign policy at least. The unity of Roman society had previously been guaranteed by norms founded on a religion and morality created by a tradition-conscious aristocracy. These determined the behaviour pattern of the citizen masses and, of course, of the aristocracy in accordance with the rules of the *mos maiorum*. After the Second Punic War and in the period of Mediterranean expansion that followed, these bonds were considerably weakened. Rupture threatened. Since the aristocracy no longer enjoyed the support of the mass of the peasantry as it had done in the First and Second Punic Wars, the old political system had been destabilised – '*coepere nobilitas dignitatem, populus libertatem in lubidinem vortere, sibi quisque ducere, trahere, rapere*' (Sall., *Bell.Jug.*,41.5). At the same time, the age of expansion had made the old political system an anachronism. It was still a system of rule and government designed originally for the city-state. This system, hardly changed, was called upon to hold together a world power – an impossibility in the long term. Its inadequacy was revealed most clearly by the administration of the provinces, which was in fact not administration at all – it was exploitation.

At the same time, the ideological foundations of the Roman state were also under attack. It was not only Hannibal who took belated revenge upon Rome. There were also the Greeks. Roman expansion and, in particular, the intellectual influence of defeated Greece inevitably broke down the old norms. 'The very people who had easily endured hardships, dangers and uncertain and difficult situations now found that leisure and wealth – desirable at any other time – became burdensome and destructive. The love of money grew first: the love of power followed. This was, so to speak, the root of all evil. Greed undermined loyalty, honesty and the other virtues. In their place it taught arrogance, cruelty, disregard for the gods and the view that everything was for sale' (Sall., *Cat.*, 10.2ff.). The old Roman value system – duty, loyalty, justice and generosity – which had come into being under the conditions of an archaic social order, could only appear out-dated at a time when Rome was becoming a world power and Roman society was being significantly restructured. At the same time, in conquered lands – especially in Greece – Rome encountered religious and philosophical ideas whose tenets often contradicted the *mos maiorum*. In this changed society the *mos maiorum* meant virtually nothing from the first for most strata in society – the many business-minded *nouveaux riches*, the despairing proletariat, the oppressed populations of Italy and the provinces and, above all, the slaves, many of whom were of foreign origin, pressed into obedience by the Romans. But the actual 'revenge of the conquered' resided in the fact that Greek philosophy, the intellectual innovation so very dangerous for Rome, found most favour precisely in the social strata which should have been the guardian of the *mos maiorum* – the aristocracy with its various groupings, especially the Scipionic circle. A degree of education and experience of the world were required to open the mind to such intellectual influences: these were only to be found within the aristocracy. Enlightened aristocrats did not consider Greek philosophy to be an ideological danger in any way: they saw it, rather, as an opportunity for the legitimation of claims to world rule and of their own pre-eminence in society through an ideological system adequate for the new age. But the effect of these influences was the disturbance of the traditional order of Roman society.

The social conflicts which had brought about the end of the archaic social system in Rome could be solved through the reforms of the Licinian–Sextian laws. The situation was now quite different. In the past, expansion in Italy had made it possible for social problems of the lower strata to be resolved at the expense of others. Now Mediterranean expansion had become a source of social tensions in Roman society. In the past, the common interests of the aristocracy and the various groups within the *plebs* had made the influential well disposed towards reform. Now the rulers were not prepared to countenance reforms in favour of the disadvantaged and repressed strata in society. No single attempt was made to resolve Rome's grave social problems – for example, through the improvement of the position of the slaves or through the integration of the Italians into the political system: such an attempt would have conflicted with the interests of the ruling social strata. Other problems were recognised and a few attempts were made to deal with them. But by and large these attempts only sought to return to earlier conditions. Such a return was impossible under the given economic, social and political circumstances. These attempts lacked impetus and were not carried through, yet they had unforeseen, fatal consequences.

There is nothing more indicative of the myopia of many influential men in the Roman elite in the second century BC than the outlook of Marcus Porcius Cato. On the one hand, he strove with all his might to re-direct the leading strata towards new economic methods – large estates and slave production, investment and profit-making. But, on the other hand, he clung on to the old Roman virtues – frugality and moderate living in particular – and regarded Greek philosophy as incompatible with Roman ideals. He regarded the other achievements of the Greek mind, such as scientific medicine, in the same light. Given an outlook as contradictory as this, the solution of even only a few of the problems of Roman society through reforming legislation was impossible. Legal measures designed merely to hinder the process of social development misfired. A senatorial decree of 186 BC against the cult of Bacchus in Rome and Italy succeeded in checking this orgiastic cult, but it could not succeed in halting the decline of the *mos maiorum* as the system of reference of Roman society. The measures taken by Cato in his famous censorship of 184 BC against luxury were as irrelevant to the real problems as were the laws passed against high living in the second century BC. The *lex Villia Annalis* of 180 BC sought to prevent the sudden rise of particular outstanding personalities from within the oligarchy through regulation of the senatorial career structure. The elder Scipio was the sort of personality at issue: only a generation later the law was ignored by Scipio Aemilianus. The memory of the Licinian Sextian laws was similarly useless as a protection for the peasantry against the large landowners, for no one observed them. Gaius Laelius (*consul*, 140 BC), who mooted significant measures of reform to the benefit of the poor, did not venture to introduce any of them (Plut.,*Ti.Gracchus*, 8.7). Before the Gracchan crisis only one law of the second century had any far-reaching consequences – and that unintentionally. Under the *lex Calpurnia* of 149 BC standing commissions were set up to investigate the excesses of Roman magistrates: this was thus a law for the protection of the provincials. Yet, while these commissions of inquiry by no means put an end to violence and extortion in the provinces, they did provide a suitable stage for the intrigue and internal struggles within the dominant strata: they thus undermined further the existing order.

Roman society was therefore heading relentlessly towards a crisis which was to be settled in the end only by violence. But this use of violence came about in accordance with the laws generated by the structure of the crisis. A general, more or less homogeneous revolutionary uprising was an impossibility: the nature of the various conflicts differed through the multiplicity of social and political problems; the interests of the various strata were different and so too were the various connections between particular groups and strata. Rather, the structure of the crisis dictated that the struggle be fought out in a series of bloody social and political conflicts, which were not interrelated from the first. In the end these conflicts only achieved the destruction of the outdated political framework of the

social system, namely the Republic: they emended the social structure but they did not bring about fundamental change. The slave
revolts were genuine social movements, but they pursued aims
which were discordant with the interests of other disadvantaged
social strata, even those of the urban slaves. They were therefore
condemned to failure. The oppressed provincials identified their
enemy as Roman rule itself, but they could only rise against it with
foreign support. The Greeks did just this with the support of Mithridates, but even then without lasting success, because the upper
strata of the provincials had increasingly become the upholders of
Roman rule. The only such revolt to achieve success was that of the
Italians. But that revolt did not destroy Roman rule: it only made it
stronger still through the integration of the upper strata of the Italians into the leading orders of Roman society. The decisive conflicts
were fought out between the various leaders of well-organised, self-
confident, armed followings: between the oligarchy which
depended upon its position of power and its connections with a wide
body of support, and individual nobles (with their own particular
aims), who emerged as spokesmen for the proletarian masses whom
they knew to be on their side, just like mighty armies. These conflicts alone could change the very foundations of the existing social
system. But even the 'progressives' strove against the oligarchy, at
best, only to put right the existing social system: their aim was not
its abolition. The grounds of the armed conflicts that followed
shifted from the problems of society ever further towards the quest
for political power. In the resulting civil wars social strata and groupings were no longer ranged against each other. The camps were composed of political groupings and regular armies under the command
of leading individual politicians. Their achievement was the
downfall of the Republican state: '*res publica, quae media fuerat,
dilacerata*' (Sall., *Bell.Jug.*, 41.5).

4 THE CRISIS OF THE REPUBLIC AND ROMAN SOCIETY

Conflicts in Roman Society during the Late Republic

The crisis precipitated by the sudden change in the structure of Roman society after the Second Punic War reached a phase after the mid second century in which the eruption of more open conflicts was inevitable. The social and political conflicts which suddenly flared up were the results of the intensification of polarities within the structure of Roman society and of the ever more apparent weaknesses of the Republican system of government. The history of the last century of the Roman Republic – from the First Sicilian Slave Revolt of 135 BC and the first tribunate of Tiberius Sempronius Gracchus in 133 BC down to the end of the civil wars in 30 BC – was overshadowed by the repeated eruption of intense, brutal and bloody conflicts. Accordingly this period of some hundred years of Roman history is generally described as the 'period of revolution', a formulation wherein the concept of 'revolution' has been applied to the different manifestations and different phases of these conflicts by scholars from Th. Mommsen to R. Syme.[67] It is of course obvious that the concept of revolution cannot be used as a characterisation of these conflicts in the same sense as it is used in modern history after the English and, especially, the French Revolution: the social and political movements of the Late Republic neither strove for nor brought about violent change in the existing Roman social system. Moreover, these movements varied so much in their causes, their supporters, their histories and their effects that they can only be brought under a single conceptual heading to a limited extent. To ensure that our terminology does not mislead it seems better to replace 'the Roman revolution' with 'the social and political crisis of the Republic which manifested itself in open, violent conflicts'.[68]

The heterogeneous nature of these conflicts is apparent from their typology and from the fluctuation in their whole character during the last hundred years of the Republic.[69] By and large the open conflicts of this period can be divided into four principal types, though it is not always possible to draw clear distinctions. Three of these are the following: the slave wars, the resistance of the provincials against Roman rule and the struggle of the Italians against Rome. In the case of the slave wars the battle lines were clearly drawn: the rural slaves, above all, faced the slave-owners and the apparatus of the Roman state which protected them. But resistance to Roman rule by provincials and Italians cannot be conceived as opposition by broadly homogeneous social strata. Very different social groupings were involved. Moreover, their objective was not the emancipation of an oppressed social stratum: rather, they sought to win the freedom of once independent communities, states and peoples from the oppression of the Roman state. But they were not without a social aspect, for it was often the lower strata in the population that mounted the fiercest opposition against Rome. The fourth principal type of conflict is the most important: the struggles of the late Republic, which for the most part occurred within the Roman citizen body between different interest groups. At first, particularly in the Gracchan period, social causes were pre-eminent or at least important in these conflicts. The (or at least, a) central objective of one camp, namely the reformist politicians and their supporters, was precisely the solution of the social problems of the proletarian masses of Rome in the face of opposition from the other camp, the oligarchy with its equally broad support. These two interest groups were labelled, in the prevailing terminology of the late Republic from the beginning of the first century BC, as *populares* and *optimates*. From the start, these conflicts were played out as political disputes which were at first conducted, by and large, within the framework of political institutions and through the political medium of the popular assembly; they concerned political power in the state from the beginning. In these conflicts the battle lines between social fronts were not clearly drawn and the social heterogeneity of the two opposing groups increased steadily as time passed. Moreover, the social substance of the conflicts between *optimates* and *populares* was thrust ever further into the background, while the quest for political power became ever more important until, finally, the issue became simply the predominance of particular political groupings and, especially, of their leaders. It was with the struggle between the Marians and Sullans in the 80s BC that the issue of political power finally came to the fore in the disputes between the various warring interest groups, whose composition changed constantly and quickly.

The old conflicts ebbed away in the 80s and 70s BC. In the Social War of 91-89 BC the Italians achieved their objective, Roman citizenship. With Sulla's defeat of Mithridates in 85 BC opposition to Rome in Greece and Asia Minor came to an end. And with the bloody suppression of the rebellion of Spartacus in 71 BC the great slave wars also came to a close. In the subsequent 40 years the issue was simply power in the state – that is, whether power should be exercised by the oligarchy or by an autocrat and, if the latter, which politician should be that autocrat. The final consequence of these conflicts was therefore not a change in the structure of Roman society, but in the form of the state supported by it.

Uprisings of Slaves, Provincials and Italians

The slave revolts of the Late Republic deserve special attention: at no time in the course of the whole of ancient history was the antithesis between slaves and their masters expressed to the same degree or with the same ferocity as in the last third of the second century and the first third of the first century BC, the period which began with the First Sicilian Slave Revolt and ended with the rebellion of Spartacus.[70] These revolts came as a complete surprise to Roman society. No one saw the danger which the first revolt on Sicily posed for Rome (Diod., 34/35.2.25). The uprising of Spartacus was at first ridiculed at Rome as a gladiatorial spectacle (App., *BC*, 1.549). Of course it was no accident that all these great revolts were played out in the short space of time from 135 to 71 BC. Diodorus set out the reasons clearly in his account of the background of the First Sicilian Slave Revolt (34/35.2.1ff. and 2.27ff.). They were the products of the development of Roman slavery after the Second Punic War. The importance of slavery in the Roman economy had increased massively, as had the numbers of slaves, within a short time. The masses of slaves were brutally exploited and appallingly mistreated, especially on the estates: slaves could easily be replaced, thanks to warfare, the slave trade and abduction. The slaves were thus very deeply embittered. At the same time masters were careless in controlling their slaves, among whom were many intelligent and educated men who had once been free citizens in Hellenistic states. Before the mid second century and after the mid first century BC the conditions for mass slave revolts did not coincide so markedly. The consequences were inevitable. Of course, there was no uniform revolutionary movement. The circumstances were not right for such a movement. Most important, there was no uniform revolutionary ideology. Moreover, opportunities for communication between slaves in different parts of the Roman world were very limited. Further, the interests and objectives of the various slave groupings were often very different. Thus, besides the slaves in revolt – especially in the cities – there were always many others who sought to gain their freedom by legal manumission, not revolt (Diod., 36.4.8). Political objectives ranged from the establishment of an independent state within the Roman world to the repatriation of slaves to their erstwhile homelands outside the imperial frontiers. For these reasons slave revolts could only flare up in virtual isolation in time and space.

The first slave war took place in Sicily in 135-132 BC.[71] It was begun by relatively small groupings of particularly badly mistreated slaves, including armed herdsmen, who formed uncontrolled bands of brigands. They captured the city of Enna by surprise and made their leader – the Syrian prophet and wonder-worker Eunus – their king. When they had joined forces with the slaves in revolt under the leadership of Cleon, a Cilician, the followers of Eunus amounted, we are told, to 200,000 men. At first they achieved remarkable success; they could only be put down after quite a lengthy war. The uprising found an echo among slaves at Rome, Sinuessa and Minturnae, in the mines at Laurium in Attica and among the slaves on Delos (Diod., 34/35.2.19). At almost the same time, in 133-129 BC, the revolt of Aristonicus flared up in western Asia Minor. Upon the death of the last king of Pergamum, Aristonicus, the illegitimate son of the penultimate ruler, laid claim to rule the state of Pergamum which had been bequeathed to the Romans. Since the cities remained loyal to Rome, he mobilised the slaves and the poor peasantry. He could only be beaten after a long and bloody war.

The next wave of revolts came some 25 years later. Revolt broke out first in southern Italy, in Nuceria and Capua, where there was unrest among the slaves. Another revolt began when a Roman *eques*, Titus Vettius, armed his slaves against his creditors (Diod., 36.2.1ff.). This last case, which had its roots in a romance between the *eques* and a female slave, indicates, as clearly as the arming of Sicilian herdsmen by their masters three decades earlier, the incredible irresponsibility of slave-owners. Immediately after these revolts the second great Sicilian slave uprising occurred in 104-101 BC. Its cause is typical of another aspect of the attitudes of Roman *domini*. In the context of a crisis in Roman foreign affairs, the Cimbric Wars, the Senate passed a decree that the abducted and enslaved citizens of states allied to Rome should be set free. But slave-owners on Sicily sabotaged the implementation of this decree. Thereupon the island was consumed by another slave war which was in many respects a re-enactment of the first. The uprising was begun by two groups of slaves with Salvius, a Syrian, and Athenaeus, a Cilician, at their respective heads. Salvius was a prophet as Eunus had been in his time; and Salvius too was made king. The number of their followers had grown to at least 30,000 and a hard war was once more required before Rome gained control of the situation in Sicily.

The uprising most dangerous for Rome broke out a generation later – the rebellion in Italy led by the Thracian gladiator Spartacus from 74 to 71BC. It began with a conspiracy of gladiators at Capua. They had no communication difficulties and ready access to arms. After initial successes the number of Spartacus' followers rose, it is said, to 120,000 men. Their rebellion was only put down after a long war during which Rome experienced defeat as well as victory. To achieve final victory the Romans had to send no fewer than eight legions against the slaves, under the command of Marcus Licinius Crassus.

Although the various slave uprisings differed from each other in many ways, they shared a series of common structural features which clearly reflect the nature of these conflicts. The uprisings began with various, relatively small groups of slaves. Being herdsmen or gladiators they were difficult to control and had arms at their disposal. After initial successes, due largely to the element of surprise, these revolts grew very quickly into mass movements as thousands of fugitive slaves streamed into the camp of the rebels. The majority of the rebels were slaves from the estates - thus, they were those slaves who had received particularly bad treatment. Groups of the poor peasantry also joined the rebels, as in the case of Aristonicus and also in that of Salvius (Diod., 36.11.1f.) and Spartacus (App., *BC*, 1.540). On the other hand, the cities were hostile both to Aristonicus and to Spartacus. The urban free poor gave almost no support to the slaves: they looked to their own interests (Diod., 36.3). Even the slaves of the cities conspicuously failed to make outright common cause with the rebels (Diod., 36.4.8). But even without this support the rebel masses achieved remarkable successes. They quickly organised themselves under suitable leaders whose authority was generally acknowledged, because of their organisational and military abilities and also because of their sacral charisma. On Sicily and at Pergamum at least they aimed as high as the creation of their own state on the Hellenistic model with a king at its head. In these cases they also developed the rudiments of a theoretical base for their own state entity which drew its religious content from the Hellenistic east:[72] this was the homeland of many slaves. But nothing was further from their minds than radical change in the ancient social system. Their objective was either the foundation of their own slave holding state with roles reversed or, as in the case of Spartacus, to break out of Italy and make for Gaul and Thrace, the homelands of many slaves. Accordingly the rebels did not reject slavery as an institution: rather, they merely turned the tables and treated their erstwhile masters as slaves by, for example, putting them to work in chains in workshops producing arms (Diod., 34/35.2.15). That is why these uprisings were not of a sort to change the structure of Roman society. Moreover, they lacked the necessary support from other groups in that society, they lacked a coherent revolutionary organisation and they lacked a positive revolutionary programme: these shortcomings condemned them to failure. Their methods of struggle were as cruel as the methods of their opponents, yet their heroism was recognised even by leading Romans. But its fate was sealed from the first.

Accordingly, the historical consequences of the slave wars for the subsequent history of Rome were not of very great importance. It has been argued that the Principate was created in the interests of the slave-holders in order to prevent a repetition of the Sicilian slave revolts and the rebellion of Spartacus through its strong system of government.[73] But that is to misconceive the importance of the slave wars and also of the other conflicts in Roman society during the Late Republic. Perhaps the most important consequence of the great slave revolts was that they made the slave-owners understand for the first time that brutal treatment and ruthless exploitation were not viable means of maintaining a slave economy, for reasons that were political as well as economic. The fact that there were no great slave revolts in the last 40 years of the Republic, when the Roman system of government was shaken more than once, indicates how the position of the slaves slowly improved after the rebellion of Spartacus. Of course, many slaves were ready to ally themselves with politicians who proffered them freedom and prosperity. Slaves were amongst those who streamed into the camp of the political adventurer Lucius Sergius Catilina (Sall., *Cat.*, 56.5). Many thousands of fugitive slaves supported Sextus Pompeius with the result that the emperor Augustus could describe the war against Sextus as a *bellum servorum* (*Res Gestae*, 25).[74] But in these conflicts the main concern was no longer the relief of the plight of the slaves: it was now the solution of political problems. Slaves were now no more than a means to an end. Thus, in the final analysis, the effects of the slave revolts on Roman society were no different from those of all the other conflicts of the Late Republic: they brought about an adjustment in the Roman social system, but not fundamental change.

Effects somewhat similar to those of the slave wars resulted from the clashes between the oppressed provincials and the beneficiaries of Roman rule. Of course, as with the slave revolts, conflicts of this type could rarely develop into great uprisings and then only through the coincidence of a variety of factors. Moreover, the multiplicity of social and political circumstances in the various parts of the Roman Empire meant that these revolts were even less coherent than the slave rebellions. The uprising of Aristonicus shows that provincial opposition could be closely allied with a slave rebellion: Aristonicus' uprising was at once a slave rebellion and the revolt of the poor rural strata of the population of western Asia Minor for whom foreign oppression was especially burdensome. It is significant that this uprising occurred at a time when Rome was only beginning to establish firmly her system of government in western Asia Minor and that its leader based his claim to rule on his royal descent. Four decades after the defeat of Aristonicus there was another mass revolt against Rome in western Asia Minor and also in Greece . It could only break out with foreign support: Mithridates, king of Pontus, attacked the Roman sphere of supremacy at a time when the Roman state was embroiled in civil war and thus vulnerable. In 88 BC, at the king's command and under the protection of his troops, 80,000 Romans and Italians were killed in western Asia Minor by the rebellious provincials. The revolt against Rome now spread to Greece and to Athens in particular. The rebels were drawn mostly from the lower social strata of the free population, whose hatred was directed principally at the merchants, entrepreneurs and tax-collectors of the equestrian order.[75]

Of course, in consequence, movements of this type did not bring about a structural change in the Roman social system, for they were not concerned with changing this social system from inside but with shaking off the rule of the Roman state. They failed, as did the slave uprisings. Aristonicus died in 129 BC in a prison at Rome. Athens surrendered to the troops of Sulla in 86 BC after a lengthy siege. In the long term these conflicts ushered in the gradual alleviation of the brutal oppression of the provinces and the realisation that the local upper strata, who had for the most part remained loyal to Rome, could be incorporated in the Roman system of government through grants of citizenship and other privileges to be pillars of the social and political order of the Roman state.

There was a social as well as a political basis to the opposition of the Italian *socii* to the leaders of Roman society, a conflict which could have been especially dangerous to Rome. Rome's Italian allies had been ever more ill-used and discriminated against from the end of the Second Punic War. From the middle of the second century BC relations between the Romans and the Italians became particularly fraught. The arbitrary behaviour of the officers of the Roman state challenged the upper strata of the population of the *socii* most strongly, while the lower strata – especially the masses of the poor peasantry – suffered from political as well as from economic oppression. As early as 125 BC these growing tensions precipitated an uprising which broke out at Fregellae (Livy, *Epit.*,60; Plut.,*C.Gracchus*,3.1) after the *consul* Marcus Fulvius Flaccus had striven in vain for the expansion of the citizenship. Thereafter the Italian problem had a place in the political battle at Rome between *optimates* and *populares*. After Gaius Sempronius Gracchus and Lucius Appuleius Saturninus had attempted reform and the programme of reforms advocated by the tribune Marcus Livius Drusus had failed against the opposition of the oligarchy, the hostility of the Italian allies manifested itself in a great uprising against Rome (*bellum sociale*), which from 91 to 89 BC turned almost the whole of Italy into a battle ground (App.,*BC*, 1.69ff.).

The uprising was not a movement aimed at social revolution, for the rebels included the Italian upper strata and were primarily concerned with the attainment of Roman citizenship (Vell. Pat., 2.15).[76] Yet the masses of the Italian population, the *ingens totius Italiae coetus* (Seneca., *De brev.vit.*,6.1), were also concerned with the solution of social problems. The treatment meted out by the Italians to their defeated enemies in conquered Roman colonies is significant. Romans from the upper strata were killed, while members of the lower strata and slaves were enrolled in the rebel armies (App.,*BC*, 1.186 and 190). Rome eventually succeeded in putting down the rebellion but only after Roman citizenship had been extended, under the *lex Julia* of 90 BC, to all Italians who had remained loyal to Rome and, under the *lex Plautia Papiria* of 89 BC, to all rebels who gave themselves up. Where the slaves and provincials had failed, the Italians thus managed to achieve their own particular objective. But this did not generate a change in the Roman social system. The social distinctions which had previously existed within the society of the *socii* were not removed, nor were the distinctions which pervaded the Roman social order. Rather the existing social order was reinforced as the Italian upper strata became beneficiaries of Roman rule with equal rights. But all conflicts were not ended at a stroke. The new Italian citizens had become members of the popular assembly but there they were discriminated against, for, at first, they were only registered in eight electoral tribes, and many were persecuted and killed by oligarchic reactionaries in the civil wars of Sulla and the Marians. But the ban had been broken: when the population of northern Italy received citizenship in 49 BC, the heart of the *imperium Romanum* was no longer only Rome with her colonies, but *tota Italia* (cf. *Res Gestae*, 25).

The Principal Conflicts of the Late Republic and Their Social Context

The conflicts of the Late Republic most important for the history of Roman society were fought out between political groupings within the Roman citizen body, beginning with the Gracchi and ending with the civil wars of the failing Republic. Appian, who described the history of these conflicts in great detail and with a sharper eye for social context than other ancient historians, clearly stresses the steady increase in the seriousness of these conflicts during the last hundred years of the Republic. They began with the murder of Tiberius Sempronius Gracchus, with the first bloodshed in the assembly at Rome which prefaced recurrent clashes which were ever more frequently armed (App., *BC*, 1.4f.). These clashes grew into outright civil war which finally ended with the creation of a monarchy (App., *BC*, 1.6ff. and 269ff.). This chain of armed conflicts exhibits a series of common structural features which are extremely instructive. Their catalysts, the composition of the opposing camps, the origin and role of the leaders of the participating masses, the programme they championed, the nature of the settlement of the conflicts, the reaction they generated and, finally, the effect of particular conflicts display many recurrent features which exhibit quite clearly the problems, power structure and future options of Roman society in the Late Republic. At the same time, the equally clear differences between the various conflicts allow us to trace the progressive displacement of social issues by political issues in these disputes. As a result of this displacement the chain of conflicts changed only the political framework of the Roman social order, not the order itself.[77]

As with the other social and political conflicts of the Late Republic, the causes of the clashes within the Roman citizen body lay in the structural change that occurred in Roman society from the time of Hannibal, a change which generated new tensions within that body. Of course, given the heterogeneous social composition of the Roman citizen body, the nature of these tensions was far more complex than that of the tensions between masters and slaves, Romans and Italians and Romans and provincials. The former tensions lay within the senatorial aristocracy, particularly between the various groupings inside the ruling nobility supported by the masses of their clients, between the senatorial aristocracy and the newly created equestrian order with rich entrepreneurs and contractors in its ranks, and between the rulers of the Roman state and the proletariat cooped up in Rome, between rich estate-owners and poor peasants. In the 130s these tensions reached such an alarming pitch that some aristocrats were induced to attempt reform. Significantly, the attempt only began when reform seemed necessary in the interests of the aristocratic state. At issue was the agrarian question, for the impoverishment of the many peasants threatened the continuing recruitment of the Roman army and thus the maintenance of the Roman system of government (App., BC, 1.43ff.). Moreover, the most apparent political threat was presented by the dissatisfaction of the proletarian masses who had streamed into Rome and took part in the popular assembly. It is also significant that the agrarian question was not to be solved by a peaceful reform, that the failure of the first attempt at reform aggravated other social tensions and that the dispute over social issues immediately generated a conflict between political interest groups.

The first open conflict within the Roman citizen body broke out in 133 BC.[78] The tribune Tiberius Sempronius Gracchus, a descendant of the elder Scipio Africanus on his mother's side and brother-in-law of Scipio Aemilianus, was prompted by his concern for the need to provide recruits for the Roman army to pass an agrarian law in the assembly against the most fierce resistance from the Senate, a law which was designed to restore the Roman peasantry. The old Licinian–Sextian legislation was recalled: no one could hold more than 500 iugera of land (in larger families, up to 1000 iugera) on the *ager publicus*, though, at the same time, these plots of land became the property of their present occupants. This limitation of land-holding released land which could now be distributed among the poor in plots of some 30 iugera. But this land was to remain the property of the state, as was made clear by a peppercorn rent, so that it would not be bought up by rich estate-owners. A commission of three men was put in charge of the implementation of the reform: Tiberius, his father-in-law Appius Claudius Pulcher and his younger brother Gaius Sempronius Gracchus. And the commission set about its work: in the following years many peasants were provided with land. But the opposition of the rich, depicted so vividly by Appian (BC, 1.38ff.), was stronger than expected. When Tiberius Sempronius Gracchus sought to stand for election to the tribunate of the next year in order to protect himself against the indictment he expected, his enemies staged a riot in which Tiberius and many of his supporters were killed. Yet the new commission was able to continue distributing land until 129 BC and could thus claim partial success in realising the programme of reform. But, for all that, the actual objective of Tiberius Sempronius Gracchus was not achieved.

The failure of the first attempt at radical reform did not prevent the recurrence of similar attempts. Nor did the memory of the sad fate of Tiberius stand in the way of recurrent measures of bloody repression. Rather, in many respects, a model had been created for future attempts at reform and for their repression. At the same time, the figure of Tiberius Sempronius Gracchus – and later that of his younger brother Gaius – became for the poor a symbol of enlightened reform in the interests of the people, of 'popular' politics. For the champions of the privileges of the oligarchy, on the other hand, Tiberius became the paradigm of the troublemaker. In accordance with their moral evaluation of their own social position they were soon termed *optimates*. In the following decades there was a periodical recurrence of episodes similar to the affair of Tiberius Sempronius Gracchus, repeatedly interrupted by periods of restored oligarchy, until, after the tribunate of Marcus Livius Drusus in 91 BC, they graduated into civil wars.

The second stage of the conflict began with the tribunate of Gaius Sempronius Gracchus in 123 and 122 BC, after the work of the agrarian commission had been halted in 129 BC and after Marcus Fulvius Flaccus' attempt at reform in favour of the Italians had failed in 125 BC. Gaius had a much broader programme of reform than his elder brother. This programme was embodied in no less than 17 new laws. In order to protect himself and his followers from the violence of the oligarchic magistrates Gaius had a law passed under which a Roman citizen could only be condemned to death by the people. In order to extend his support he renewed the tax contracts of the equestrian *publicani* in the province of Asia: the latter thus received a free hand in the exploitation of that province. He also transferred to the *equites* the right of inquiry into instances of maladministration, that is, of trying in court guilty senators, especially senatorial provincial governors. This reform proved to be of the greatest consequence, for it meant the politicisation of the equestrian order and its entry into the conflict from a position which inevitably brought about trouble with the Senate. Gaius Sempronius Gracchus' measure by which the people were permitted to buy grain at a reduced price also had a long-term effect. And his measures for the improvement of the Italian road system and for the provision of granaries improved the position of the urban *plebs* in particular. But rather less effective was the heart of his reforms, namely the improvement of the position of the peasantry, including the rural masses of the Italian allies. The implementation of the agrarian reform of Tiberius Sempronius Gracchus was resumed with measured success: as a result of the shortage of land in central Italy Gaius sought to provide for the landless masses by colonisation in Africa, but failed. He also failed in his attempt to gain Roman citizenship for the Latins and at least the right to vote in the assembly at Rome for the *socii*. As with Tiberius Sempronius Gracchus' earlier attempt at reform, Gaius' programme galvanised reaction – it was unpopular with many Roman citizens precisely because of the benefits which were to be bestowed upon the Italians. In 121 BC Gaius Sempronius Gracchus and his supporters met violent deaths. The implementation of agrarian reform was continued, albeit half-heartedly, until in 111 BC a new *lex agraria* abolished the regulation on rents introduced by Tiberius Sempronius Gracchus: with this was lost the main objective of his programme of reform – to secure the economic survival of the peasantry by protecting their parcels of land against purchase by the rich.

After the death of Gaius Sempronius Gracchus it was roughly two decades before open conflict again broke out, stimulated by the fact that Gaius Marius, a *homo novus* hostile to the nobility, was *consul* each year from 104 to 100 BC. But the tribune of 103 and 100 BC, Lucius Appuleius Saturninus, was the actual leader of the reformers, not he. The programme of the reformers had much in common with that of the Gracchi, whom the *populares* consciously followed. Their use of the tribunate and the popular assembly as vehicles of reform was founded upon the Gracchan model. The 'popular' themes of their policy were, as before, the solution of the agrarian question, the distribution of grain to the poor and measures in favour of the Italian allies. However, the agrarian question was now new to its very core. In the serious political disputes of 103 and 100 BC the principal issue was the provision of land for Marius' veterans, land to be provided by colonisation in the provinces: since many of these veterans had no property at all new smallholdings had to be created, yet Italy could no longer satisfy the need. Another new feature was that the *populares* too had now to resort to demagogy and violence from the first, thus placing their natural allies, the equestrian order, on the side of senatorial reaction. In 100 BC, as before in 121 BC against Gaius Sempronius Gracchus and his supporters, a public emergency was declared. As *consul*, Gaius Marius had to deal with it and thus take action against his own side. The murder of Saturninus and his followers proved to be the final scene in a chain of recurrent acts of violence.[79]

But the far-reaching consequences of Marius' most important measure were not yet visible. This was the reform of the army which he carried out during his campaigns. Hitherto the Roman army had been recruited from peasant smallholders who provided their own equipment. By contrast, Marius filled the ranks of the army with unpropertied proletarians (*capite censi*) whose equipment was provided by the state. This form of recruitment was not completely new: in time of crisis the unpropertied had been called upon before. Nor did Marius' reform put a total end to recruitment from the *census* classes of the propertied. Nevertheless, Marius' reform brought a torrent of unpropertied citizens into the army: its consequences were crucial to the history of the Late Republic. This reform laid the foundation for the settlement of conflicts through civil warfare with regular armies. Moreover, the new system of recruitment posed once more the agrarian question, for the principal objective of new recruits was the attainment of land after their military service. The discontented masses had been moved away from Rome, but they could now back up their demands with armed force. At the same time, very close bonds were forged between the soldiers and the leading politicians who commanded the armies. Only these commanders could ensure, thanks to their wealth, that the soldiers received regular pay. Most important, only they could gain, thanks to their political power, plots of land for their discharged soldiers in Italy or in the provinces.[80] Leading politicians thus received an instrument which was as powerful as it was loyal: to use it against political enemies was tantamount to civil warfare.

This change in the nature of the conflict within the Roman citizen body soon became manifest. After the fall of Lucius Appuleius Saturninus, in 91 BC, when the tribune Marcus Livius Drusus undertook the solution of the acute problems, the conflict entered a decisive new phase.[81] The multi-faceted programme of Drusus, which embraced all the social strata involved in the conflict, indicates the complexity of these problems. To the Italian allies he proffered Roman citizenship, to the proletariat the solution of the agrarian question, to the *equites* access to senatorial offices and to the senators a part in the juries reserved for the *equites* since Gaius Sempronius Gracchus: *tribunus plebis Latinis civitatem, plebi agros, equitibus curiam, senatui iudicia permisit (Viri ill.,*66.4). That Drusus, like earlier reformers, fell victim to reaction was no longer extraordinary. But after his murder the situation was quite new in so far as the fall of this popular politician was not followed by ten or twenty years of revived oligarchy as had happened in previous cases of the sort. Rather, the conflict now degenerated into a permanent political and military polarisation of interest groups ranged against each other. The Social War of 91-89 BC, unleashed by the fall of Drusus, was itself a full civil war, in which the *optimates* and *populares* were compelled to unite in defence of the overriding interests of the Roman system of government. But immediately thereafter began the civil war between the *optimates* and *populares* with all its might.

At first the *populares* grouped themselves behind Publius Sulpicius Rufus, tribune of 88 BC, behind Marius, who had surfaced once more from the depths of political oblivion, and, most important, behind Lucius Cornelius Cinna, the *consul* of 87 BC. The *optimates* settled for Lucius Cornelius Sulla.[82] But the scales were tipped by the armies which supported the respective political groupings. Marius was able to mobilise many of his veterans, while Sulla had the troops assigned him for the war with Mithridates in the east. The *optimates* emerged victorious from a vicious civil war in which Rome was occupied first by Sulla's supporters, next by those of Marius and, finally, by Sulla's troops once more. Their reaction was no longer that of earlier phases in the conflict. Sulla disposed of his opponents by mass execution and he assumed public powers as *dictator* from 82 to 79 BC to safeguard the oligarchic regime by drastic measures of reform. His laws were designed to resurrect the rule of the Senate. The Senate was enlarged by the addition of 300 new senators drawn from the *equites*. Senatorial office and the senatorial career structure were regulated once more. Legislation was made dependent on senatorial ratification. The powers of tribunes were drastically curtailed. The jury courts were transferred from the *equites* to the senators and became senatorial courts. And to prevent the emergence of military power in Italy, military commands were no longer given to consuls and praetors in office: they were given only to ex-consuls and ex-praetors who were to exercise that power for one year as governors of their respective provinces. Yet these reforms undermined several pillars of the aristocratic Republic. Sulla's autocracy was in reality the first decisive step on the road to monarchy in the Roman state.

Sulla's regime lasted for almost ten years after his retirement and death shortly after. But this constitutional system could not offer a lasting solution. It was designed to preserve the pre-eminence of the disjointed oligarchy: many of the problems which had characterised earlier disputes between *optimates* and *populares* remained unsolved. Moreover, after the civil war between Marius and Sulla, the only means for the long-lasting solution of the crisis became apparent, namely the monarchical power of the leaders of political groupings with their own armed forces. The restoration of the old Republic ceased to be an opinion after the partial rescindment in 70 BC of Sulla's measures in support of the rule of the Senate by means of a judicial reform and the removal of restrictions on the tribunate. Significantly, the jury courts were divided between senators and *equites* (and a third group of well-to-do men from the tribal organisations), and in the last four decades of the Republic tribunes were only of political importance as the agents of the holders of extraordinary commands. The future belonged to these powerful politicians and generals, for the rise of whom Marius' army reform had set the course. The last 40 years of the Republic, the era of the 'last generation', proceeded in the shadow of a struggle over two issues. First, whether the oligarchic Republic was to be saved or to be converted inevitably into a monarchy. Second, the question of which of the leading rival politicians should become the autocrat.[83] In the first two decades after the fall of the Sullan system two politicians rose to prominence with dazzling speed. One was Gnaeus Pompeius, who owed his pre-eminence above all to his brilliant victories in the east from 67 to 63 BC. The other was Gaius Julius Caesar, who won his military laurels in the conquest of Gaul from 58 BC. The civil war between these two rivals (from 49 BC) was a struggle about constitutional form in as much as Pompey set himself on the side of the Senate. The result of this war, Caesar's autocracy, meant the evident victory of the monarchy over the Republic. This victory was not to be reversed by the murder of Caesar in 44 BC. With the downfall of Caesar's murderers, the last champions of the oligarchic system, at the hands of Mark Antony and Octavian, the future Augustus, in 42 BC, the Republic finally went under. The only question now was who should be Caesar's political successor. After the elimination of peripheral figures, like Sextus Pompeius and Marcus Aemilius Lepidus and after the Battle of Actium (31 BC) and the death of Antony (30 BC), the future Augustus was left as victor, *qui cuncta discordiis civilibus fessa nomine principis sub imperium accepit* (Tac., *Ann.*, 1.1).

The features common to the conflicts within the Roman citizen body from Tiberius Sempronius Gracchus to the Battle of Actium, which shed light on the structure of the crisis, are as noteworthy as the mounting distinctions which illustrate the displacement of the substance of the crisis from the sphere of the largely social to the sphere of the purely political. The first point to notice is the fact that conflicts between the various interest groups in the Roman citizen body usually flared up at times when the Roman state found itself in particular difficulties. Such occasions of weakness in the oligarchic system had first made it possible for the leaders of the *populares* to pursue a policy of reform. The elder Gracchus began his attempt at reform shortly after crushing Roman defeats in Spain, at a time when the first Sicilian slave revolt was in full swing and when the uprising of Aristonicus was just beginning at Pergamum. The younger Gracchus came on the scene shortly after the first revolt of the Italian allies at Fregellae. Marius and Saturninus exploited the impotence of the nobility in the conduct of the war in Africa against Jugurtha and the consequences of the war against the Cimbri and Teutones, together with the difficult position of the oligarchic system during the second Sicilian slave revolt. In the pursuance of his programme of reform Marcus Livius Drusus sought to exploit a situation intensified by topical political scandals. The most serious instance of popular politics began some years later at a time when the Social War had just ended and when, in the east, Mithridates, supported by provincials in revolt, was beginning his attack upon the Roman provinces. The disintegration of the Sullan constitution coincided with the uprising of Spartacus. The oligarchic system was still strong at Rome in the first decades of the crisis of the Republic, at least: at first, it could only be attacked during temporary periods of weakness.

But these observations cannot obscure the fact that the various conflicts in Roman society during the Late Republic were not directly interrelated. Neither the slave wars nor the provincial rebellions nor the uprisings of the allies against Rome were fought in alliance with, for example, the *populares*. The interests of the rebellious slaves and the popular movements were fundamentally different. The slave revolts had no support from the masses of the Roman proletariat – rather the contrary: the *populares* often called upon the slaves to help them in their cause, though usually without success, as in the case of the younger Gracchus (App.,*BC*,1.115), of Marius (App.,*BC*,1.262f.) and at first in the case of Cinna (App.,*BC*,1.293; it was otherwise later, *BC*,1.316). Nor could there be any alliance between the *populares* and the provincials who fought against Roman rule. The Spaniards who supported Quintus Sertorius, a Marian, in his struggle against the oligarchy were not enemies of Roman rule: they fought for Sertorius, who treated his regime in Spain with its own Senate as the legal Roman government. On the other hand, there were definitely close relations between the *populares* and the Italian *socii*: the espousal of political and economic reforms in favour of the Italians formed part of the programme of 'popular' politics from Gaius Sempronius Gracchus to Marcus Livius Drusus. But it is significant that in the Social War *optimates* and *populares* fought side by side against the rebellious Italians. As soon as a social or political movement threatened the Roman ruling system, the various political interest groups at Rome rejected it unanimously. In the history of the hundred years of crisis in the Roman Republic this factor alone would have sufficed to prevent the transformation of the multi-faceted conflicts of this period into a unified social movement with the aim of changing the existing social order. In the major conflicts of the Republic no social camps of oppressors and oppressed faced each other: thus these conflicts did not result in violent change in the Roman social order.

The history of the warring camps in the long series of conflicts within the Roman citizen body reveals the nature of these disputes most clearly. Appian rightly stresses that in the time of Tiberius Sempronius Gracchus there were still the rich landowners on one side and the poor on the other and that the ordinary population accordingly identified its own interests either with one camp or with the other (*BC*, 1.39ff.). But even then there were senators on the side of the poor and, on the side of the oligarchy, strong groupings of simple citizens personally dependent upon the aristocracy, while the *equites* were divided between both camps (Vell., 2.3.2). Thus Cicero was close to the truth when he affirmed that Rome was divided into two camps after the Gracchi in such a way that one could speak of '*duo senatus et duo paene iam populi*' (*De re p.*, 1.31). At the latest, it was after the civil war between Marius and Sulla that the conflict became quite clearly no more than a struggle between opposed and fluid political interest groups, whose membership could change suddenly with the passing interests of particular politicians and groupings.[84] Sallust characterised the *populares* and *optimates* of the 60s BC very aptly: when young men entered the tribunate, 'they began, with a recklessness commensurate with their age and type, to incite the masses against the Senate by their antagonistic rhetoric, to inflame them still further by their gifts and promises and thus to consolidate their own prestige and power. Most of the aristocracy opposed them with all its might, ostensibly for the sake of the Senate, but in reality for the sake of their own dominance.... The one side posed as champions of the rights of the people, while the other espoused a desire to increase senatorial prestige as much as possible – they claimed a concern for the common good but they fought only for their own influence' (*Cat.*, 38.1ff.).

Thus members of one and the same social group ever more frequently took up opposed political stance. It is of prime significance that not only the leaders of the *optimates* but also those of the populares were always senators, that is men who sought to realise their own aspirations in their struggle with the oligarchy.[85] Their origins and personal motives might be very different. Many came from the high aristocracy, as did the Gracchi, Marcus Livius Drusus and Caesar. Others, like Marius and Gaius Servilius Glaucia, a companion of Lucius Appuleius Saturninus, were embittered enemies of the high aristocracy – ascending as long-disadvantaged *homines novi*. Some, for example the Gracchi, were inspired by disinterested motives, while others, like Publius Sulpicius Rufus, were scoundrels (Plut., *Sulla*, 8.1). Some had had to endure heavy political defeats earlier in their public careers, as had Saturninus, while very many were deeply in debt, as were Sulpicius Rufus (Plut., *Sulla*, 8.2), Caesar (App., *BC*, 2.3 and 2.26f.; Plut., *Caes.*, 5.8f.) and Antony (Plut., *Ant.*, 2.3). But all these differences did not alter the fact that the leaders of the *populares* were as much members of the senatorial aristocracy as were those of the *optimates*. Moreover, there were plenty of other senators who supported the cause of the *populares*: Sulla, a champion of the cause of the aristocracy, had more than 100 senators who had opposed him killed or exiled (App. *BC*,1.482). In the power politics fought out after Sulla the political stance of the senators was still less unified and stable: in the civil wars of the failing Republic there were senators who changed sides more than once. Only a very few nobles could take up a political stance as consistent as that of the younger Marcus Porcius Cato, who always supported Republican ideals. Far more typical were the vacillations of Pompey and Cicero in their long political careers.

Nor did other social strata display consistency in the conflicts of the Late Republic. In 133 BC part of the *equites* supported the oligarchy, while part supported Tiberius Sempronius Gracchus. A decade later they were mobilised by Gaius Sempronius Gracchus against the Senate through the institution of equestrian jury panels, but they participated, nevertheless, in the crushing of the Gracchan movement in 121 BC. Later there were repeated conflicts between the *equites* and the senators, but it was *concordia ordinum* – the harmony of senators and *equites* – that Cicero affirmed to be the foundation of the Republic.[86] The distance between the political positions of particular *equites* is most clearly illustrated by the fact that Sulla executed 1500 *equites* as his enemies, but appointed 300 other *equites* into the Senate. The masses of the urban proletariat could easily be manipulated by demagogy and by largesse, a method particularly favoured by the *populares*.[87] Antony's incitement of the masses against Caesar's murderers clearly shows how they could be directed by a skilled politician (App.,*BC*,2.599ff.).The *optimates* could use the same tactics to mobilise the masses in their own interests. The particular strength of the dictatorship of Sulla resided (his 120,000 faithful veterans apart) in the loyalty of the 10,000 *Cornelii*, who were his freedmen and who supported his cause among the urban *plebs* of Rome in particular (App.,*BC*,1.489). The veterans always supported their erstwhile commander: he had led them to victory and had secured land for them. From the time of Marius and Sulla veterans – together with serving soldiers – constituted the backbone of the political factions which formed around particular leading personalities.[88] The conspiracy of Catiline against the state system in 63 BC clearly shows how heterogeneous the social com-

position of a political interest group might be, especially in the conflicts of the Republic from the time of Marius and Sulla. The leader
of this uprising was a failure from the old aristocracy, in debt and
scarred by political misfortunes. Among his supporters were men
from every possible social group, who were united only by their discontent with the *status quo* – senators, *equites*, members of the
upper strata of the Italian cities, craftsmen, proletarians, freedmen
and slaves.[89]

The composition of the hostile camps within Roman society in the
Late Republic changed as the issues in dispute became different.
Tiberius Sempronius Gracchus strove to bring in a social reform to
benefit the poor peasantry and the proletariat by political means.
His younger brother went further in his pursuit of this aim: at the
same time he brought the *equites* and the Italian allies into the conflict and, with them, corresponding new political aims. Social issues
– particularly the provision of land for the poor and for the veterans
after Marius by land redistribution and colonisation – always played
a part in the programme of the *populares*, even later, but from the
end of the second century BC the crucial issue was the distribution
of power and thus the constitutional question. The agrarian question, like the other central socio-political problem of the Late
Republic, namely *frumentatio* (that is, the distribution of food
among the masses of Rome), became increasingly no more than a
pretext as ambitious politicians struggled for power in the state. The
change from a movement with social and political aims to a
purely political power struggle is revealed by the manner in which the
conflicts between the interest groups were fought out. From the Gracchi to Sulpicius Rufus in particular, though also to an extent after
Sulla, the *populares* made use of the institution of the popular tribunate and the popular assembly as the means and framework of the
struggle. Accordingly political blows were struck, escalating from
incident to incident, by means of demagogy, breaches of the constitution, riots, political murders and the brutal annihilation of
defeated political opponents, though not yet in the form of outright
civil war.

These means of conflict remained in use even later, especially in
the notorious conflicts in Rome in the late 50s BC which paved the
way for the civil war between Caesar and Pompey. But from the 80s
BC the means of the struggle had changed markedly. The *populares*
mobilised armies to achieve their goals and, like Cinna in 87-84 BC,
instituted harsh political regimes in Rome. But the *populares* were

not alone in this: the oligarchic reaction also took to new ways of using force. The oligarchs had once been satisfied, by and large, with the persecution of the most active *populares*: seldom did they go so far as to revoke reform legislation, content with the illusion that the situation would be restored to order by itself. But Sulla's dictatorship was an attempt at total repression, though not without a series of notable political reforms which indicate an awareness that the old forms of the Republic could not now be restored without change. Yet the greatest innovation was the civil wars as fought between Marius and Sulla, Sertorius and Pompey, Pompey and Caesar, the Republicans and the political heirs of Caesar, and finally between the various political heirs of the *dictator*. In these wars regular armies stood against each other, the whole Roman Empire was the battleground and the political contestants were killed in droves in bloody battles and proscriptions. In these brutal wars there could be no more talk of a movement for social reform: they were about power and their consequences impinged upon the political, not the social, system of Rome.

The Consequences of the Crisis for Roman Society

In accordance with the structure of the conflicts of the Late Republic and the manner of the change which took place in Roman society from the Gracchi to the rise of the Principate, the social system was not fundamentally changed in this century. It was only modified. It was only the political system that was fundamentally changed, the system which held Roman society together.[90] By and large the economic foundations of the social system remained as they had been since the Second Punic War. As before, economic activity was founded upon agrarian production above all else: agrarian production took place on large estates, but also on the smaller plots of the peasant colonists and on the smallholdings of poor peasants. However, also as before, the rural economy was only part of the economy in which well-developed craft production and trade also played an important part, allied with vigorous entrepreneurial activity, long-distance trade, finance and mining. Expansion, which provided the opportunities for the further development of this economic system, was proceeding apace, notably through Pompey's conquest of Syria, through Caesar's conquest of Gaul and through the further extension of Roman rule in Spain, in the Balkan peninsula and in Asia

Minor. Thus the stratification of society underwent minimal change. Yet in the period of open conflict some social strata suffered while others managed a considerable advance. Moreover, in some cases, their composition changed markedly. However, no entirely new social strata came into existence and none of the social strata which had evolved previously disappeared. Thus the model of a society ruled by a narrow elite with some characteristics of orders remained largely intact. Though the tensions within this society were only solved to a limited extent in the century of crisis, all the tensions and conflicts of the Late Republic could not explode the social system. Nor was a new ideology developed in order to hold the fabric of society together. Although the *mos maiorum* was no longer a common value system even for the senatorial aristocracy, most contemporary theorists nevertheless deeply regretted its disintegration: the dominant intellectual direction was towards its revival, not its replacement by totally new ideals. It was only the bonds which had previously held Roman society together within one political system that were completely destroyed: these were the Republican state and its institutions. Yet in the last decades of the Republic a solution was already in sight, promising to secure the old social system within a new political framework – monarchy.

The criteria which determined the various positions within society and thus the social stratification of the Late Republic, were hardly different in nature from the foundations of the social stratification of the period from the Second Punic War to the Gracchi. These criteria constituted a complex system which took into account, as before, social background, personal ambitions and ability, landholding and financial resources, political privileges and political training, citizenship or lack of rights, personal freedom or slavery, ethnic or regional affiliation and economic activity, whether in urban or in rural production. The former factors brought individuals the *dignitas*, rank and honour, necessary for a better social position. Cicero clearly defines its social significance: *dignitas est alicuius honesta et cultu et honore et verecundia digna auctoritas* (*De inv.*, 2.166). There was only innovation in so far as these factors could operate in the instability of ongoing, outright conflicts in a different way and to a different extent than in the past when the aristocratic Republic was in its heyday. The scion of a noble family enjoyed the privilege of political participation by virtue of his prestige, connections and, usually, inherited land and wealth: even one deeply in debt was by no means compelled to forfeit his political

ambitions on that account. Thus it is very far from the case that
homines novi achieved parity with the *nobiles* in entry to the highest
office after the consulships of Marius. In the period of more than 60
years from the first consulship of Marius to the death of Caesar we
know of only eleven consuls who were *homines novi* in the senatorial order. The social position of the 'new men' only really changed
in the period from 43 to 33 BC, when they provided 18 consuls in eleven years.[91] But in the Late Republic the personal ability and ambition of the 'new men' were more likely to come to fruition than in the
century before Marius thanks to contemporary circumstances. The
best example of this is Marcus Tullius Cicero, like Marius a *homo
novus* from Arpinum, who owed his political career and his general
recognition as *princeps senatus* to his multi-faceted abilities.[92]

Most important, opportunities were to hand for astute and ruthless persons to amass almost unbelievable riches within a short
space of time. These were provided not only by entrepreneurial
profits and ongoing expansion, but also by political upheavals, especially from Marius and Sulla on: these upheavals brought about the
eradication of leading families and the confiscation of enormous fortunes. Marius began his career as a relatively poor man, yet, according to Plutarch, he acquired estates fit for a king (*Mar.*, 34.2ff. and
45.11). Sulla, once poor, became the richest man of his day (Plin.
NH, 33.134). Marcus Licinius Crassus, the third member of the First
Triumvirate, increased his inherited wealth from 300 to 7,100 talents
(about 42,000,000 denarii), which he invested in estates, mines and
slaves (Plut.,*Crass.*, 2.1ff.). The standard for 'wealth' was thus quite
different from that obtaining in the time of the Scipiones, for example. That portion of Pompey's bequest which his son could claim a
decade after his death, alone amounted to 17,500,000 denarii (Dio,
48.36.5). Caesar gave his mistress jewellery worth 1,500,000 denarii
(Suet., *Caes.*, 50.2), while Lucius Licinius Lucullus, who had successfully waged war against Mithridates, gave meals worth 50,000
denarii (Plut., *Luc.*, 41.7). A more ordinary Roman senator or
eques who had just reached the necessary property qualification for
his *ordo* (100,000 denarii) could not match these fortunes. Cicero
owned estates and villas in various parts of Italy – in his homeland
Arpinum, in Tusculum, Lanuvium, Antium, Astura, Caieta, For-
miae, Sinuessa, Cumae, Puteoli and Pompeii – but he was never one
of the richest Romans of his day. Of course, there were rich *equites*
as well as rich senators: a case in point is Cicero's friend, Titus Pom-
ponius Atticus, who made his money from the purchase of land in

Italy and in Epirus, from moneylending, from renting houses in Rome and even from publishing: as a businessman he was respected as successful and judicious (Nep., *Att.*, 13). But the opportunities of the time of civil war could be seized by men of humbler origin too: so, for example, Chrysogonus, a freedman of Sulla, who acquired the auctioned property of a proscribed citizen so cheaply that he could boast of a profit of more than a hundredfold (Plut., *Cic.*, 3.4). Freedmen also had the opportunity of acquiring political influence and power, not just through their wealth, but also through their valuable connections with powerful *patroni*: Chrysogonus was for Cicero *potentissimus hoc tempore nostrae civitatis* (*Rosc.*,6), while Demetrius, an influential freedman of Pompey, was treated like a leading senator in Syria (Plut., *Cato Min.*, 13.1ff.).

That landownership and wealth should secure political power and influence was nothing new for Roman society. All that was new were the escalating aspirations and the improved opportunities for the acquisition of wealth and thus of power and influence. Moreover, political experience, skill in manipulating the masses and the qualities of military leadership made extraordinary careers possible. The Roman citizen was given largesse, was wooed politically, entered the army where he gained pay and booty, and received land, whether as a veteran or a proletarian. Even the simple personal freedom of a provincial, who otherwise had no rights, might mean more than it had before, since the members of the provincial upper strata, at least, had a greater hope now that they might be awarded Roman citizenship.

Of course, in the period of open conflicts wealth and prominence might not only be gained quickly – they could also be lost quickly: even the most powerful politicians and generals could fall victim to their enemies. As a result of the vast losses in the civil wars and in subsequent bloody encounters, most strata in society were decimated. But at all levels new groups always arrived. The changes in the composition of particular strata on account of this fluctuation were quite the most important social consequence of the conflicts of the Late Republic for Roman society. Very many senators fell victim to the civil wars and the proscriptions – 300 in 43 BC alone: their places were taken by ever more *homines novi* from the equestrian order and from the elite of the Italian cities. Sulla brought 300 *equites* into the senatorial order and thus raised the number of senators to 600 (App., *BC*, 1.468). Caesar, who even resorted to provincials, took this policy still further (Suet., *Caes.*, 41.1 and 80.2), so that in the final years of the Republic the Senate had 900 members (Dio, 43.47.3). The equestrian order alone lost at least 1,600 mem bers in the proscriptions of Sulla and 2,000 in the proscriptions of 43 BC. Nevertheless by the mid first century BC the number of mem-bers of the equestrian order had risen to about 20,000 (Plut., *Cic.*, 31.1). Among the many new *equites* were men from the provinces in considerable numbers – from Sicily, from Africa and especially from Spain (*Bell. Alex.*, 56.4). There were also considerable changes in the composition of the elites of the cities of Italy and, in part, also of those of the provinces. This was largely due to the settlement of veterans after Marius in Italy and in the provinces. Ex-soldiers, who had land under cultivation in the territory of the colonies, constituted the upper strata of these cities. In the municipalities social climbers, such as freedmen and their progeny, also rose into the local elites where they took over from older families who had lost their prop-erty in the period of crisis or had been exterminated in the civil wars.

But members of the Roman proletariat were also often settled in colonies: under Caesar the number of the poor in Rome officially recognised as recipients of grain declined from 320,000 to 150,000 (Suet., *Caes.*, 41.3). Yet the proletarian body was constantly renewed by the influx of new groups and especially by large-scale manumis-sions in the last century of the Republic; Sulla's 10,000 *liberti* alone meant a very important new force (App., *BC*, 1.469). At the same time, the many freedmen were constantly replaced by new slaves. In his war against the Cimbri and Teutones Marius apparently took no less than 150,000 prisoners, who were enslaved (Oros., 5.16.21). In his Gallic wars Caesar enslaved 53,000 prisoners after a single battle (*BG*, 2.33.6), while the total number of his prisoners is said to have amounted to 1,000,000 (Plut., *Caes.*, 15.6). Moreover, there were other sources whence slaves might be gained. Most important was abduction which reached remarkable heights in the east until Pom-pey annihilated the pirates in 66 BC. In 104 BC the king of Bithynia refused to send military assistance to Rome against the Germans on the grounds that the majority of his subjects had been carried off to be slaves of the Romans.[93]

Thus Roman society was constantly in a state of upheaval in the Late Republic as the composition of its strata repeatedly changed. The most important consequence of this change was that a founda-tion was laid for the integration of society in the various parts of the Roman empire into a more or less coherent social system and for the evolution of upper strata constituted according to broadly uniform criteria. The Italians were brought fully into Roman society. From the last generation of the Republic the great legal divide no longer lay between Romans – that is, the inhabitants of Rome and of the various Italian cities with Roman citizenship – and non-Romans, but between Italians and provincials. But even in the provinces the first steps were taken towards integration. One path was Italian colonisation in the provinces, particularly in southern Gaul, Spain, Africa and in some parts of the east.[94] The other – still more important for integration – was the extension of Roman citizenship to members of local elites in the provinces, particularly in areas where there was most Italian colonisation. Provided they fulfilled the appropriate economic requirements and had performed well in the service of a leading politician, these new citizens from the provinces might even be accepted into the equestrian order, indeed, in some cases, even into the Senate. In Augustan Spain, in the city of Gades alone there are said to have been 500 *equites* (Strabo, 3.5.3). This was the city of Lucius Cornelius Balbus, who had gained Roman citizenship in 72 BC and in 40 BC became the first provincial to attain the consulship (*primus externorum*: Plin., *NH*,7.43).[95]

But this development came about, by and large, within the framework of the social stratification which had evolved as early as the second century BC: it did not entail a social system that was really new. In the Late Republic the social apex remained the senatorial aristocracy, with the nobility and certain social climbers at its very peak. Its composition had certainly changed and its prestige had been diminished accordingly: Florus was later to speak of a '*senatus … debilitatus*' in this period, which '*omne decus maiestatis amiserat*' (2.5.3., on the year 91 BC). But the fact remained that political and economic power lay pre-eminently in the hands of its members. The *equites* also gained a leading position, though the offices of institutionalised public leadership were open to them only upon their entry into the Senate. As Florus rightly stressed (*ibid.*), their political and especially their economic power all but gave them the opportunity to rule the state. It was into these two orders that the dominant strata in Roman society were organised: when Cicero speaks of *ordines* at Rome he means particularly these two *ordines*.[96] In the local civic elites the rich landowners joined together: the extension of Roman citizenship to the Italians in 90 BC began to generate a greater coherence in the peninsula, while these elites were enlarged in the provinces through the accretion of the colonial upper strata. Below these strata there were rich and poor freedmen, craftsmen, traders, proletarians and slaves in the cities who were engaged not only in trade and craft production but also in a wide range of other occupations besides (cf. especially Plut., *Crassus*, 2.5ff.) – from peasants on the land (sharply distinguished from the prosperous colonists) to poor day-labourers, like Varro's *mercennarii* and *obaerati* (*De re rust.*, 1.17.2), and the masses of slaves put to work on the estates. All in all this was a social model much the same as both that of the second century BC and that of the Early Empire.

Of course, this social system was fraught with tensions which repeatedly erupted into open conflicts. In these bloody conflicts the number of victims amounted to several millions. In this period Roman society never once achieved a real solution of its problems. In fact, there were only a few social problems which the Republic was in a position to master: no one encapsulated its impotence more clearly than Livy in the classic phrase, '*nec vitia nostra nec remedia pati possumus*'.[97] In reality it was only the Italian question that was solved and that by a concession which was only made after a bloody war, though the best forces in Roman society had long recognised it as imminent and in the interests of the system. There was less oppression of the provincials and even the slaves were better treated in the last decades of the Republic. Varro held, in contrast to the elder Cato, that they were to be encouraged to greater efficiency not by brutal exploitation but by rewards and privileges.[98] But the provinces remained the *praedia populi Romani*; Cicero considered the Gauls of Narbonensis to be barbarians. At the same time, Varro made no secret of the fact that he viewed slaves as labour, not human beings. Thus the gulf between the beneficiaries of Roman rule and the oppressed was only closed a little: it was not eliminated. The agrarian question and thus the provision of land for the proletariat came near to solution, particularly through the colonisation of the provinces and through the redistribution of land in Italy after the various civil wars. But this solution was very different from that proposed by the Gracchi and its price was very high. Finally, there were similarities also in the outcome of clashes within the dominant strata of Roman society – between *equites* and senators, between 'new men' and families of the nobility and between particular groupings within the oligarchy. Conflicts led not to a real solution of issues but to mutual slaughter. The Late Republic was unable to deal with its crisis either by reform or by social revolution: it could only evade its gravest problems by the abolition of its traditional political system and leave the definitive solution to a new political system.

To a large extent this impotence was a function of the inability of Roman society in the Late Republic to find ideals which might check its conflicts or help to mitigate them and, at least, bring the dominant strata together on a common ideological foundation. The ideological and moral standard of the *mos maiorum* was disappearing. There is no clearer indication of this ideological crisis than the oft-lamented decline of the good old standards in the Late Republic, a decline exemplified by the lifestyle of leading men – the notorious luxury of Lucullus, for example (Plut., *Luc.*, 39.1ff.), or the corruption without which Caesar's career would not have been possible (Suet., *Caes.*, 13). Sallust traced the whole crisis of the Roman Republic back to these moral weaknesses. Once Rome no longer had Carthage to fear 'there began an unrestrained and carefree existence, as so often follows in the wake of good fortune' (*BJ*, 41.1ff.). Of course, the actual roots of the crisis lay in the inadequacy of the city-state constitution and in the social change which had followed the Second Punic War. Yet Sallust was quite right to stress the importance of the loss of the old ethical standard, for with it fell the value system of Republican society. His concern is indicative of the fact that the Republic was unable to replace the *mos maiorum* with a new ideological and ethical system, for all that the Late Republic could boast minds as creative as Cicero, Sallust and Caesar. The one acknowledged benchmark remained ancestral custom which was generally recognised as the generator of the best state form in history (Cic., *De re p.*, 1.70). The only future course was the restoration of ancient tradition in a form appropriate to the times – not, after all, through resort to the tenets of Greek philosophy to any significant extent.

It was only the traditional political system that was lost forever in the conflicts of the Late Republic – an aristocratic system of government with its roots in the constitution of an archaic city-state. Even Cicero admitted that this system had broken down: *'rem publicam funditus amisimus'* (*Ad Q.fr.*, 1.2.15). The political and military disputes fought out between the interest groups within the Roman citizen body, made still graver by broader contemporary conflicts, destroyed the Republican regime based on the co-operation of magistrates and assembly under the guiding authority of the Senate and thus of the oligarchy. Moreover, the Roman empire, which at the end of the Republic stretched from Gaul to Syria, was no longer to be held together and ruled for any length of time in the framework of the old, quite anachronistic political system. All these factors point together towards the only possible political solution of the crisis. Cicero came to favour the idea of the replacement of the oligarchy by the monarchy: the next generation knew no alternative. The way out of the conflicts of the Late Republic led inevitably towards the rule of one man. The Scipiones as an example of how, even earlier, individuals who were particularly active and successful in warfare and politics might gain pre-eminence within the oligarchy has already been remarked upon. The political struggles from the time of the Gracchi offered still more scope, as particular nobles put themselves at the head of the discontented masses in opposition to the oligarchic regime. The *populares* and the *optimates* too, hot on their heels, massed behind particular politicians, who became the leaders of interest groups. After Marius' army reform these leaders also had at their disposal a reliable and decisive weapon in the struggle for power, namely the proletarian army, closely and personally bound to them. Foreign wars and victories (as that of Marius over Jugurtha and over the Germans, of Sulla over Mithridates, of Pompey in the east, of Caesar in Gaul, of Antony further east and of Octavian in Illyricum) also gave scope for them to test their army, to provide booty for the soldiers and to bolster their own personal *dignitas* with military glory. Thus the power of these leaders continually grew and the future belonged to that leader strong enough to thrust aside all rivals on the road to autocracy. Augustus' monarchy, created by these means, finally furnished Roman society with the political framework and the ideological orientation that it had so long been seeking in vain.

5 THE SOCIAL SYSTEM OF THE EARLY EMPIRE

Conditions Old and New

The first two centuries of the Empire, from the rule of Augustus (27 BC – AD 14) approximately to the reign of Antonnus Pius (AD 138 – 161), were more than the acme of Rome's political history when the *imperium Romanum* reached its greatest geographical extent and when, for the most part, peace reigned both within and on the frontiers of the empire. There is a certain sense in which this period is also the peak in the history of Roman society. Entirely new forms of social relations, fundamentally changing the social structure of the Roman world, were as little in evidence in this period as in the dying Republic, largely because the most important features of the economic structure remained broadly unchanged. Only two factors pertaining to social development were new. They did not appear together under Augustus, but had been in part prepared and in part introduced under the Late Republic. The first new factor was the establishment of the imperial monarchy as the most suitable political framework for Roman society. In consequence the positions and functions of the various social strata were to an extent defined anew and the social pyramid of the Empire acquired a new summit in the imperial house. The other new factor derived from the integration of the provinces and the provincials into the system of the Roman state and Roman society. In consequence, the 'Roman' social order was also extended to the populations of most of the provinces. This amounted to the development of a broadly homogeneous imperial aristocracy and the unification of local elites, together with some assimilation of wider strata of the population.[99]

These circumstances indicate why the Early Empire can be considered the acme of Roman social development. The very much divided orders-strata model of Roman society, which had developed in the Late Republic from the Second Punic War, was not replaced by a really new social system in the period from the reign of Augustus to the mid second century AD. But it was in this period that it reached its 'classic' form. It did so on the one hand through a vertical modification in the political framework under the rule of the emperors (that is, through the emergence of a clearly defined internal hierarchy) and, on the other, through a horizontal development (that is, through its extension over the population of the whole empire). Naturally, during the more than 150 years from Augustus to Antonnus Pius this social system was not static: rather, it was subject to slow but perpetual change. The position of the various social strata, for example, of the senatorial aristocracy or of the slaves on the estates, did not remain unchanged during this period, while the integration of the provincials through the extension of Roman citizenship and through urbanization proceeded gradually and at different speeds in the various parts of the empire. At the same time, even before the mid second century there were symptoms indicating the direction of the crisis and of the fundamental change in the Roman social order. Yet in the Early Empire all change occurred within the framework of the traditional orders-strata system and the omens of the great change became only after the reign of Antonnus Pius symptoms of a deep crisis in Roman society.

If the social structure of the Early Empire differed relatively little from that of the Late Republic, then this continuity depended particularly upon the nature of the Roman economic system which changed hardly at all in the transformation from Republic to Empire.[100] Certainly the Early Empire might be described as the acme of Roman economic activity. There was an apparent and considerable economic up-swing which lay in an increase in the quantity and, to an extent, also in the quality of produce. Under the favourable conditions of the *pax Romana* the development and urbanisation of the provinces generated higher productivity in wide areas of the empire, particularly in the west. Agrarian production flourished not only in traditionally important agricultural areas (such as Egypt, Roman from 30 BC, or the province of Africa), but also in formerly backward areas (such as the northern provinces of the empire). The latter phenomenon was not so much due to the transferral of southern genera of plants and animals as to the introduction of more profitable methods of cultivation with specialised labour on medium-sized and large estates. Roman mining tapped new resources of raw materials, as, for example, the gold deposits discovered in the interior of Dalmatia under Nero or the gold mines of Dacia conquered by Trajan. The control of production was regulated afresh through the introduction of a central imperial administration over the most important mines and mining areas. Craft production benefited, particularly in the west, from the high level of demand from urbanisation and from the army, a demand which could only be satisfied by mass production in large work-places with specialised craftsmen. The best example is pottery production, especially the production of *terra sigillata* ware in the workshops of Etruria, northern Italy, Spain, southern Gaul, central Gaul and, later, in northern Gaul and on the Rhine. And there was an equally clear up-swing in trade, with a lively exchange of goods between the various parts of the Roman empire, as shown, for example, by archaeological and epigraphical finds from the trade centre on the Magdalensberg in Noricum, which bear eloquent witness. The general extension of financial activity over the whole Roman empire, accompanied by investment and banking, put the final touch to this economic system.

But this up-swing took place within the framework of the economic structure which had developed earlier in the Late Republic. The Roman economy did not generate entirely new forms in the Early Empire. The only fundamental innovation was the extension of the Roman economic system over the whole Roman empire. A consequence was the replacement of backward forms of production in under-developed provinces by a gradual shift to production on municipal estates. A case in point is the replacement of the common cultivation of the land by village communities or extended families in the north Balkans and in Pannonia. Another consequence of the economic development of the provinces was of still greater historical importance. Italy lost its economic importance – in agriculture as much as in craft production and trade – to other parts of the empire approximately from the mid first century AD onwards: in the west, in particular, to North Africa, Spain and Gaul. But, on a broad view, this development did not lead to fundamental changes in the structure of the mode of production. There were no radical changes, for the technological development which might have brought about a proper revolution stagnated, by and large, in the Early Empire after a remarkable up-swing in the Later Republic (particularly in the Hellenistic east). Thus the economic prosperity of the Early Empire was limited – all the more so because expansion, which had secured continual new sources of raw materials, new labour forces, new markets and thus new opportunities for development for the Roman economy, was slowly coming to an end. Whereas Augustus had added to the Empire Egypt, north-west Spain, the German Rhineland, the Alpine territories, the Danube region and the northern Balkans as well as central Asia Minor, his successors annexed only a few new provinces, in accordance with the realistic foreign policy traceable to the Augustan notion of a '*coercendum intra terminos imperium*' (Tac., *Ann.*, 1.11). Of the provinces created after Augustus only Dacia was of really great importance for the Roman economy by virtue of its mineral wealth, while, for example, Britain, conquered by Claudius, was of hardly any economic value to the empire according to Appian (*BC*, praef., 5). All in all the economic up-swing lasted only as long as the development and urbanisation of the provinces newly annexed in the Late Republic and at the beginning of the Empire offered opportunities for growth first to the Italian and then to the provincial economy.

Thus, by and large, Rome of the Early Empire took over the economic system of the Late Republic and abandoned the search for new forms of production. For all that, the Roman state enjoyed circumstances which might have permitted the evolution of a new – indeed, an early capitalist – economic system: there were almost inexhaustible sources of raw materials, more than 1,000 urban centres of production, a uniform currency throughout the empire, a developed system of banking and credit, entrepreneurs in search of lucrative transactions and financial might, large quantities of cheap labour, a very widespread system of wage labour and, finally, a degree of technological expertise that should not be underestimated. What was probably lacking was the demand for sufficient nourishment and full employment of the broad masses which brought in the industrial revolution in eighteenth-century western Europe. In the case of Rome the interdependence between technological advance and the population problem is stood quite on its head. The clearest indication of Roman economic thought is the behaviour of the emperor Vespasian, who prohibited the spread of technological innovations on the argument that many craftsmen would lose their opportunities for work through such innovations (Suet., *Vesp.*, 18). Thus the economic structure of the Roman empire remained relatively simple, indeed backward when compared with its complex political and social structure. Despite the great up-swing in craft production and in trade, Rome remained under the Empire an agrarian state.

The crucial importance of agrarian production is immediately apparent from the fact that the overwhelming majority of the population was employed in the agrarian sector. Of the more than 1,000 cities in the Roman empire the majority probably had, at most, 10,000 to 15,000 inhabitants, as did most African cities. Some had 20,000 inhabitants, like Pompeii, a city of medium size by ancient standards while there were also small cities with 2,000 or 3,000 inhabitants at most, like Petelia in southern Italy. Only a few larger cities, like Pergamum, had a population of 50,000 to 100,000 or a little more. Apart from Rome with its population estimated at perhaps 1,000,000, Alexandria in Egypt and Antioch in Syria, at best, can be counted as large cities proper with their population of some hundreds of thousands. In other words, of the total of perhaps 50 to 80 million inhabitants of the empire after Augustus, nearly 90 per cent lived on the land and directly from the land. Apart from this, many city-dwellers – for instance, many inhabitants of veteran colonies and smaller municipalities – are to be regarded as peasants who cultivated plots in the immediate vicinity of the cities.[101] Moreover, it can be shown that it was not so much crafts, trade and banking as agrarian production that constituted the principal source of the gross national product and of wealth in general.[102] Many rich Romans – most senators, like the younger Pliny or Herodes Atticus, many *equites* and most urban decurions – owed their wealth to their lands. It seems that only a few major entrepreneurs, largely *equites* and freedmen, amassed their enormous fortunes through trade and financial dealings, as did Trimalchio, the literary figure whom Petronius immortalised as the type of the *nouveau riche* of humble origin. Lastly, it is beyond doubt that the correlation between the agrarian economy and the other branches of the economy at large was a function of the predominance of agrarian production. A significant part of craft production was carried out either to satisfy the demands of agriculture (implements, for example) or in processing agricultural products (textiles, for example) or for the transport of agricultural products (for example, amphorae for the transport of wine and olive-oil). At the same time, the most important trade goods were agrarian products: thus Trimalchio, slaves apart, traded, significantly, in wines, meat, fruit and perfume. And the wealth thus acquired was typically invested in land: quite naturally, Trimalchio did just this.[103]

But the social structure of the Early Empire was not simply a reflection of this relatively backward economic structure: it was also dependent upon social, political and legal factors which had no direct economic connection – thus upon the organisation of society into orders with its emphasis upon the origin of individuals, upon the political context of the imperial monarchy and upon the possession of or lack of Roman citizenship. Nevertheless, the importance of the aforementioned economic situation for the social structure of the Roman empire is evident. In accordance with the role of agriculture, the most important economic criterion for the division of society was not simply money, but the possession of land (whose value, of course, could be most easily expressed as a monetary sum). Accordingly the upper strata proper consisted not of entrepreneurs, great merchants and bankers, but of rich landowners (who were concerned in trade and finance, all the same), who also formed the upper strata of the cities, the centres of economic activity. Nor is it surprising that members of the lower strata of the population worked, for the most part, in agrarian production, whereas urban craftsmen and traders were a relatively small minority. A further corollary of the nature of the economy was that a true middle order could not evolve, for it would have required its own economic functions, dealing with the care of a considerable technological machinery. Finally, we must observe a direct connection between the fundamentally conservative character of the Roman social system and the structure of the Roman economy. The scope for radical change in the distribution of wealth was limited by the relatively stable nature of the agrarian economy. In consequence, the social hierarchy remained fairly constant, social mobility was restricted and the ideas which determined the thought and actions of the dominant groupings were very much bound up with tradition. All this shows once more how little difference there was between the social system of the Early Empire and that of the Late Republic. The existence of the imperial monarchy as a new political framework and the integration of the provinces reinforced this social system: it did not change its foundations.

The consolidation of the imperial monarchy from Augustus onwards completed the social system in a clear manner. In the person of the emperor and the imperial house the social hierarchy gained a new summit, supervening the old apex of the social pyramid – the small circle of oligarchic families at each other's throats. From Augustus onwards there were no longer several *principes civitatis* with their *factiones*, as in the Republic, but only one *princeps* of the Senate and of the people, and of the whole *genus humanum*. His leading position in Roman society was founded upon the factors which had secured social pre-eminence from time immemorial – power, prestige and wealth.

The *princeps* enjoyed power which was, in practice, unlimited: there was no power in the Roman state which could be employed as an alternative to that of the emperor. The contemporary view is revealed by Tacitus' account of the behaviour of the 'weak' Claudius when conservative senators took a stand against his policy of admitting the Gallic aristocracy to senatorial offices. He duly heard the contrary arguments but did not allow himself to be swayed by them and immediately contradicted them. Thereupon, the Senate passed a decree in accordance with his proposal (Tac., *Ann.*, 11.23ff.). Through his possession of *tribunicia potestas* the ruler could take the legislative initiative at any time or introduce any measure he chose in the name of the interests of the Roman people's protection. As holder of *imperium proconsulare maius* he governed the so-called senatorial provinces together with the magistrates appointed by the Senate, he governed the imperial provinces alone, through his legates, and he was commander-in-chief of the Roman army. Moreover, as the guardian of good *mores* he had the right to admit suitable persons into the equestrian order and 'new men' into the senatorial order or to expel *equites* and senators from their respective orders. There were no higher offices in the bureaucracy or in the army which could be filled without his express or tacit approval.

At the same time, the emperor possessed the highest *dignitas* in Roman society by virtue not only of his constitutionally secured power, but also of his personal position. He could invoke his personal *auctoritas*, in which alone, says Augustus, he surpassed other men ('*auctoritate omnibus praestiti: RG,*34). The ruler stood as the ideal embodiment of all the old Roman virtues, especially *virtus, clementia, iustitia* and *pietas*. His singular prestige was expressed in the imperial titulature which gradually developed (*Imperator Caesar Augustus* with an enumeration of his particular titles of office and power), in his special dress and insignia and through the ceremonial associated with his person. It was further reinforced by his religious charisma which won him cult honours and in the Greek east direct deification. At the same time, the emperor was the wealthiest man in the Roman empire. He had the *patrimonium Augusti* (the imperial crown property) and also his own *res privata* (his personal property), both of which consisted principally of lands, mines and workshops.[104]

But it was not only the existence of this new social summit which completed Rome's social hierarchy. Close social connections necessarily existed between the man at this summit and the various groupings in society, most particularly between the emperor and individual orders and other corporatively organised groups in the population. The varied nature of these connections, generated by the dif-

74838

ferent positions of the various groups in the population, brought it about that the position and function of these groups, and thus also their mutual relationships, were to an extent defined still more precisely than before.

The social connections between the emperor and particular groups in the population were in part based on Republican precedents, though, of course, in the context of the imperial monarchy their nature was modified. Under the Republic social relationships between persons and groups of persons – to set aside that between masters and slaves – rested on two pillars. On the one hand, *amicitia* operated where those involved were of comparable status or, at least, of a fairly similar social position. On the other, the *patronus–cliens* relationship applied where those involved were obviously very different in power, prestige and wealth. Accordingly, the *princeps* treated leading senators and *equites* as his *amici*, men with whom he had social intercourse as did Hadrian, for example, who was concerned to eat with his friends (SHA, *Hadr.*, 9.6f.) – and men who might be called upon to consider weighty matters in his 'privy council' (*consilium principis*), like the *proceres* among the senators and the praetorian prefects under Domitian (Juvenal, 4.74ff.). By virtue of the prestige of this friendship the *amicus Caesaris* stood apart from ordinary men; its loss amounted to loss of social status or even political ruin.[105] The relationship of the subject masses to the emperor approximated to that of *clientes* to a powerful *patronus*. When Augustus took the title *pater patriae* in 2 BC the whole empire became almost clients under his 'fatherly' protection. Social connections of this sort might assume a concrete form, particularly in the close relationship between the ruler and urban communities, regions, provinces and other organised groups in the population. Thus the emperor was also the *defensor plebis* who bestowed upon the *plebs* of the city of Rome largesse of grain and money and public games, too. The subjects not only took part in his cult honours – as, for example, did the inhabitants of Narbo in the case of Augustus (*'qui se numini eius in perpetuum obligaverunt'*: *ILS*, 112) – but also swore an oath of loyalty to him, as did the whole of Italy in the case of the future Augustus as early as 32 BC and as all communities did later when a new ruler began his reign (so, for example, the Spanish Aritienses to the emperor Caligula upon his accession in 37 BC: *ILS*, 190).[106]

A further consequence of the fundamental change in the structure of the Roman state that had occurred through the introduction of the imperial monarchy was that various groups in society gained new functions and thus, in part, newly-defined positions. In particular the public functions of the highest groups in Roman society – the members of the senatorial and equestrian orders – were established anew, a contribution to the further consolidation of the orders-strata system with its peculiar social hierarchy. The members of the senatorial order had long held the most important offices in the civil administration, the judiciary and the military. This remained the situation in the Early Empire, apart from the fact that certain top posts were created for the cream of the equestrian order, most importantly the praetorian prefecture. But the public activity of the senators took on a totally new character, for the service of the state increasingly came to mean the service of the emperor. The *legati Augusti* at the head of the legions and of the imperial provinces and the other officials appointed by Augustus (for example, the curators of roads and prefects of the treasury) considered their *officium* to be the imperial service. Moreover, even the consulship, the magistracy most symbolic of the aristocratic Republic, was treated as a reward of outstanding importance for service to the person of the ruler. According to Fronto it was considered an honour for those senators who had distinguished themselves in the service of the emperor (*Ad M. Caes.*, 1.3.3.). And these close dealings between the emperor and the senatorial order did not lose their importance in the face of political conflicts which came to a head spasmodically between certain emperors and particular senatorial groupings, especially under Tiberius, Caligula, Claudius, Nero and Domitian. This usually occurred because some emperors broke certain rules of the game in the relationship between the monarchy and the senatorial aristocracy with its consciousness of tradition and its great concern for its own prestige – in part, the result of personal temperament, in part the result of political necessity.

Much more apparent was the new arrangement for equestrian functions. In the Late Republic the *equites* could only hold public office as judges and officers. From Augustus onwards, particularly able *equites* – upon the completion of their military service – were employed as *procuratores Augusti* for the administration of imperial property and for the economic and financial administration of the empire at large. Through the establishment of these roles the different social positions of the senatorial order and the equestrian order respectively were precisely fixed, as were the differences between the members of these two leading orders and other groups in society. Moreover, within the two leading orders the social hierarchy was regulated more precisely than before. The position of a senator within his order no longer rested simply upon his family, wealth and tenure of traditional offices: it also depended upon whether he had been admitted to an official career in the imperial service or not. Among the *equites* distinctions were drawn according to whether or not they held any public offices and, moreover, according to the level they had reached in the equestrian *cursus honorum*. But the introduction of new hierarchies by the imperial regime went beyond the senatorial and equestrian orders. A new hierarchical structure was even created among the slaves and freedmen through the genesis of an influential elite – the imperial *servi* and *liberti*.

Social circumstances changed in the *imperium Romanum* as the Roman social system gradually extended itself over most parts of the empire. Through the spread of the Roman economic system in the Latin west and through the integration of the Greek east into the economic activity of the empire, a division of society occurred in most provinces in broad conformity with that in operation in Italy. The consequence was that the higher strata of the empire were no longer identical to the upper strata of Italy, as had been the case by and large even at the end of the Republic: rather, the former increasingly admitted men from the leading families of the provinces. At the same time, the lower strata in the various parts of the empire had a more coherent character than before. These developments are most readily observed in the advance of provincials to the commanding heights of the empire. As early as the Flavian emperors (69-96) men from the provinces, particularly from Spain and southern Gaul, formed a very influential grouping in the senatorial order. In the person of the emperor Trajan (98-117), who came from an Italian colonial family in the province of Baetica, the first provincial ruler gained the throne, and as power was being transferred to Trajan there was only one serious rival – Marcus Cornelius Nigrinus who was himself from Spain. Hadrian (117-138) was a close fellow countryman and relative of Trajan. The family of Antonnus Pius (138-161) came from southern Gaul and the family of the emperor Marcus (161-180) was another from Baetica. In the latter's reign provincials for the first time constituted a majority in the consular elite of the senatorial order.[107]

The integration of the provinces and the provincials was advanced in a variety of ways – through the construction of a road network, through the introduction of a coherent administration, through the admission of provincials into the Roman military service, but above all through the extension of Roman citizenship (for which, in principle, a knowledge of Latin was a requirement) and, still more important, through urbanisation. Citizenship was awarded either to individual persons and families – mostly the members of local elites – or to entire communities. As we know from Augustus' account, there were 4,063,000 Roman citizens in 28 BC, 4,233,000 in 8 BC and 4,937,000 in AD 14.[108] After Tiberius' policy of restraint (14-37), the number of citizens rose under Claudius (41-54), to whom Seneca attributes the extension of the citizenship to 'all' Greeks, Gauls, Spaniards and Britons (*Apoc.*, 3.3), by at least another million (5,984,072 citizens in AD 48: Tac., *Ann.*, 11.25). From the time of the Flavian emperors the citizenship was increasingly extended in hitherto backward areas. The conclusion of this development came with Caracalla (211-217), who gave citizenship to all free inhabitants of the Roman empire by the *constitutio Antoniniana*. Urbanisation was still more important, for the integration of the western provinces at least. It came about either through the planned settlement of legionary veterans (and sometimes also of proletarians from the city of Rome) in *coloniae* or through the extension of civic autonomy to local communities, which thus became *municipia*. In the Greek east, which could look back upon a long tradition of urban development, only a few cities were founded: the Greek-Hellenistic *poleis* were promoted instead. Those emperors who distinguished themselves through a particularly active policy of urbanisation are precisely those who extended the citizenship over large numbers of the population, namely Augustus, Claudius, the Flavians, Trajan and Hadrian. In the mid second century the Greek *rhetor* Aelius Aristides could state that the Roman empire possessed a dense network of cities, while at the beginning of the third century Tertullian stressed that the whole Roman world had been opened up through civilisation and that there were civic communities everywhere (*'ubique res publica'*).[109]

By virtue of the existence of more than 1,000 cities in the Roman Empire conditions were ripe more or less everywhere for the assimilation of social structures. Society was divided into two parts. On the one hand, there were the upper strata, who were also the elites in the cities and the rich landowners of the city territories and whose wealthiest members were admitted to the equestrian and the senatorial orders. On the other, there were the lower strata in the cities or on the land, whose members lived under different forms of social dependency as free men, freedmen or slaves. Of course this social system was not homogeneous, for the development of the various parts of the empire took place under very different local circumstances: in particular, the lower strata of the population in the various parts of the empire were, to an extent, quite different. Economic, urban and social conditions like those in Italy (where particular areas also displayed considerable variations) actually existed only in Roman North Africa, in southern and eastern Spain, in southern Gaul, on the Dalmatian coast and – to set aside legal and cultural differences – in Greece and Macedonia, in western and southern Asia Minor and on the coast of Syria – in other words, in the Mediterranean area. But in the northern provinces – as in Britain, Gaul, Germany, Raetia, Noricum, Pannonia, the Dalmatian hinterland, Dacia and Moesia and also in the northwest of Spain – the number and importance of cities was less than in the south and, by and large, the division of society was simpler. A clear indication is that in these areas in the Early Empire there were, significantly, only very few senatorial landowners and slave masses (though the latter were also largely lacking from the African provinces). A north–south divide in the empire was recognised by contemporaries: for example, Vitruvius, at the beginning of the Empire was convinced that southerners were more intelligent and northerners more warlike, mainly in view of their different levels of civilisation (*Arch.*, 6.1.9ff.). None the less, there were also often very great structural differences between neighbouring provinces, indeed even within one and the same province (as, for example, in Dalmatia between the coastal lands, urbanised at an early stage, and the backward hinterland). Yet there were only a few parts of the empire where the Roman economic model and the Roman division of society hardly gained entry. The most important example is Egypt, which Augustus took over as patrimonial property and where the traditional local social system (with its different categories of peasants and absence of slaves in agrarian production, *inter alia*) was changed only slightly. On the whole, the Roman empire was characterised by a uniform economic and social system in the sense that this system, albeit different according to province or region, was either clearly defined or, at least, indicated the direction of the process of economic and social development, whereas no really clear alternative models were available.[110]

The Social Stratification

In accordance with the conditions of its development, Roman society was not divided essentially differently in the Early Empire than in the Late Republic. Rather, it was simply that the traditional system of division received its most clearly defined forms. As always, this society was divided into two main parts of unequal size, for the dividing-line between the upper strata and the lower strata was the clearest social division. Aelius Aristides expressed this social division through the polarities of rich/poor, large/small, prestigious/ nameless and noble/ordinary: although he stressed the parity of all men under imperial justice, he took it for granted that the 'better' should rule and the 'masses' should obey. The Roman legal sources, from the mid second century AD at least, speak of *honestiores* on the one hand – the holders of elevated social and economic status and of the appropriate prestige (*condicio, qualitas, facultas, gravitas, auctoritas, dignitas*) – and, on the other, the *humiliores* and *tenuiores*.[111]

Four principal criteria can be found for membership of the higher echelons, which broadly correspond to the polarities of Aelius Aristides. One had to be rich, hold higher offices and thereby power, enjoy social prestige and, above all, one had to belong to a leading *ordo*, a corporately organised and privileged order which comprised men of wealth, higher offices and prestige. It was only the man who fulfilled all these conditions who really belonged in the full sense to the upper strata of society, namely – the imperial house apart – the members of the *ordo senatorius*, the *ordo equester* and the *ordo decurionum* of the various cities. But rich freedmen, who might be very wealthy, or the imperial slaves and freedmen, who, as well as enormous wealth, sometimes possessed great power as grey eminences, did not display all these characteristics. They could not be accepted into the leading *ordines*: they were despised for their lowly origin and, in theory, they served only in subordinate positions. Soldiers in no way belonged to the upper strata, though the military – as the events of the year of the four emperors made particularly clear – were an important power factor (Tac., *Hist.*, 1.4) and although the soldiers of the elite units (praetorians and legionaries) enjoyed a variety of privileges. Nor should the low social status of the *plebs* of the city of Rome be misjudged, although the *plebs* occasionally appeared a political power factor as late as the beginning of the Empire. The true polarity to membership of the higher echelons is evident, of course, in the interdependence of poverty, powerlessness and exclusion from higher public offices, together with low prestige and an existence only outside the privileged orders. In consequence, the members of the lower strata are broadly – though not entirely – identical with the producers at work in the rural and urban sectors of the economy. Membership of and exclusion from the upper strata were determined by the coincidence of various factors which can be listed as follows: lofty or lowly origin, possession or lack of citizenship, freedom or slavery, ethnic or regional affiliation to the population of one region of the empire or another, individual ability, background and loyalty to the imperial monarchy.[112]

Trimalchio clearly expresses the importance of wealth as a qualification in Petronius' Satyricon (Chapter 77) – '*credite mihi: assem habeas, assem valeas; habes, habeberis*'. Money alone was not the crucial factor so much as the ownership of land as its main source: but the enormous gulf that might exist between rich and poor was clear, nevertheless. The inequality of the distribution of land among owners, for example, in the environs of Veleia and Beneventum in Italy under Trajan is revealed by the evidence of the so-called alimentary tables from these cities. These show that 65 per cent of landowners held land valued at less than 100,000 sesterces, while only 7 per cent of owners held land valued at more than 500,000 sesterces and only 3 per cent held land worth more than 1,000,000 sesterces.[113] And yet the concentration of landholding in Italy in the Early Empire steadily proceeded, so that the elder Pliny could speak of the destruction of the land by *latifundia (NH*,18.35). Development proceeded in much the same way in the provinces, too, particularly in the Mediterranean lands, as in Africa, where half the land was the property of six great landowners in the mid first century AD (Plin., ibid.). The greatest documented fortune amounted to 400,000,000 sesterces, a fortune owned by the senator Gnaeus Cornelius Lentulus at the beginning of the Empire (Seneca *De ben.*,2.27) and also by the freedman Narcissus, the powerful secretary of Claudius (Dio, 60.34.4). At the other end of the scale there is evidence of quite incredible cases of poverty – for example, in Egypt, where 64 peasant families came to share a plot of one *aroura* (2,200 square metres) and six families held a single olive-tree as common property. There was a corresponding difference between the lifestyle of the rich and that of the poor. Wealthy families possessed luxurious palaces and villas at Rome and on their estates, buildings which Martial describes as kingdoms (12.57.19ff.) with furniture, *inter alia,* worth millions (Plin., *NH*,13.92): their wives wore jewellery worth 40,000,000 sesterces, as did Lollia Paulina under Augustus (Plin., *NH*,9.117f.). On the other hand, Egyptian peasants, for example, lived crowded into huts and primitive houses: in one attested case ten families lived in this way, in another, 42 persons: often they owned almost nothing.[114] And of course the gulf between rich and poor was expressed in the contempt to which the latter were continually exposed, a contempt bitterly denounced, for example, by Juvenal (3.126ff. and 5.1ff.). Moreover, the rich could quickly become still richer, as did Seneca who amassed a fortune of 300,000,000 sesterces within four years (Tac., *Ann.* 13.42), while the poor, the great majority according to Seneca (*Helv.*, 12.1), only very seldom had the luck of a Trimalchio.

The boundaries between those who possessed power and influence and the subject masses were also clear. Higher offices were open only to privileged groups. The high offices in the administration of the empire and in the command of the military were reserved for senators and *equites*, while the administration of the civic communities was reserved for the local elites gathered in the *ordines decurionum*. Of course the actual power base of most civic magistrates and community councillors was very limited, as was that of the holders of the lower equestrian and senatorial offices. At the same time, on occasion, greater power could certainly be exercised in ways other than through the offices of the three leading *ordines*, namely through the offices of the imperial freedmen, who were in principle subordinate, but in practice of the highest importance at the head of the court bureaux, especially under Caligula, Claudius, Nero and Domitian. And there was also bribery (Plut., *Galba*, 24.1, for example) and influential women (for example, Suet., *Otho*, 2.2) and manipulation of every sort. Under the aforementioned emperors, at least, emperors who constantly came into conflict with the elite of the senatorial order and, to an extent, also of the equestrian order, the court personnel were deliberately used as a counterbalance to the power of the leading orders. But under Augustus, Tiberius and Vespasian the situation was quite different and from Trajan onwards the influence of the imperial freedmen was greatly restricted. The Senate was still regarded as the most important organ of the legislature. Through offices in the executive and the judiciary leading senators and *equites* had a share in supreme power as members of the imperial *consilium*, as governors of the most important provinces, as military commanders, as praetorian prefects and as officers in the administration. Imperial power was largely exercised through the power extended to them. Of course they were always under constraints and like the younger Pliny in Bithynia, they acted in accordance with the directions of the emperor. Nevertheless, we have a particularly clear indication of the power which a consular governor and military commander might possess: in the Early Empire, emperors-to-be who had no dynastic claim to the throne could most easily proceed to sole power from the position of a senatorial legate. Galba was proclaimed emperor while governor of Hispania Citerior, Vitellius while commander of the forces of Lower Germany, and Vespasian while the head of the expeditionary forces sent against the rebellious Jews. Moreover, Trajan was designated the successor of Nerva while governor of Upper Germany and Hadrian gained imperial power on the death of Trajan while legate of the expeditionary forces sent against the Parthians. The praetorian prefects also enjoyed a great deal of power, as the position of Lucius Aelius Seianus under Tiberius makes clear enough.

Still more clear-cut was the dividing-line between upper strata and lower strata fixed on the criterion of prestige. The social distinction gained very clear and significant expression in the ever more well-defined legal notions of '*honestior*' and '*humilior*', The 'better' were treated with special respect by the lower strata and by the state on the basis of formal and informal privileges. By a decision of Vespasian, a senator might never be insulted by an *eques*: at best, the *eques* could offer an insult through a member of the first order, since the *dignitas* of the first and the second *ordo* were not the same (Suet., *Vesp.*,9.2). Important persons were also accorded a special reverence by the masses (for example, Tac., *Ann.*,3.23). The increasing bestowal of privileges upon the 'honourable' in the course of the second century in the field of criminal law contradicts Aelius Aristides' claim that all groups in the population were equal before the law. Even veterans and decurions were exempted from punishments of a shameful nature. Members of the equestrian order convicted of crimes which would have brought ordinary persons a sentence of forced labour were only required to go into exile. Senators convicted of capital crimes were spared the death penalty and were only required to withdraw into exile. By contrast ordinary mortals suffered the full severity of the Roman criminal law, namely flogging and torture, forced labour, condemnation to gladiatorial shows and beast-hunts and execution by crucifixion. At the same time insults offered by an ordinary man to an important personage were dealt with with particular severity.[115] Moreover, the distinguished were very much aware of their status. Tacitus, for example, was particularly fervent in his condemnation of the adultery of Livia, the daughter-in-law of Tiberius, with the praetorian prefect Seianus, an *eques* from Volsinii, in view of the gulf in status that lay between them. This lady from the highest family had brought shame to her ancestors as well as her descendants through her liaison with a mere 'municipal' (*Ann.*, 4.3).

Apart from the special case of the rich freedmen and the wealthy and influential personnel of the court, in the Early Empire an elevated social status was identical with membership of one of the privileged *ordines*. This was broadly the same as the coincidence of privileged social status through wealth, high offices and prestige, according to rank within the senatorial order, the equestrian order and the decurional order in the various cities. This meant that one did not become a member of the leading social strata as a matter of course after fulfilling certain social requirements, as is the case, for example, in a modern class-based society, where the requirements may be wealth of a certain size, a respected job or a prestigious place of residence. One was only admitted into an *ordo* after a formal act and membership was expressed through symbols and titulature particular to the order. Of course, the son of a senator was 'automatically' a senator himself, for, after Augustus, the status was hereditary in principle: just like the adult members of the order he could claim the title *clarissimus* (*clarissima* in the case of the wives and daughters of senators). But 'new men' were admitted into this order by the emperor. If they were below the age of 27 or 28, he conferred upon them the *latus clavus*, the broad stripe of purple, to be worn as a status symbol. Having gained this they could stand for the lower senatorial offices. Older men received the status of the appropriate senatorial rank. Admission into the equestrian order occurred when the emperor granted the *equus publicus*, often followed by entry into an equestrian post. As symbols of their order the *equites* wore a narrow purple stripe, the *angustus clavus*, on their tunic and a gold ring: they also bore the title *equo publico* or *eques Romanus*. Admittance to the decurional order in the various cities was gained by tenure of a civic magistracy or at least by official entry into the list of decurions (*album decurionum*). Expulsion from an order was a similarly formal procedure: it meant clear social demotion (for example, Tac, *Ann.* 12.59). Thus the upper strata were corporatively organised in such a way that entry and membership were readily controlled. In this fashion the hierarchy of the social system was carefully preserved.

As was appropriate to the aristocratic structure of this society, the first criterion in determining whether an individual belonged to the privileged upper strata or to the lower strata, was birth. Once a family attained social position it was largely hereditary: thus membership of the senatorial order was in principle hereditary for three generations, while hereditary membership of the equestrian order operated at least *de facto* and hereditary membership of the decurional order was entirely the norm, from the second century at least. Moreover, the emperors deliberately fostered this continuity in the composition of the leading *ordines*: for example, like Augustus (for example, at Dio 55.13.6), they came to the financial aid of impoverished senators and thereby allowed them to display the required minimum census of their order. Of course Roman society was not a caste system: personal merit was valued and some, like Juvenal, criticised the concept of nobility of birth (8.1ff.). But for all that, it remained the case that the son of a distinguished family had to do very little to maintain the position he inherited. One might even 'earn' the highest offices '*sola generis claritate*' (Plin., *Paneg.*, 58.3). Thus every senator descended from a father of consular rank (or from more distant consular forebears) was inherently a candidate for the consulship (under the Antonines at least): this important office brought with it the highest social prestige and was duly coveted by many senators in vain. Moreover, a man whose father had held the particularly prestigious position of *consul ordinarius* (eponymous consul of the year), had an unwritten right to the same privilege.[116] By contrast, humble origin was always regarded as a taint: the *humiliore loco natus* was always at a disadvantage and to rise into the higher orders the *homo novus* had to break through strong social barriers by his '*industria vel fortuna*' (Tac., *Ann.*, 3.55).

The social position of an individual was also very much dependent upon his legal status. Only citizens – still a privileged minority in the view of Aelius Aristides – had the rights adjudged necessary at Rome for elevated status (that is not to say that in communities without Roman citizenship, like the Greek *poleis*, rich and influential non-citizens were not pre-eminent among the local population). Even within the citizen body there were two categories, namely the full citizens (*cives Romani*) and the 'half-citizens' of communities with Latin rights (*ius Latii*). The members of these last communities, wherein either the magistrates alone or the decurions, too, possessed full Roman citizenship, were distinct from full citizens in that they lacked certain rights.

Subordinate offices apart, positions in the public service and in the administration of cities organised as municipalities or colonies were open only to Roman citizens. Only citizens were permitted relatively prestigious service in the Roman legions and only they enjoyed various privileges in private law, *inter alia* the bequest of property by legal will. Of course, citizenship did not automatically bring wealth, influence and greater prestige, but the superiority of the citizen to the non-citizen (*peregrinus*) was, on the whole, evident.

Another legal distinction might be equally crucial, namely whether a man possessed freedom by free birth or manumission or had the status of a slave, in principle the property of another. The slave was usually subjected to particularly bad treatment. He could not choose his occupation or his domicile and he had very little chance to amass wealth: apart from subordinate positions (for example, as policeman, administrator of the public archives, customs officer, etc.) he could hold no public offices. Moreover, the freedman was also often at a disadvantage to the free-born. The hierarchy of *ingenui*, *liberti* and *servi* was considered so important that Martial recommended that the favours of a free-born woman were to be preferred to those of a freedwoman and those of a freedwoman to those of a slave-woman (3.33.1ff.). Certain measures of the emperors make very clear the taint which a slave origin gave a family, even generations later: Tiberius prohibited the sons of freedmen from holding equestrian rank (Plin., *NH*, 33.32), Claudius only allowed the son of a freedmen to enter the senatorial order after his prior adoption by a Roman *eques* (Suet., *Claud.*, 24.1) and Nero put an end even to this concession (Suet., *Nero*, 15.2). Even the powerful imperial freedmen were despised as 'slaves' by the elite, though the latter often enough behaved in a servile manner towards them (for example, Tac., *Ann.*, 14, 39). By contrast, on the whole, free birth was an incomparably favourable point of departure.

Also significant, by and large, was the part of the empire and the people from which an individual came. A long-standing principle of Roman society was that even its commanding heights lay open to *alieni* and *externi*, as Claudius stated (*ILS*, 212). In his speech on Rome (Chapter 60) Aelius Aristides stressed that outstanding and cultured persons were to be found in all parts of the empire, without distinction between east and west. With regard to broader strata in the population Trajan declared that '*nulla provincia est, quae non et peritos et ingeniosos homines habeat*' (Plin., *Ep.*, 10.40.3). Nevertheless, prejudices and ingrained attitudes were shed only slowly and never completely in the course of the Empire.[117] Under the early emperors, at least, the pre-eminence of Italy and of the Italians was taken for granted. Tiberius expressly pointed out that Italy enjoyed a privileged position through the import of goods from the provinces (Tac., *Ann.*, 3.54). Claudius' measures to integrate the provincials more closely through the extension of citizenship and admission to the Senate led to criticism in conservative circles. After Claudius' reforms discrimination was largely ended, at least with regard to the inhabitants of the Latin provinces (cf., for example, Tac., *Hist.*, 4.74 on the equality of the Gauls), though certain prejudices survived down to the Late Empire – for example, that the Gauls were hotheads and the Africans untrustworthy. But, as regards the inhabitants of the eastern half of the empire, the old prejudices were more deeply ingrained: they were foreign to the Romans through their language, Greek, and through their customs which were considered un-Roman. Juvenal, for example, the descendant of a freedman, looked with deep contempt upon *equites* from Asia Minor (7.14f.): he felt unhappy in Rome, where the city swarmed with Syrians, as if the Orontes had flowed into the Tiber (3.60ff.). Martial spoke with similar disdain of Cappadocians and Syrians (10.76.1ff.). Particularly marked were prejudices against the Jews and, above all, the Egyptians, who were typecast even in the Late Empire as greedy, undisciplined, irresponsible and unpredictable (for example, SHA, *Q.*, 8.1ff.). And there were clear social consequences of this sort of discrimination against various minorities. We seldom hear of Jews with high honours, like Tiberius Julius Alexander, an apostate equestrian Jew from Alexandria in Egypt under Nero and Vespasian: the first Egyptian senator, Aelius Coeranus, gained admittance to the senatorial order more than two centuries after Egypt had become a part of the Roman empire.

Straightforward personal ability and merit, skill, training and political experience were important, even so, but their role in determining social status was evidently restricted. The personal advantages to be derived from financial skill and hard bargaining is best shown by the fabulous wealth that Trimalchio amassed, despite setbacks, from his business activities. Training could also play a major part, as, for example in the case of doctors, who were often of servile origin: from their *honoraria* they often amassed huge fortunes. A case in point is Publius Decimius Eros Merula, a freedman at Assisi, who, after considerable public expenditures, left a fortune of as much as 500,000 sesterces (*ILS*,7812). Knowledge of the law was also an aid to advancement, as in the case of the senator Salvius Julianus, a 'new man' from Africa in the mid second century, who, while *quaestor*, drew a double salary from Hadrian in consideration of his *doctrina* (*ILS*, 8973). Among the leading senators there were highly educated orators and lawyers, like the younger Pliny, and – in the east in particular – philosophers, like Herodes Atticus and many others.[118] Tacitus remarked on two leading senators of the Flavian period, Titus Eprius Marcellus and Quintus Vibius Crispus, that they had risen from poor and lowly circumstances ('*sine commendatione natalium, sine substantia facultatum*') to join the *potentissimi civitatis* through their *oratoria eloquentia* alone (*Dial.*, 8.2f.). Political and military service to the emperor and the loyalty thereby displayed might be of crucial importance, especially at times of internal political crisis. An example is Lucius Tarius Rufus, a *consul* under Augustus, who rose from *infima natalium humilitas*, probably as a Liburnian seaman, to the commanding heights of Roman society for the particular reason that he had especially distinguished himself in the battle of Actium. Vespasian admitted to the senatorial order at least 20 *equites* who had given him active support in AD 69.[119]

But personal *meritum* could only modify and reduce the importance of other factors in the determination of social position: it could not nullify them. Economic success did not play the large part that it does in modern industrial society: because of his servile origin Trimalchio could not overcome the critical social barriers before him. Much the same was the case with training. In general terms it was a requirement for elevated social status and it was useful for a political career, but the stigma of servile origin was not washed away by training: the doctor Merula was excluded from the privileged *ordines* as much as Trimalchio. Moreover, there were only a few fields of training which were of direct political use – in particular, in the law and in oratory, which actually brought great social advantages. But there were limitations even here. The best indication of their nature is the fact that, under Domitian, the chair of a professor of rhetoric was deemed appropriate for a senator *who had left* his order (Plin., *Ep.*, 4.11.1f.). It was only in the political and military service of the emperor that personal merit and achievement counted really decisively (Plin., *Pan.*, 70.8), though, at the same time, high birth did not lose its importance altogether. This ambivalence was entirely typical of the Roman social system. On the one hand, it held to the precedence of noble birth and to the determination of social position according to origin, on the aristocratic principle, yet, at the same time, it offered scope for personal qualities and ambitions. Tacitus realised that this ambivalence produced great differences in quality among the leading groups of Roman society between *nobiles* and *homines novi*.

The Senatorial Order

From the beginning of the Empire the *ordo senatorius* closed its ranks still more tightly than in the Late Republic. At the time of the Second Triumvirate the number of senators had been increased to more than 1,000. After he had purified the Senate of 'unworthy' elements Augustus fixed the number of senators at 600.[120] In the following two centuries the figure hardly changed: each year only 20 senators could begin a senatorial career as *vigintiviri* or enter the Senate as *quaestores*. In addition – as happened under Vespasian and regularly from the time of Domitian – there were those persons of equestrian background who were admitted to the senatorial order with the rank of ex-*quaestor* or higher. In consequence the number of senators may have increased slightly from the end of the first century, but at the end of the second it was still not much greater than 600. Thus the senatorial order was a small and exclusive *ordo*. The fact that it was more clearly distinguished than before from the equestrian order below was important for its exclusivity too.[121] At the end of the Republic and still to an extent under Augustus the boundaries between the senatorial order and the equestrian order were still fluid. In principle, the son of a senator had the rank of *eques*. Sons of senators could stand for senatorial offices as could *equites*. There were even some offices which could be held by a senator or an *eques* without any change in their respective order. Augustus drew the boundaries tighter. The sons of senators were formally included in the senatorial order (Suet., *Aug.*, 38.2; cf. *Dig.*, 23.2.44) and thus separated from the *equites* proper. At the same time the minimum property qualification for a new senator, which had previously been the same as that of an *eques* (400,000 sesterces), was raised to 1,000,000 between 18 and 13 BC (Dio, 54.17.3 and 54.26.3f.). Caligula put the final touch to the separation of the senators from the *equites* by a measure of AD 38 (Dio, 59.9.5): an *eques* who attained senatorial office or was permitted to wear the broad purple stripe, the symbol of the senatorial order, formally belonged thereafter to the first order and relinquished all formal ties with his erstwhile order. Senatorial and equestrian offices were thus separated definitively.

The actual wealth of most senatorial families far exceeded the prescribed minimum *census*. A fraction of their wealth was derived from moneylending, from the sale of craft products made on their estates and from the salaries paid by senatorial offices (the highest annual salary, that of the *proconsul* of Africa and of Asia, amounted to 1,000,000 sesterces). But it was income from the land that was crucial. Each senator was also a great landowner. Many senators had estates in Italy as well as in the provinces. When the number of provincial senators had increased markedly the emperor Trajan brought in a measure whereby senators were required to invest a third of their wealth in land in Italy, so that they might regard Rome and Italy as their homeland (Plin., *Ep.*,6.19.1ff.). The wealth of the younger Pliny, acquired by inheritance and marriage and by moneylending and the administration of large bequests, lay almost exclusively in land (*'sum quidem prope totus in praediis'*: *Ep.*, 3.19.8). His estates were situated around his home town, Comum in northern Italy, and in the region of Tifernum Tiberinum in Umbria. Although he could lavish considerable amounts of money upon his fellow townsmen and dependents, he was not one of the richest senators. His total wealth may be reckoned at perhaps 20,000,000 sesterces. There were senatorial families who were much richer (cf.p.111): their expenditures on the public were sometimes vast, especially in the east. It was a small thing for the father of Herodes Atticus to lay out 4,000,000 denarii for the water supply of Troy: he regularly bestowed money, wine and meat for sacrifices upon all the citizens of Athens. His son (whose full name was Tiberius Claudius Atticus Herodes), in addition to his many other benefactions in Greece, Epirus and Italy, had the stadium decorated with marble and the Odeum built at Athens, a theatre at Corinth, a stadium at Delphi and an aqueduct at Olympia.[122]

But the possession of wealth and the generosity and luxurious lifestyle that it made possible was characteristic not only of senators but also of many *equites* and of the cream of the freedmen. It was therefore not so much economic as social, legal, political and ideological factors which promoted the corporate identity and exclusivity of the first order. Many senators were united by complex family relationships and friendships, complicated further by multiple marriages and by adoptions. The correspondence of the younger Pliny and that of Marcus Cornelius Fronto makes the extent of such connections clear. Characteristically, many senators took the names of relatives. The 'record' in polyonomy is held by Quintus Pompeius Senecio, consul in AD 169, whose full nomenclature contains a total of 38 separate names.[123] It was also important that the public functions of the senators were of a relatively uniform nature. Their uniformity derived, on the one hand, from the character of their offices, which demanded the skills of a jurist, an administrator and a military commander, and, on the other, from their privilege of taking part in senatorial debates and in the decisions of the Senate, which required the same skills as were necessary in the tenure of senatorial offices. Accordingly, the training received by senators was also uniform. Young senators were trained in law, oratory and warfare through a purely private education within the circle of the family and relations and through the tenure of the lower senatorial offices. However, it was still possible for able and interested young men to acquire a knowledge of history, literature and philosophy.[124]

This system of induction imbued the senator both in the ideals of the Roman state and in the tradition of his own family: the uniformity of the patterns of thought and behaviour among members of the first order was thus greatly promoted. This senatorial identity manifested itself first in proud confidence in belonging to the noblest order (*amplissimus ordo*) and also in the conviction that the senator who met the requirements for membership of his order was unsurpassable, like Aufidius Victorinus, of whom Fronto, his father-in-law, said that he was '*omnium optimarum artium praecipuus vir*' (*De nep. amisso*, 2.3). Part of this identity was readiness to serve the Roman state (Plin., *Ep.*, 4.23.3), or at least to pursue a political career, though also the desire to offset the exertions and dangers of high office by a high standard of living (Tac. *Ann.* 2.33). The feeling of belonging among the senators was very marked, despite various rivalries and frictions between individuals, families and groupings. As Juvenal put it, when the house of a noble burned down the whole aristocracy took pity and all helped the victim, whereas no one came to the aid of an ordinary mortal (3.209ff.).

This unity of the senatorial order is all the more remarkable since the *ordo senatorius* was composed of a heterogeneous body of men and was subject to constant change in the course of the Principate.

Many marriages within the senatorial aristocracy were childless: the privileges accorded to a father of three children did not change the fact. Under the Antonines only one in two of the consular senators at most had an adult son who could follow in the footsteps of his father.[125] This meant that, of the senatorial families of a given time, only about half would exist a generation later. And the ranks of the senators had been depleted still further by the sacrifices made by the order under Tiberius, Caligula, Claudius, Nero, in the year of the four emperors and under Domitian. Whereas at the end of the Republic there were some 50 families of the most ancient lineage, who claimed descent from the 'Trojan ancestors' of the Romans (Dion. Hal.,1.85.3), as early as the reign of Claudius only a very few really old families remained (Tac., *Ann.*,11.25). In the mid second century Apuleius stated (Flor.,8) that only a few senators were to be found among the many ordinary men and only a few *nobiles* among those. At the end of that century Manius Acilius Glabrio (*consul,* probably in 173) was reckoned to be the most distinguished senator through his ancestry: he traced his family tree back to Aeneas (Herod. 2.3.4.) and his family had provided a *consul* as early as 191 BC.[126] Thus the senatorial order had always to be replenished with *homines novi.*

'New men' played a very important role within the senatorial order under the Principate. As early as the reign of Augustus a number of important *homines novi* stood out from the senatorial elite, as, for example, Marcus Vipsanius Agrippa or Titus Statilius Taurus. After Vespasian (who was himself a new man) new men constituted the majority of senators entrusted with the most important positions in the administration of the empire, in the command of the army and in the governorships of the imperial provinces.[127] Moreover, it was often the *homines novi* who, like Cato and Cicero, articulated most clearly the attitudes of their new social home, a home with which they identified totally. Tacitus and Pliny are the best examples. The coincidence of two factors meant that men of this sort were over-represented at the commanding heights of the senatorial order. First, the *homines novi*, who were often selected to become members of the senatorial order through consideration of their outstanding abilities, were usually eager to bring about their full integration into the Roman aristocracy through sterling service in the administration of the empire. Second, they enjoyed the energetic patronage of the emperor, since they were considered especially loyal supporters of the monarchy through their close connection with the imperial house.

Homines novi came largely from the upper strata of the cities of the empire. They were very often the sons of meritorious *equites*. Most of them gained at an early age the right to wear the toga with a broad purple stripe and to attain a low senatorial office, once chosen by the Senate (*ius honorum*). In addition there were erstwhile *equites*, who had begun an equestrian military and administrative career and who might be admitted into the senatorial order at a rank appropriate to their age (*adlecti in amplissimum ordinem*). It was always the emperor who decided who should receive such a privilege and social advancement. Nevertheless, the patronage of powerful relatives and friends played an extremely important part, especially in the recommendation of young men for admission to a senatorial career. There was usually a great future for a man praised by a senator as influential as Pliny as '*iuvenis probissimus, gravissimus, eruditissimus, omni denique laude dignissimus*' (*Ep.*, 2.9.2ff.).

At the beginning of the Empire many 'new men' still came from Italy. But the recruitment of new senators from the Italian peninsula became ever more infrequent during the first century: in particular, the economic difficulties of Italy increasingly stood in the way of the emergence of new families of great landowners. In their place provincial *novi homines* came into the Senate in ever increasing numbers, as the process of integration of the provinces into the empire continued. In the Antonine era there were hardly any more new men from Italy, except those from the north of the peninsula between the Alps and the Po, an area which was like a province in many ways and wherein there was always an aristocracy of great and powerful landowners. The realignment of the senatorial order was only accelerated by the extinction of many older senatorial families from Italy. The process was taken further by a variety of imperial measures to promote the integration of the provincials, like Claudius' extension of the *ius honorum* to the aristocracy of the Tres Galliae in AD 48.[128] Under the early emperors the number of provincial senators was still quite small: we know of only about a dozen senators of provincial origin under Augustus and Tiberius. Most of these came from the most Romanised and urbanised provinces, especially from southern Gaul and Baetica. Under Nero the number of attested provincial senators had risen to about 50. From the reign of Vespasian their numbers rose far higher. Besides southern Gaul and Spain there were also senators in ever increasing numbers from other parts of the empire, especially Africa, Asia, and Galatia. Under Antoninus Pius the number of provincials matched the number of Italians, among consulars at least, and under Marcus provincials constituted the majority at the summit of power for the first time.[129] Yet this process of realignment did not have any radical social or political results: the provincial senators – like Gnaeus Iulius Agricola from Forum Julii or Marcus Cornelius Fronto from Cirta – championed the ideals and attitudes of the Roman senatorial aristocracy as much as their fellow senators who came from Italy.

The internal hierarchy of the senatorial order was not constituted by the grouping of its members according to ethnic or regional criteria. It derived from the status of particular offices, which the senator could attain through the various opportunities embodied in the *cursus honorum*. The career open to a senator under the Empire was quite different from the Republican *cursus honorum* through the accretion of many new offices in the service of the emperor. Normally, a senator began his career at the age of 18-20 as a *vigintivir*. He usually proceeded thence to become a *tribunus legionis* in a province. He gained formal membership of the Senate at the age of 25 when he became *quaestor*. Thereafter he became *tribunus plebis* or *aedilis* and, at the age of 30, *praetor* (the age limits, which could sometimes be breached by personal privileges, functioned in practice more as lower limits). At praetorian rank one might hold certain offices in the sphere of competence of the Senate, in particular, as *proconsul* in a senatorial province. But many posts lay in the imperial sphere and were appointed directly by the emperor, posts which included that of legionary commander (*legatus legionis*) and that of governor in an imperial province (*legatus Augusti pro praetore*) without a legionary garrison or with only one legion. At about the age of 40 – in most cases, about 43 – the senator could become *consul*. There were several pairs of consuls each year – usually four or five pairs under the Antonines, for example – so that the consulship did not remain the privilege of a small group of senators as it had been in the Late Republic. The most important offices in the administration of the empire were bestowed upon consular senators, as were responsibilities in the city of Rome, governorships in imperial provinces with more than one legion and proconsulships in the most important senatorial provinces, Africa and Asia. Really outstanding senators might conclude their careers with a second consulship and the prefecture of the capital (*praefectus urbi*).[130]

The various types of career were different: they reflected the

internal stratification of the senatorial order. They are best distinguished in the Antonine period, when – after a long development
with a variety of experiments – they had achieved a fairly set form.
A small elite, consisting of the descendants of the older families
ennobled in the Republic or under the early emperors and of the
closer relatives of the ruling emperor, enjoyed patrician rank which
brought them important privileges. Normally the patrician began
his career in the top class of the *vigintiviri* as mint-master (*triumvir
monetalis*). He gained the quaestorship and the praetorship often
through imperial commendation. He did not pass into the essentially plebeian – and expensive – offices of the popular tribune and
the aedile, but rose to the consulship at only 32 or 33. He could
forego the often difficult tenure of praetorian and consular offices in
the provinces. His social prestige was such that he did not need
them. Other senators, especially *homines novi* whose ability had
been recognised early, gained as much advancement in their careers
from the emperor, but in a rather different way. Once they had
gained praetorian rank (having often had imperial support in
senatorial elections for the lower offices) they were placed in key
offices in the administration of the empire as commanders and governors and passed through a lengthy career. One example among
many is that of Sextus Iulius Severus, the best general of Hadrian
(Dio, 69.13.2; *ILS*, 1056).[13] A similar mechanism operated in the
case of other senators who were not pushed so hard by the emperors
and who held senatorial offices between those of *praetor* and *consul*.
These privileged senators – under the Antonines somewhat less
than half of all senators – constituted as consulars (or as senators
destined for the consulship) the elite in the empire. Ordinary
senators, distinguished neither by particularly high birth nor by
their capacity and ability, received scant backing from the emperor.
After the praetorship they held senatorial offices, if they were lucky,
and had virtually no prospect of attaining the honoured rank of *consul*.

The result of this arrangement was that there was a clearly defined
social hierarchy even within the first order – and also that only a
quite small selection of men was available for the appointment of
the most important commands and offices. This aristocratic system
of selection worked well for the most part so long as Rome did not
encounter any great external or internal political problems. But in
extraordinary situations – as, for example, in the Batavian revolt of
AD 69 – its shortcomings were evident. Under the new conditions in

which the Roman world found itself from the second half of the second century the crisis of this system, especially in the upper echelons of the social hierarchy, was inevitable.

Other Elevated Orders and Strata

The *ordo equester* had many more members than the senatorial order.[132] Under Augustus up to 5,000 *equites* took part in the equestrian parade at Rome on 15 July (Dion.Hal., 6.13.4). And these constituted only a minority in the equestrian order, for many *equites* did not travel to Rome for the festival and *equites* over the age of 35 were not required to participate (Suet., *Aug.*, 38.3). According to Strabo (3.5.3; 5.1.7) the number of the members of the second order at Gades and Patavium, the two cities with the most *equites* at the beginning of the Empire, reached some 500. In the theatre at Arausio in southern Gaul there were three rows of seats for *equites* (*ILS*, 5655). The total number of *equites* under Augustus may perhaps be estimated at 20,000, much as it had been towards the end of the Republic (cf.p.101). In the first two centuries of the Empire the number doubtless increased considerably through the constant admission of ever more provincials to the equestrian order.

As members of a leading *ordo* the *equites*, too, had an identity, as is apparent, for example, from the painstaking recitation of their titulature in honorific inscriptions and epitaphs or from their solidarity within the society of particular cities (*ILS*, 7030). But the *ordo equester* was not as homogeneous an order as the *ordo senatorius*. When most of its members showed a common spirit and common modes of behaviour, this was because they had borrowed the ideals and the traditions of the senators, for they had none that were specifically their own. This was especially the case with those who entered the public service and received the same legal and military training. The structure of the equestrian order – loose in comparison with that of the senatorial order – the economic circumstances of its various members – which were often different – its heterogeneous composition and the occupations of various *equites* – which were also often very different – did not permit the equestrian order to emerge as a social group as close-knit as the senatorial order.

It was of prime importance that membership of the equestrian order was not hereditary, in formal terms at least. Admission followed the elevation of the individual not the family: the equestrian order was thus not an aristocracy of birth but an aristocracy of individuals ('*Personenadel*'). Yet it often happened in practice that the son of an *eques* was also admitted to the equestrian order (for example, *ILS*, 6335): hence the phrase 'equestrian families' (for example, Tac., *Hist.*, 1.52). But it was hardly possible for equestrian families like the senatorial families, to maintain membership of their order for many generations and that not just because of the childlessness of many equestrian families. There are attested cases of sons of *equites* who did not attain the same rank (*ILS*, 6496, for example). But there is, understandably, more evidence for the elevation of the son of an *eques* into the senatorial order. The equestrian families constituted the most important source of ongoing recruitment for the replenishment of the senatorial order. For example, the family of the future emperor Septimius Severus left the equestrian order because its members were repeatedly admitted into the senatorial order (cf.SHA, *S.*,1.1ff.). In general, the connections between the members of the senatorial order and those of the equestrian order were very close as a result of marriages, family links and friendships. The younger Pliny, for example, corresponded with many *equites* as well as with senators. And the equestrian order was still more open from below, to the decurional order of the various cities. Very many *equites* – especially those who did not aspire to a career in the public service or could not enter upon one through a lack of ability and connections – held civic offices and belonged both to the *ordo equester* and to the *ordo decurionum* in one city or even in several cities at the same time.

Moreover, the economic circumstances of the *equites* might be very different. According to Martial, the minimum required property qualification of 400,000 sesterces allowed only a modest existence when set against the demands of an equestrian lifestyle; there were even *equites* who had hardly enough to eat (Gellius, *NA*,11.7.3). But most were far better placed. So, for example, the author Columella, who had lands in various parts of central Italy. And we also know of *equites* who were enormously rich, men who were much more wealthy than many senators, as was Vedius Pollio, the friend of Augustus, whose immeasurable wealth was famous (Dio, 54.23.1ff.). The sources of the wealth of the *equites* were also different. Those who held higher public offices as procurators drew an annual salary of 60,000, 100,000 and 200,000 sesterces and, from the reign of Marcus, 300,000 sesterces according to their rank. The holders of the top equestrian offices, like the praetorian prefecture, were still better paid. But it was their private sources of income that were crucial. Among the *equites* there were many great merchants, great entrepreneurs and bankers, like Cornelius Senecio, who, according to Seneca, exhausted all opportunities for gaining income, including the customs contracts so popular with the *equites* (*Ep.*, 101.1ff.). By and large the members of the equestrian order were more concerned in non-agrarian sources of income than were the senators. But even among the *equites* the main source of wealth remained land. According to Quintilian (4.2.45) the jurors of the city of Rome (*iudices*), of whom the majority (3,000 of a total of 5,000) had equestrian rank, were owners of estates. So too were the many *equites* in Italy and the provinces who also belonged to the decurional order in the cities there.

The social composition of the equestrian order was also heterogeneous. Some *equites* were of relatively lowly origin. Among them were the sons of freedmen, like Vedius Pollio. They gained advancement through their economic ability or they owed it to their valuable connections with powerful Romans, as did the future emperor Publius Helvius Pertinax (SHA,*P.*, 1.1ff.). Even freedmen were sometimes admitted into the equestrian order, as was Antonius Musa, the doctor of the emperor Augustus (Dio, 53.30.3): later, too, freedmen in the imperial service were rewarded in this manner, as was Icelus under Galba (Suet. *Galba*, 14.2). But these were the exceptions, for the taint of servile origin was not reconcilable with the ideology of the order. Even Horace, *libertino patre natus* (*Serm.*, 1.6.6), suffered from this slur. In the Early Empire equestrian rank was also given on occasion to the leading members of tribal aristocracies in the provinces. To the latter category belong the Cheruscan Arminius[133] and also several leaders of the north Gallic-German uprising against Rome in AD 69, like the Treveran Iulius Classicus and also apparently the Batavian Iulius Civilis. Many *equites* rose into the equestrian order through their personal merits, after a long military career. This happened through promotion from the post of centurion to the rank of *primus pilus* (with a salary of 60,000 sesterces), as in the case of Quintus Marcius Turbo from Dalmatia, who began his career as a centurion under the Flavians and attained the highest equestrian offices under his friend Hadrian.[134] But most *equites* belonged to the *ordo decurionum* of the cities of the empire and owed their rank, essentially, to their wealth. Of the 53 securely attested or probable *equites* from the province of Dalmatia at least 20 held civic offices and belonged to the upper stratum of their respective cities. Of the 22 attested *equites* from Noricum most are known to have come from the leading families of their respective cities. There were many *equites* in the colonies and municipalities of the province of Hispania Citerior, who furnished the provincial high priests appointed each year under the Flavians, Trajan and Hadrian, at least.[135]

The ethnic composition of the equestrian order was also more varied than that of the senatorial order, though the admission of provincials to the second order had as little radical social and political consequence as their admission to the first order. Since many provincials could attain the minimum equestrian *census*, the inhabitants of the provinces were more strongly represented in the *ordo equester* than in the senatorial order as early as the reign of Augustus: the existence of 500 *equites* at Gades in southern Spain indicates as much. Nevertheless the ethnic realignment of the equestrian order in the Principate took the same course as the change in the composition of the senatorial order. Within the equestrian military tribunate the proportion of Italians to provincials was 90:29 in the period from Augustus to Caligula, as far as our evidence goes, 25:20 under Claudius and Nero, 21:30 under the Flavians and 117:143 in the second century. As with the majority of provincial senators, most *equites* of provincial origin in the first century AD came from certain more urbanised areas, like Spain, southern Gaul and Asia. In many provinces urbanisation, with its social consequences, only gradually created the conditions for the evolution of rich families oriented towards Rome, whose members might be distinguished with the *equus publicus*. The earliest attested *eques* from Africa, who engaged in imperial service, was admitted to the *ordo equester* in the fourth decade of the first century; of the 162 attested African *equites* with a normal *cursus honorum* only six attained their rank before Hadrian. Of the 22 Norican *equites* the first is attested under Trajan and the first attested Pannonian *equites* appear at the beginning of the second century.[136]

The final point of diversity was the different nature of equestrian occupations. Many of the *equites* held civic offices or the position of a *iudex* at Rome, while others completely rejected a public role. Those who achieved elevation into the second order from the post of centurion were career officers, but in the final phase of their *cursus honorum* they could pass into the highest equestrian offices in the administration of the empire as procurators. In most cases, the careers of *equites* admitted to public service began with military posts which were themselves of equestrian rank *(militia equestris)*. In such a career an *eques* first served as the commander of a body of infantry 500-strong *(praefectus cohortis)*. Thereafter he served as a staff officer in a legion or as the commander of a body of infantry 1,000-strong *(tribunus legionis, tribunus cohortis)* and, finally, as the commander of a body of cavalry 500-strong *(praefectus alae)*. From the second century this last post might be followed by the command of a body of cavalry 1,000-strong.[137] Particularly well-qualified and ambitious *equites* could pass thence to high posts in the economic and financial administration of the empire or to the governorship of some smaller provinces with the title of *procurator Augusti*. Finally, the best-fitted were appointed to the highest offices at court (particularly from the Flavian period and, still more so, after Hadrian when these offices were no longer allotted to imperial freedmen). Thereafter they might hold the posts of commander of the fire service of the city of Rome *(praefectus vigilum)*, of the highest official in charge of the grain supply of Rome *(praefectus annonae)*, of viceroy of Egypt *(praefectus Aegypti)* and of praetorian prefect, the highest equestrian appointment *(praefectus praetorio)*.[138]

The *equites* who entered public service constituted 'an aristocracy of office'. The majority of *equites*, however, were not involved in such service – indeed, in the mid second century, for example, there were only about 550 equestrian military posts and (under Antonnus Pius) there were only a little more than 100 procuratorial positions. This meant that the equestrian order was not involved in the political government of the Roman empire *en masse*, as was the senatorial order, wherein the majority, who could not aspire to the consulship, could at least gain admittance to the lower senatorial offices. But the *equites* in top positions, together with the leading senators, belonged to the elite of the empire and the praetorian prefect was often the second man in the state. There was hardly any difference between the functions, the rank and the privileges of the cream of the senatorial and equestrian orders. Both groups together constituted the dominant military and political grouping in the empire: even in the view of contemporary Roman society the two elites were hardly distinguished. Thus the crucial distinction in the social and particularly in the political hierarchy within the highest groups in Roman society lay not simply between senators and *equites*, but between the particular echelons within these two leading *ordines*.

Still more diverse than the equestrian order were the social elites in the cities. By contrast with the senatorial order and the equestrian order, there was no umbrella institution to unite the members of this status grouping – there was no 'empire order'. The organisation of the civic elite into an order, with the title *ordo decurionum* in communities organised on the Roman model, created an autonomous body in each separate city. In each city it comprised the members of the council and the magistrates, deliberately set apart from the *plebs* of the city. In principle membership of this sort of local *ordo* was no more hereditary than was membership of the equestrian order. Admission was granted to those rich citizens who, having achieved the age of 25 or 30, gained membership of the council *(decurionatus)* through the tenure of civic magistracies – without actually performing any functions, from the second century onwards. Yet since the sons of decurions inherited the property of their fathers it was common in the Early Empire for the members of a family to belong to the *ordo decurionum* of their city over several generations. Further, since, in the second century at least, there were no more radical realignments in the cities (for example, through the rise of freedmen), the decurionate became ever more hereditary in practice, so that the sons of decurions were brought into the *ordo*.[139]

The *ordo* of a particular city had some 100 members at most. There were only a few exceptions to this rule, mostly in the east, where the council of elders *(gerousia)* in the larger cities might have a membership numbering several hundreds, and also in small cities which could not find 100 men able to bear the expenses of the decurionate. In some Italian cities, as in Cures and Veii, the councillors were known, significantly, as *centumviri*. In the *album* of AD 223 from Canusium (*ILS*,6121) 164 *decuriones* are indeed listed, but once one deducts the 39 honorary decurions of the senatorial and equestrian orders, who were the *patroni* of the community, and the 25 sons of decurions (*praetextati*), the actual number of councillors becomes precisely 100. We can therefore estimate a total of 100,000 to 150,000 decurions in the more than 1,000 cities of the Roman empire. According to R. Duncan-Jones, the number for Africa was some 25,000, perhaps 2 per cent of all adult males in the cities.[140]

Paradoxically the uniform organisation of the civic elites generated a marked heterogeneity in their composition. The importance and the size of population of particular cities were often very different, as was, therefore, their social structure. Accordingly there were great differences from city to city in the actual social status of the 100 or so leading men of the *ordo decurionum* in respect of their wealth, economic role, training and origin. This is immediately apparent from the disparity of the amounts fixed as minimum property qualifications for the decurions. In many larger and average-sized cities the minimum required was 100,000 sesterces, as in Carthage and in Comum in northern Italy. In communities of less importance the figure was lower: in the small African municipalities it was only 20,000 sesterces. Since in second century Africa a fortune of 60,000 sesterces was regarded as only modest (Apul., *Apol.*, 101), the decurions in many small cities were only 'rich' by local standards.

And there could be great differences between the *ordines* of particular cities even within the same province. At Tarraco, for example, the rich capital of the province of Hispania Citerior, most civic worthies known to us possessed the equestrian property qualification; admission to the *ordo* of this city meant social elevation in the case of rich foreigners, such as landowners from the interior. By contrast, the decurions of the smaller cities of the peninsula only seldom attained the *ordo equester* and were only regularly successful in gaining the high priesthood of the province at Tarraco from the time of Hadrian. Although most decurions were the owners of estates in the civic territories, where they often had villas, as, for example, in Noricum, the size and rentability of their estates might be very different. Thus the lands of the rich citizens of the cities of Gaul might be as extensive as ten square kilometres, whereas the estates of the rich decurions of Aquincum were at most three to four square kilometres in size and on the territory of many cities there were estates still smaller.[141]

And there were many other differences between the local *ordines*. In the great centres of trade there were many merchants and entrepreneurs among the decurions, as at Ostia, Aquileia and Salona, for example. In larger cities the *ordo* was also often miscellaneous in other respects. Thus, at Salona, for example, in accordance with the structure of the population of this colony, the *ordo* consisted of the descendants of early Italian settlers, veterans, the descendants of rich freedmen, immigrants who increasingly flooded in from Italy and various provinces and immigrant locals from the Dalmatian mountain country. By contrast, at Aquincum, for example, the decurions attested from the second century were Romanised Celts. In the small municipalities of Pannonia and the Dalmatian hinterland the decurions were also locals – frequently peasants who were only relatively prosperous and who were far behind the decurions of the large cities not only in respect of their economic position, but also with regard to their political connections and their education.[142] As a rule the *ordo decurionum* in one and the same city was never homogeneous. This was not simply because the groupings of the rich encompassed differences in origin and occupation, as at Salona. As with the social hierarchy within the senatorial and equestrian orders, the *ordo* of the various cities also displayed an internal stratification – all the more so from about the beginning of the second century, when many decurions were gradually confronted by financial difficulties and ever less able to bear the burdens of membership of their order.[143] Thus, as early as Hadrian, a distinction was drawn within the *ordo* of a city like Clazomenae in Asia Minor between the *primores viri* and the *inferiores* (*Dig.*, 50.7.5.5.). And earlier still there were certain eminent families in many cities, whose members gained prestige through benefactions and expenditures and held the magistracies disproportionately often. Such families are often attested in the second century, as, for example, are the *Valerii* at Poetovio in Pannonia, a family which furnished several *equites* and also, significantly, the first attested Pannonian senator.[144].

But the separate *ordines decurionum* in many cities of the empire-cities with structures which were in some respects very different – also had important features in common, for all their differences. Decurions in the various cities shared common rights and duties and, thus, had uniform functions. It was not only the privileges of the decurions in criminal law that were uniform: so too were their duties – the administration of their cities in the fields of justice and finance, the food supply, construction and the maintenance of public order. These duties were carried out by means of both the decrees of the decurions meeting as a council and the activities of the magistrates, who entered the *ordo decurionum* – at least in the Early Empire – through their magistracies, in theory. The members of this order thus had the chance of a career structure specific to themselves. Normally, a *decurio* became first *aedilis* and then *duumvir* (in many cities with the titles *quattuorvir aedilicia potestate* and *quattuorvir iure dicundo*), that is, vice-head and then head of the community, each for one year. Yet he could also hold other offices, like the quaestorship in the city, or could repeat his headship and hold municipal priesthoods.[145]

No less important was the economic role of the decurions in the community. Together with the rich freedmen they met most of the public expenditure of the cities. Thus a decurion was expected to pay the community a price for his position (*summa honoraria*) or to bear the cost of the construction of public buildings. The same applied to the receipt of the honorific office of civic priest, which in the African city of Mustis, for example, cost 5,000 sesterces, an office in which rich incumbents paid as much as twice that sum. In the other African cities the price of various offices usually ranged between 2,000 and 20,000 sesterces.[146] Rich civic worthies some-times expended much higher sums and gained lustre through their frequent acts of beneficence. Aulus Quinctilius Priscus, for exam-ple, who passed through a civic career at Ferentinum in Italy, put his lands, worth 70,000 sesterces, at the disposal of the community and endowed annual distributions of food from the income from these estates (*ILS,* 6271). But his *munificentia* was still rather modest when set beside the sometimes very lavish expenditures of other members of the order of decurions. A decurion of eastern origin, Gaius Domitius Zmaragdus, financed out of his own pocket the con-struction of an amphitheatre in the municipality of Carnuntum in the second century (*ILS,*7121), while the sum of about 2½ million sesterces, which the famous Opramoas of Rhodiapolis bestowed upon the cities of Lycia in the first half of the second century (*IGRR*, III, 739), matched the beneficence of rich senators and *equites.*[147]

In the first century AD this system of liturgies rested by and large on the basis of free choice: the economic activity that flourished in the many newly founded cities, in particular, afforded financial opportunities to the local upper strata which were often outstand-ing. But from about the reigns of Trajan and Hadrian the *inferiores* among the decurions found it increasingly difficult to make such expenditures. It was then that a process began which led to increas-ing state control of the system of liturgies: its consequence was that the decurionate started to become a burden for some of the rich. The tendency is already visible in the Antonine period, most clearly so in the repeated submissions of city-dwellers in search of exemp-tion from the burden. But it was after the emperor Marcus that really serious consequences manifested themselves as a result of this process. In the Principate, on the whole, civic elites were able to ful-fil the economic functions that were so important for the empire. Moreover, their political role made them the backbone of the sys-tem of Roman rule: by administering their communities they bore the burden of the state. Further, despite all their ethnic and social differences, they were the common elite both of the cities and the civic territories, where they were the champions of Roman ideals and customs: as such, they contributed to the furtherance of the unity of the Roman Empire.

These community elites did not include another, equally wealthy social grouping in the cities, which – at least in respect of the economic status of its members – should be counted with the upper strata of Roman society, namely the rich *liberti*.[148] The sources of their income very often lay in the fields of trade, banking and craft production, but also in the ownership of land. And these wealthy men, too, usually invested their profits in land. In consequence they were often as much owners of land in the civic territories as were the decurions. Yet, because of the taint of their servile origin, even the richest freedmen could not enter the *ordo decurionum* of a city, except in a few exceptional cases. More commonly their merits were rewarded with the insignia peculiar to a decurion (*ornamenta decurionalia*), though these did not make them members of the *ordo*. Normally they formed their own body which constituted a 'second order' in civic society beside the *ordo decurionum*, as did the equestrian order beside the senatorial order in the society of the empire at large. The members of such a body usually called themselves *Augustales* (with a range of variations), in accordance with their role in the imperial cult. Occasionally the body was expressly called an *ordo Augustalium*, as at Ostia (*ILS*,6141; 6164). Such organisations were to be found everywhere, except in small agrarian cities which had hardly any rich *liberti*. Here and there these bodies included *ingenui* (often including the sons of freedmen), but in the larger cities at least the *Augustalis* was a rich parvenu of servile origin like the social type embodied in Trimalchio.[149]

The economic concerns of these freedmen were much the same as those of the decurions. They contributed an important part of the money needed for urban development and for the welfare of the urban population by paying a cash sum or by erecting cult statues to gain admission to the *Augustales* or other honours and also by financing public construction work and embellishment. Publius Decimius Eros Merula, for example, the rich doctor of servile origin at Assisi (p.114), paid that city 2,000 sesterces for membership of the organisation of wealthy freedmen and he donated a further 67,000 sesterces for the erection of statues and the paving of roads (*ILS*,7812). Other freedmen could provide much greater sums for public purposes, sums which, in the first century at least, sometimes exceeded the expenditures of decurions. The economic flourishing of many cities in the Early Empire was largely due to this social grouping. But its importance suffered a marked decline from the beginning of the second century. The result of this decline was a heavier burden for the decurions and increasing difficulties in civic finances.

The position of the rich freedmen in the cities was in some respects comparable to that of the imperial slaves and freedmen. In view of their favourable economic circumstances and their position of power, the slaves and freedmen of the emperor (*familia Caesaris*) can also be counted, by and large, with the upper strata of the Roman empire, despite their own stratification.[150] Through their activities in Rome and in other administrative centres they often belonged to the upper strata in the cities, though they were not linked to these communities by any formal ties, for the most part. Further, their wealth allowed them to lend financial support to the cities. One Publius Aelius Onesimus for example, a freedman of Hadrian, donated 200,000 sesterces to his home city of Nacolea in Asia Minor for the purchase of grain. The fact that in making this expenditure he made explicit reference to his modest means is significant of the financial resources of his kind (*ILS*,7196). The great gulf between the social status of these *liberti* and *servi* and that of ordinary freedmen and slaves is revealed by the fact that they often had wives of free birth. They even gained a certain measure of prestige from their service to the person of the emperor, in the central chancelleries of the administration of the empire at the imperial court, in the bureaux of the provincial capitals and the imperial estates. But the stigma of servile origin limited them in much the same way as it limited the rich freedmen of the cities. Despite their greater services and despite their power and wealth they seldom entered the equestrian order, save in a few exceptional cases, and they never entered the senatorial order. This limitation applied even to the highest members of the *familia Caesaris*, even to the three most powerful *liberti* in the imperial court, who under Claudius largely held the conduct of Roman affairs in their hands through their enormous influence over the emperor, that is, the general secretary (*ab epistulis*) Narcissus, the head of the office for petitions (*a libellis*) Callistus and the financial secretary (*a rationibus*) Pallas. Even Pallas, who was in a position to refuse the 15 million offered him for his services by the Senate, only had the particular status symbols of a *praetor*, which did not bring him formal admission to the senatorial order of Rome (Plin., Ep., 8.6.1ff.).

Lower Strata in the Cities

The social composition of the lower strata of the population in the Roman empire was even more heterogeneous than that of the upper strata. This was largely a corollary of the great economic, social and cultural diversity of the various parts of the empire. Indeed, this diversity also affected the leading strata in important ways, yet the members of the latter were for the most part brought together in organised orders and had their particular ranks therein marked out by uniform status symbols. A process of integration also occurred among the lower strata during the Empire, but – especially in rural areas – it could never proceed as far as in the higher echelons of Roman society. Thus at the turn of the first into the second century there were slight differences at most between the decurions of Italy, Africa and Pannonia, for example, in view of their numbers, wealth and level of education. But whereas the rural population of Italy still included many slaves, in Africa it already consisted of *coloni* to a significant extent and in Pannonia, by contrast, it was largely made up of independent peasants.

At the same time, the lower strata were not divided by hierarchical distinctions as clear as those among the upper strata. The only clear divisions were not horizontal, like those between senators, *equites* and decurions without equestrian rank, but vertical. First, there was the obvious division between the *plebs urbana* and the *plebs rustica*, founded upon their differences in place of habitation, occupation, economic activity, lifestyle, opportunities for advancement, culture, traditions and customs.[151] This division was made all the more obvious by contrast with the structure of the upper strata, which had no division of this sort. The concepts of *urbanitas* and *rusticitas* immediately express the general view of the difference in the level of culture between the population of town and country. Strabo divided the population into city-dwellers and country-dwellers, with an intermediate category (13.1.25). Galen observed a great social gulf between the well-provided city-dwellers and the disadvantaged country-dwellers (6.749f.). Moreover, the different legal status of free-born, freedmen and slaves were also clearly defined. These differences had important social consequences, for the legal categories reflected different forms of dependency upon the upper strata among the lower strata. Yet the boundaries between all these groups were not obvious social divisions, despite the gradation from *urbanus* down to *rusticus, ingenuus* to *libertus* and thence to *servus*, a gradation of which there are many signs. It was not inclusion in one of the aforementioned categories that determined whether one possessed the means of production or not, whether one was prosperous or poor and whether one was partially or wholly dependent upon members of the upper strata. Rather, the latter factors were the basis of a pervasive internal stratification within each of the aforesaid groups, though this was always only a graduated stratification with no clear boundaries.

The lower strata in the cities tended to display more uniformity than the lower strata of rural areas. Moreover, by and large, they enjoyed a better social position than the masses of the rural population. In the cities there were usually better prospects for employment, better opportunities to change occupation, more scope for a public life, more largesse and, not least, better chances of entertainment than in the countryside. It is significant that the rich freedmen who formed the bodies of *Augustales*, usually came from the *liberti* of the cities. Of course, most members of the *plebs urbana* were not so lucky. Nevertheless, in the large cities, at least, especially at Rome, many of them were able to find a secure living. It should be noted that even when they owned a fortune of 20,000 sesterces and four slaves they were still counted among the poor (Juv., 9.140ff.). Even for slaves life was essentially rather better in the cities than on the land. Seneca observed a marked difference between the less oppressive position of urban slaves and the hard work of the rural slaves (*De ira*,3.29.1). Columella reviled the urban slaves for being habituated only to pleasure, unlike the hard-working slaves on the estates (1.8.1f.).

It was also important that the members of the urban lower strata might be organised in associations (*collegia*). These collegia controlled by the state or by the civic administration, allowed even quite simple folk, slaves even, to come together in guild associations (for example, in the *collegium fabrum*, a guild of craftsmen which existed in many cities) or in associations of the devotees of the same god.[152] The members of such associations enjoyed a certain corporate identity: in the government of these associations they might imitate the role of civic dignitaries. At the same time these associations could finance better meals and a proper burial for their members out of membership dues and the donations of wealthy citizens.

Moreover, the operation of the civic fire brigade was put in their hands. But still more important than these associations was the fact that the *plebs urbana* was regularly provided with grain – in Rome often by the emperor, in the other cities mostly by rich private persons. A bonus was the availability of entertainment, particularly at shows in the amphitheatre, circus and theatre (at Rome, again, often financed by the emperor and in the other cities by rich citizens). And there were also the other opportunities for the pleasure-seeker provided by a city – like a visit to a brothel: 28 brothels are attested at Pompeii alone.

But, for all that, the life of most members of the *plebs urbana* was a hard one. The urban *plebs* – particularly its lowest strata – was despised in more elevated circles, as Tacitus' comment on the urban *plebs* makes plain – '*sordida et circo et theatris sueta*' (*Hist.*, 1.4).[153] Their living conditions were often wretched, their working conditions often most unpleasant, their clothes and food often inferior and their belongings usually paltry.[154] They in particular suffered badly from occasional food shortages, like that of AD 32 (Tac., *Ann.*, 6.13). Beggars seeking to exact pity were an everyday sight at Rome, (for example Seneca., *Clem.*, 2.7). Hard work and ability by no means guaranteed economic and social success. Even trade, which was often profitable, did not bring security, as witnessed by a trader of the city of Rome ('*qui negotiando locupletem se speravit esse futurum; spe deceptus erat:* ILS,7519). Deep discontent was caused by the social humiliation that poor clients – free-born and freedmen alike – had to suffer in the houses of the rich, often indeed at the hands of their slaves (for example, Juvenal 3.184ff.). Of course, urban slaves, too, were often badly treated, as, for example, by the senator Larcius Macedo (Plin., *Ep.*, 3.14.1) – significantly, like Vedius Pollio, the son of an ex-slave – whose cruel treatment of slaves was notorious.[155]

The occupations of the members of the urban lower strata covered a wide range. Amongst them, in particular, were to be found the 'intellectuals' of the Roman empire (apart from the jurists, who often belonged to the higher social strata). As legal advisers, administrators of houses and other property, doctors, pedagogues, artists, musicians, actors, community scribes, engineers and, in a number of cases, as philosophers, they practised most of the intellectual pursuits, which were regarded as at about the level of the crafts. Among the slaves there were many domestic servants and slaves with luxury functions, who played no part in production. The same may be said of the many free-born and freedmen in the larger cities, especially Rome, where the broad masses of parasitic recipients of grain always constituted a *Lumpenproletariat*. In the smaller provincial cities in particular, there were many simple townsmen who were nothing but peasants, working the surrounding estates. However, in the larger cities, on the whole, the members of the urban lower strata only had an economic function as, at best, craftsmen and traders. Many of them had a small business that was their own or rented, where they worked alone or with a few slaves or freedmen. Thus, as late as the time of Augustine, there was a street of silversmiths at Rome with many workshops (*De civ. Dei*,7.4). Even slaves could carry on a small business, as, for example, at Eburacum in Britain where there was a small goldsmith's workshop (*ILS*, 3651). But craftsmen were employed in large numbers in the workshops of wealthy business owners: for example, the many slaves in the *terra sigillata* workshops at Arretium at the beginning of the Empire, the freedmen in the *sigillata* factories of northern Italy in the first half of the first century AD and, especially, the craftsmen of free origin in the *sigillata* concerns of Gaul in the period thereafter. The structure of trade was similar. Many small traders possessed their own shops, as did, for example, freedmen at Rome who opened shops selling metalware, where they also employed their own freedmen (*ILS*,7536). As representatives (*institores*) of their master, at least, slaves could conduct a business (*ILS*, 7479). However, very many freedmen and slaves were employed as the agents of greater business houses, like, for example, the many *liberti* and *servi* of the family of the *Barbii* from Aquileia, who worked as agents in the cities of Noricum and Pannonia.[156]

These cases suggest a certain social distinction between *ingenui, liberti* and *servi* based on their respective legal status, but the social differences between these groups are by no means always clear-cut. In general the boundaries between them were quintessentially vague, for they – in the cities, as distinct from the countryside – very often derived simply from the reproductive structure of particular categories within the population. The slave usually had the prospect of manumission: he gained his freedom at about the age of 30 (a maximum in most cases), provided he lived that long. Every freedman was an erstwhile slave. And very many of the free-born were descendants of erstwhile slaves, for the child of a *libertus* born after his *manumissio* was regarded as an *ingenuus*. One consequence of this great internal mobility among the urban lower strata was that a very large percentage of the lower strata of the population – at least in the larger cities – consisted of persons of servile origin. Tacitus saw this very clearly when he stressed that very many of the population of Rome, even many *equites* and senators, were descended from slaves (*Ann.*, 13.27). A further consequence was the need constantly to replenish the pool of slaves.

The great extent of slavery throughout the urban centres is particularly apparent from the masses of epitaphs and dedications which indicate the presence of a very large number of *servi* and *liberti* in the many cities of the empire.[157] The percentage of slaves cannot be calculated. P.A. Brunt's hypothesis that the total population of Italy was about 7,500,000 under Augustus, of which 3,000,000 were slaves, is plausible, but beyond proof.[158] Our only fairly reliable figure for the number of slaves relates to Pergamum, for which Galen gives the number of citizens as 40,000 and the number of adults in total, including wives and slaves, as 120,000 (5.49). That would mean that slaves constituted about a third of the total population of Pergamum in the mid second century AD. Particularly wealthy families had many slaves. Augustan legislation envisages the possibility that one *dominus* might possess 500 slaves. In the great Roman town-house of one Lucius Pedanius Secundus, a leading senator, there were 400 slaves in AD 61 according to Tacitus (*Ann.*, 14.43). The highest recorded number of slaves in the possession of one master is 4,116 (Plin., *NH*,33.135). As Seneca puts it in his well-known observation, the number of slaves was so great that they would have constituted a serious threat to Rome, if they had been able to recognise each other by a particular manner of dress (*Clem.*, 1.24.1). But it should not be supposed from the aforementioned cases that large numbers of slaves also lived in the households of urban families of average wealth. Slave prices fluctuated in the first and second centuries AD according to the state of the market in particular parts of the empire at particular times and according to the age, sex and education of the slaves: in general, the price varied from 800 to 2,500 sesterces (though the price of a doctor as well trained as Publius Decimius Eros Merula was estimated at 50,000 sesterces upon his manumission).[159] That meant that, for example, a civic decurion, whose total property, including land, house and furniture, was only 100,000 sesterces, could afford only a few slaves, at most. In Noricum, for example, the highest attested number of slaves in one household is only six (*CIL*,III,4962). And in the northern provinces in particular, epitaphs containing references to a large number of freedmen as clients of a rich family are very rare.

Under the Empire there were no longer the unlimited opportunities for the procurement of slaves that had existed in the first and second centuries BC. Under Augustus prisoners were still often enslaved after wars of conquest, as were some 44,000 members of the tribe of the Salassi in the western Alps in 25 BC (Strabo,4.6.7). But under his successors Rome fought only a few wars of conquest and even in these the local population was by no means always sold into slavery. And since armed opposition to Rome among the conquered peoples was rare, there was a far smaller number of condemned rebels on the slave market. The enslavement of 97,000 rebellious Jews in the great Jewish War of AD 66-70 (Jos., *BJ*, 6.420) was as much an exception as their revolt itself. Trade in slaves with neighbouring peoples – the Germans, for example, or the Ethiopians – could satisfy only a very small part of the Roman need. In the Principate most slaves came from within the Roman empire and were not enslaved by force, not least because kidnapping was hardly possible in the ordered conditions of the Empire. Many slaves were the products of 'marriages' between slaves; they were the *vernae (oikogeneis)* attested in many inscriptions and papyri. But it should be observed that the natural reproduction of slave families could not maintain the number of slaves and certainly could not increase it, not least because slaves often gained their freedom at a marriageable age. The claim that 70 slave children came into the world each day on Trimalchio's estates is a deliberate literary exaggeration (Petronius, *Sat.*,53).

There can be no doubt that an important source of slaves lay in the 'voluntary' enslavement of free inhabitants of the empire. It was common practice for poor families simply to expose their children: these children were brought up as slaves (*alumni, threptoi*) by those who found them. The possible scale of this practice is revealed by a letter of Pliny to Trajan wherein the legal status of foundlings in Bithynia is described as a major issue of concern to the whole province (*Ep.*, 10.65.1). In the poor economic circumstances in which many families – nominally free, but in practice without rights and food – lived, especially in the provinces, it often happened that the children were sold into slavery or that they sold themselves into slavery as adults. This practice was very widespread among the Phrygians, for example, who provided a particularly large number of slaves under the Empire (Philost., *Apoll.*, 8.7.12). In Dio of Prusa we read the question, 'But how do you mean, I could become a slave?' and the answer, 'Because innumerable free persons sell themselves, so that they become slaves by agreement, occasionally even under conditions that were by no means reasonable and extraordinarily hard' (*Or.*,15.22f.). The jurist Marcianus treated the latter means of procuring slaves as, at least in theoretical terms, on a par with the enslavement of prisoners and the birth of *vernae* (*'si quis se maior viginti annis ad pretium participandum vendere passus est': Dig.*,1.5.51).

The latter method of enslavement was often practised not least because slaves could expect a better fate under the Empire than in the last two centuries of the Republic. The realisation that, for political and, especially, economic motives, slaves should be better treated than in the slave barracks of Cato, began to gain ground as early as the end of the Republic. Under the Empire this attitude spread farther and wider among slave-owners, with an eye to the fact that the slave population could no longer be replenished in perpetuity with new slaves. The trend was further strengthened by the humanitarian ideas conveyed by some philosophical currents. And slaves were given many privileges, mainly to spur them on to higher productivity. Columella knew very well that the profit of the owner depended not on the brutality of his exploitation of his workforce, but on their taste for work (*De re rust.*,1.7.1). At the same time, cruelty towards slaves was increasingly frowned upon. Augustus certainly disapproved of Vedius Pollio's cruel treatment of his slaves (Dio,54.23.2ff.), though, in accordance with Roman tradition, he did not interfere in the relationship between master and slave which was regarded as a private matter. Nevertheless, as early as Augustus' reign, the state began to take measures in favour of slaves. The *lex Petronia* (19 BC) prescribed that a slave could only be condemned to fight to the death with wild beasts with the agreement of the authorities. Later emperors took legislation for the protection of slaves further. Claudius treated the killing of old and sick slaves as murder and he bestowed public care and freedom upon slaves exposed by their masters. Domitian forbade the castration of slaves. Hadrian prohibited the killing of criminal slaves by their masters and, moreover, even their incarceration in private gaols.[160] Increasingly, leading Romans followed these behavioural norms, as did the younger Pliny, for example, who treated his slaves well, allowing them even the testamentary disposal of their own posses-

sions and taking an interest in their lives (*Ep.*, 8.16.1ff.). Seneca openly expresses the idea that even slaves are men: '*servi sunt?*
immo homines! servi sunt? immo contubernales! servi sunt? immo
humiles amici!' (Ep.,47.1).[161] In the *Satyricon* Petronius puts the same idea in the mouth of Trimalchio: slaves, too, are men, they drink the same mother's milk as other men, they have only fallen victim to a grim fate (*Sat.,*71).

It was of especial importance that slaves – in the cities at least – were very often manumitted: they had good prospects of *manumissio* after a certain age.[162] As early as the reign of Augustus the manumission of slaves was so commonplace that the masses of *liberti* seemed a social and political threat to the state (cf. Dion.Hal.,4.24.4ff.). The imperial government had to lead the flood in a direction in accordance with the interests of the Roman state. The *lex Fufia Caninia* (2 BC) set a limit upon the number of slaves who could be given their freedom by will at one time on the death of their master. Where a man owned 3-10 slaves, half, at most, could be given their freedom; where 11-30, a third; where 31-100, a quarter; and where 101-500, a fifth. The *lex Aelia Sentia* (AD 4) laid down the minimum age of 20 for manumission and also made it more difficult for younger slaves (below 30) to become citizens, by fixing conditions for their freedom. The real purpose of this legislation was not to limit manumission in principle and reduce the number of *liberti*. It was only meant to prevent persons of servile origin from gaining the citizenship *en masse* and without state regulation and thus exercising all too great an influence on public life. Even after these two laws it was still possible for all the slaves of a household to be freed (Gaius,*Inst.*,1.44), only not all at once by will and not with the result that all the slaves so freed would become full citizens without discrimination. Regulated exceptions apart, the latter privilege was only granted to 'mature' slaves, who had reached the age of 30. Directed at similar aims was the *lex Iunia* (perhaps AD 19), which bestowed only Latin rights, instead of full citizenship, upon persons freed at an early age or by informal means. So too the *lex Visellia* (AD 24), which prohibited the entry of freedmen into civic magistracies. Thus all these laws were not able and did not seek to restrict the general practice of granting freedom to slaves after the passage of a certain length of time (often at the age of 30 years). Rather, slave-owners usually followed this practice in the first and second centuries of the Empire as did the younger Pliny (*Ep.*, 8.16.1). According to the work of Artemidorus Daldianus, devoted to dream-reading, under the Antonines, slaves had good reason to look forward to manumission: it was only a question of time and procedure. The prospect of freedom gave many slaves hope. Under certain conditions this hope might even induce a poor non-citizen to sell his children or even himself into slavery. Provided that the master was a citizen, one automatically gained by manumission full Roman citizenship or at least Latin rights. They thus gained a privilege which a poor peasant in most provinces in the Early Empire would only obtain with difficulty – for example, through 25 no less painful years of military service in an auxiliary unit – or not at all. Moreover, during his enslavement the slave was kept in his master's house and was very often trained in a practical skill, in one of the crafts for example. In such a situation enslavement might even be 'attractive' for a peregrine: in western Asia Minor, for example, according to Philostratus (*Apoll.*, 8.7.12), nothing wrong was seen in it. For the masters this system had an advantage in the zealous labour of slaves who did not wish to put at risk their prospect of freedom and, moreover, had often to earn a little wealth (*peculium*) in order to buy their freedom at their *manumissio* through the repayment of their purchase price. Still more important were the advantages deriving from the relationship of patronage which the former master maintained with his *libertus* through economic and moral obligations. These obligations might range from a freedman's surrender of a portion of his earnings to his former master to the performance of personal services, for example, in the care of a sick former master.[163] This system was therefore in reality no more than a more refined form of exploitation than slavery without manumission. And the actual position of many freedmen was much worse than that of their small elite, whose members, like Trimalchio, for example, were freed from these social bonds by the death of their *patronus*. On the other hand, the system was only viable so long as liberated slaves could always be replaced by new ones. Yet in the Early Empire this form of slavery was entirely practicable and was the usual practice in the cities. It seems that many masters bought themselves slaves with the intention of manumitting them after a certain time and thereby creating a form of social dependency that was especially profitable for them.

Lower Strata in the Countryside

The position of slaves in the countryside was often very different from that of slaves in the cities, a distinction which applies to the lower strata of town and country in general. The social composition of the *plebs rustica*, which constituted the overwhelming majority of the population of the empire, was even more different in the various parts of the empire than that of the urban plebs. Of course, there were *ingenui, servi* and *liberti* also in the countryside, but their relative numbers were even more imbalanced in the various rural areas than they were in the cities. Moreover, these labels might cover very different social positions – for example, a free-born peasant might as easily be a smallholder or a tenant as a landless casual labourer.[164] Distinctions must also be drawn with regard to the slaves, especially between those who worked on small peasant holdings or on average-sized municipal estates in fairly small numbers and often in a patriarchal relationship with their master, and those who worked in large gangs on the *latifundia*. Particularly in those parts of the Roman world where in the Early Empire the ownership of land had not been concentrated into the hands of a few – as it had not, for example, in the Danubian lands – there was hardly a great difference between the (not very numerous) slaves of the various peasants or landowners of the decurional orders and the 'free' peasant population. Such slaves often worked beside their master and his dependents: they could start their own families and even acquire a little property of their own. By contrast, the position of slaves on the large estates was often much less favourable, though, even here, there were differences – quite apart from the fact that the overseers of the estates who were themselves servile (the *vilici* and *actores*) enjoyed a privileged position. It is significant that such a slave could be proudly proclaimed by his dependents as an *agricola optimus* (*ILS*, 7451) and that, moreover, urban slaves might sometimes be brought in to administer an estate (Plin., *Ep.*, 9.20.2, for example).

The cultivation of *latifundia* by large numbers of slaves was by no means co-extensive with the existence of large estates. In Africa and Egypt, for example, those who worked on the *latifundia* of large private landowners and of the emperor were for the most part peasants who were nominally free. In Italy slave labour on large estates was still localised, at least in the first century AD. Our best evidence is the agricultural treatise of Columella, written in the 60s.[165] By and large, Columella shared the same old attitude as Cato and Varro, that the use of slaves brought maximum profit from an estate. He stressed that, in order to increase the profitability of production, the work of the slaves should be specialised as much as possible. Although he avoided unnecessary brutality, he worked his slaves hard, partly in chains, the old method; he regarded slaves as little more than tools (*De re rust.*, 1.8.8). Yet the position of slaves improved in the Early Empire even on the *latifundia*. About a generation after Columella, the younger Pliny remarked that there were no slaves in chains on his estates, and that there were none in chains in the neighbourhood (*Ep.*, 3.19.7.).

There was also no lack of freedmen in the countryside and in agriculture. *Liberti* sometimes also worked on the smaller and average-sized properties, as, for example, on the plots of Norican peasants or on the allotments of veterans in Dalmatia and Pannonia. On the whole, slaves of masters such as these seem to have been freed more often than the slaves on the large estates. Yet the practice of manumission was not unheard of on the *latifundia*. The younger Pliny seems magnanimously to have granted freedom to his slaves without regard to their occupations (*Ep*, 8.16.1). A first-century inscription from Forum Livii in Italy contains the instructions of an estate-owner of the equestrian order to his freedmen, who worked his estate (*CIL*,XI,600). But by and large manumission was a much less common practice in the countryside, especially on the *latifundia*, than in the cities. Columella only mentions *manumissio* once: he recommends that freedom should be granted to those slavewomen who have brought more than three children into the world (*De rust.*, 1.8.19). We can see that large landowners of his calibre were not much concerned to free their slaves and, moreover, that they were very interested in the maintenance of their numbers of slaves through the birth of *vernae*. It may be supposed that the economic and social advantages which the manumission of slaves offered masters in the city were little to be expected in the countryside. Personal initiative and a certain scope were necessary for a successful career as a craftsman or trader. A slave with the prospect of manumission and, especially, a freedman with personal freedom could fulfil these requirements better than a slave without a future. By contrast, these requirements were drawbacks for an estate-owner. The potential unprofitability of the employment of free labour instead of slave labour is made quite clear by the observations of Pliny that he had to put to rights by using slaves an estate which had been run down by the previous owner who used *coloni* as *inbecilli cultores (Ep.*, 3.19.6f.).

Yet under the Empire it was increasingly difficult to find from generation to generation the large numbers of slaves needed to work the *latifundia*. Where Columella offered the mothers of three slave children a reward that was enormous by his standards, the natural reproduction of slave families was hard put to maintain the numbers of slaves. The number of free inhabitants of the Empire within the peregrine populations of the provinces was steadily declining through the gradual extension of Roman citizenship and they seem to have preferred enslavement in the cities, where they had better prospects of a future. Under the Empire slavery therefore declined constantly in the countryside, more quickly, it seems, than in the cities. On the *latifundia* the system of the colonate increasingly took over its role.[166] The *colonus* was a tenant, who rented a small part of an estate, worked that portion together with his family (so that his wife was called a *colona*: see, for example, *ILS*,7454) and gave the estate-owner a fixed share of what he produced. In the first century this system was already widespread in some provinces – particularly so in Africa and there especially on the extensive imperial estates, whose structure set a pattern for private *latifundia*. The much-quoted inscription from Henchir-Mettich, cut in the last years of Trajan, shows the colonate as the basic system for the cultivation of imperial estates: it relates not only to the contemporary period but also to an earlier one, for it refers to a *lex Manciana* passed earlier.[167] The system had long been known even in Italy, but it seemed (to Columella, for example: *De re rust.*,1.7.1ff.) essentially less productive than the slave system. For that reason Columella recommended it only for the cultivation of estates in infertile areas, where the use of expensive slaves was not economical. Yet from the second century this form of cultivation spread far and wide, even in Italy.

Most *coloni* were free men, but they also included freedmen on occasion (for example, *ILS*,7455). And even slaves were used in the tenancy system: as *quasi coloni* they lived under practically the same conditions as the 'real' *coloni*, as early as the first century AD (*Dig.*, 33.7.12.3). There was hardly any difference in their living and working conditions: the slaves used as tenants were no worse treated that the 'free' *coloni* – for example, they were no longer chained of course. Moreover, the nominally 'free' *coloni* were often little better placed than the slaves with regard to their chances of social mobility through a change of domicile or occupation. Thus the traditional differences in the respective status of free-born, freedmen and slaves gradually lost its social importance. But the *coloni* on the large estates did not constitute an entirely homogeneous peasant population, for new social distinctions developed. Thus in the inscription from Henchir-Mettich there is evidence of several categories among the workers on imperial estates: the 'normal' *coloni*, namely the small tenants, the *coloni inquilini;* landless peasants who lived on the estates and had to perform various tasks, and *stipendiarii*, other peasants, of whom some lived on the estates and others outside them, the former being required to perform stipulated tasks.

Under the Early Empire slaves and *coloni* apparently only constituted a minority of the rural population. Other widespread peasant groups lived in the various parts of the empire, different in their composition from area to area. In most provinces there were small landowners who owned property beneath the decurional *census* of the nearest city. This type of small, independent farm, lauded in the *Georgics* of Virgil, did not disappear in the Early Empire, even in Italy. The data on property sizes given by the alimentary tables highlight the fact that at the beginning of the second century there were still many small properties in the vicinity of Veleia and Beneventum, thus in two areas as different as northern Italy and Campania. Further, in most parts of the Empire there were large numbers of impoverished peasants without land, who sought to survive as day-labourers and seasonal labourers on the estates of wealthier peasants and municipal landowners and on the *latifundia*. And in many regions there were herdsmen, who – even in Italy – did not live among men and who regarded every stranger as an enemy (Fronto, *Ad M. Caes.*, 2.12). And there were the small traders, who were also to be found in rural market-places, and, especially, the small craftsmen, who worked in the villages or in the workshops on the larger estates as, for example, smiths or potters. Finally, there were also small tenants and convicts, who worked in the mines, among the rural population.

It was only in the Later Empire that coherent structures developed within the rural population of the empire, after the large-estate and colonate system had come to dominate the scene. But in one respect the position of the rural population was almost completely uniform under the Early Empire: the most oppressed social strata in the Roman empire were the fairly poor and impoverished sections of the rural population. Among these sectors those who suffered worst were not the slaves on the *latifundia*, who were of value to their masters and were at least regularly fed, but the mass of nominally 'free' peasants, who were without means of support and who, in the provinces, often also lacked the privileged status of a Roman citizen. For example, the life of the 'free' country-dwellers of Judaea or Egypt was far worse than that of the slaves on Columella's estate. Philo (*De spec. leg.*, 3.159ff.) paints a wretched picture: the rural population suffered badly under the burden of taxation and when a peasant took flight his family or neighbours were brutally mistreated and all too often tortured to death.

The Orders-Strata Structure and Its Effects

Figure 1

In short; the social structure of the empire under the Principate is best represented in the form of a pyramid (Figure 1). This pyramid neither reflects the extreme numerical imbalance between the various strata nor reflects the constant fluctuations in society in the first two centuries of the Empire. But it does illustrate, nevertheless, some particularly important features of the social hierarchy. Since the prerequisites for an independent middle order did not exist, it may be stated that society was divided into two main groups of unequal size, namely the upper strata and the lower strata. If we add up the number of senators, *equites* and decurions without equestrian status, we arrive at a total of no more than 200,000 adult males: these, together with their wives and children, amount to no more than 1 per cent of the total population of the empire. The elite proper – the holders of the most important senatorial offices and highly placed *equites* – numbered only some 160 at the end of Augustus' reign and about twice that figure in the mid second century AD. Most members of the high social strata, who stood out above the common herd by virtue of their property, powerful positions and prestige, were grouped according to clear hierarchical criteria in separate *ordines*, that is, in closed, corporate social units with specific property qualifications, offices and rank. These organisations may be considered orders by virtue of their characteristic features. In them the elite of society was united, without any sort of distinction between the urban and the rural upper strata. The rich freedmen and members of the *familia Caesaris* were not admitted to these privileged and prestigious organisations: they could be accounted members of the upper strata only in respect of their wealth and, to an extent, of their political influence. Nevertheless, even among the freedmen there is an observable trend towards imitation of the orders through the civic organisations called *Augustales*. And the *familia Caesaris* also constituted a group with a legal and functional identity, like an *ordo*.

The lower strata consisted of motley sections of the masses from town and country. Unlike the privileged *ordines*, they can by no means be termed orders. At best we can describe them as various strata, without implying that these social groups were stratified in a hierarchy. These strata shared common characteristics, particularly with regard to their economic activities in town and country and with regard to their legal status as *ingenui*, *liberti* or *servi* respectively. The border-lines between the various lower strata ran vertically in accordance with these characteristics: that is, these border-lines could only determine the social position of the individual to a certain extent. There were no clear social divisions running horizontally through the lower strata, whereas within the upper strata there were clear distinctions between the positions of the various strata. Thus positions within one and the same lower sector of the population could be very different, while the positions of particular members of different lower strata could be very similar.

Now, of course, this model cannot encapsulate every aspect of the Roman social system during the first two centuries of the Empire. Attention must be drawn to two weaknesses in the model. First, the legal and organisational criteria of division are given full weight, but it does not give due importance to the boundaries between social sectors which are based on functions and social prestige and which do not always match the boundaries between legally definable groupings and sectors. With regard to functional characteristics and the prestige that went with them, the upper strata of the Roman empire may be described as two principal strata constituting local elites and an imperial aristocracy. The local elites consisted of a separate lower stratum, containing the rich freedmen organised as *Augustales*, and a separate higher stratum, containing the 'ordinary' decurions and magistrates together with their fellows who were also members of the equestrian order but held only local, not state, offices. By contrast, the imperial aristocracy consisted of men who exercised military and political functions in the service of the state or who had at least the prospect of such functions, like senators without office. But pre-eminent within this imperial aristocracy was the politico-military elite, consisting of senators in high office and high equestrian public functionaries. The second shortcoming of this model, as here constructed, a model which emphasises *differences* between the various strata of the population, gives disproportionate weight to social stratification as a characteristic of society. In the determination of social realities in the Roman world it was by no means *only* the fixed positions within a social hierarchy that mattered, but also the personal relations between individuals placed higher and lower, which were always of the greatest importance – for example, within the *familia,* between a slave and his master, in a civic community, between a plebeian client and his *patronus* of the local elite, or on an estate, between the labour force and the estate-owner. Whereas members of a privileged *ordo* deliberately closed ranks and separated themselves in various ways from other hierarchical groups in society, the various sectors of the lower population of the empire had closer connections with their masters and patrons than with each other. Nevertheless, the social differences generated by the mechanisms of social stratification discussed more fully above (p.106) were a reality and their importance should not be mistaken. They were emphasised by ancient authors as crucial, thus, for example, the difference between rich and poor.

In view of the divisions here described, the Roman social system of the first two centuries of the Empire (and in other periods of Roman history) is best understood with reference to the concept of the orders-strata structure. On the other hand, the concept of class (in the strict German sense of *'Klasse'*) would hardly be appropriate for a definition of this social system. A social class grows up on the foundation of a common relationship between its members and economic production. In simple terms, this relationship depends upon the ownership or non-ownership of the means of production (in an ancient society, inevitably, land and workshops with the requisite equipment), on the division of labour and on the distribution of the goods produced. If Roman society had been a class society in the Early Empire, there would necessarily have been two classes. First, the upper class, whose members possessed the means of production and lived off the profits from their property, worked by others. And second, the lower class whose members owned neither land nor the means of craft production, who played a direct part in production and who fed the upper class by their labour. To a certain extent, various groups in Roman society would meet these economic criteria. Senators could be allocated to the upper class without much difficulty and slaves on the *latifundia* to the lower. But a class model of this nature cannot do full justice to the reality of the Roman social system. First, a middle class would have to be introduced between the upper and lower classes. The members of this class would have to possess the means of production, but would nevertheless play a direct part in production. Among them we would have to include social groups as diverse as independent peasants who owned their own land, *coloni*, who at least had rented land, and craftsmen with their own small concerns. But it is crucial to note that Roman society was by no means structured *only* according to the aforesaid economic criteria, but also according to social and legal criteria, which did not completely coincide. The decurions in the cities were sometimes peasants who played a direct part in production, yet, as members of a privileged order with prestige and official functions, they belonged to the upper strata. Again, rich freedmen of Trimalchio's stamp satisfy all the economic criteria of a 'ruling class', for they possessed the means of production, took no direct part in production and lived off the labour of their employees: yet they were denied entry to a privileged order, tenure of the higher offices and social prestige. It would therefore be unrealistic to define Roman society in the Early Empire as a class society (to say nothing of a 'slave-owners' society'). It was a society divided into orders and strata with a quite unique structure, which, despite common features, is very different even from other pre-industrial societies.[168]

The characteristics of this structure explain the extent of the flexibility of the social system in the Early Empire. Since the orders-strata model of Rome either took over or at least pointed the way for social development in the provinces too, the commanding heights gradually opened up to erstwhile 'non-Romans', while, at the same time, the Italians lost their earlier leading role. But this kind of permeability in the social system is not to be confused with the vertical mobility that permitted the improvement or the worsening of one's social position either within one and the same social stratum or through a change of stratum.[169]

The opportunities for upwards mobility always corresponded very closely to the boundaries which ran within the social pyramid. Those who were already privileged had many such opportunities. Provided they made skilful use of the economic means at their disposal and provided they made headway in a municipal, equestrian or senatorial *cursus honorum* up the ladder of hierarchical offices, they could bring about a considerable improvement in their social position, as, for example, did the younger Pliny, who added new purchases to the estates he inherited and who climbed the successive rungs of the senatorial ladder right up to the consulship. Nor was there any great obstacle to advancement from the decurional order of a community to the equestrian order and thence into the senatorial order, whether within a generation or over more than one generation. The gulf between the *census* requirements of the respective *ordines* was not insurmountable for many rich men. At the same time, the leading orders which were always in need of new recruits on account of their regular childlessness, always found their natural source of supply in the personnel of a lower order. And the lower strata,too, especially in the cities, had comparable opportunities for upwards mobility. Since very different social positions might be included within one and the same low category of the population, the improvement of one's position within such a category was entirely possible, especially through ability and good fortune in the economic sphere. This applies as much to urban craftsmen, who could make themselves rich men, as to rural slaves who could work their way up to become estate bailiffs. As a result of the looser structure of the lower strata, change of status was also possible – at least in the cities – for slaves were very often freed and the children born after their manumission were regarded as free-born.

But for all that, social mobility is not to be over-estimated as a relatively positive factor in the social life of the Early Empire. Those who were able actually to make use of the opportunities described above constituted a minority – in the countryside, it seems, a very small minority. For example, of the 90 or so *equites* who gained the lowest equestrian military office, as prefects of cohorts, each year, only two-thirds could reach the next stage to become military tribunes and only one-third could reach the third stage and become prefects of cavalry. But it was most important that the crucial social division between lower strata and upper strata could only be crossed with difficulty. The man who lacked the appropriate economic resources at the outset could by no means be sure of acquiring them by hard work or other personal qualities. This applies especially to the lower strata of the population in rural areas, where wealth – the ownership of land – was more constantly divided than in the cities. Certainly, upwards social mobility was also possible in the countryside: the *locus classicus* is the famous inscription from Mactar (of the third century AD), wherein a one-time agricultural labourer of little account proudly recounts the success of his endeavour (*ILS*,7457). He came from a poverty-stricken family, worked for twelve years as a seasonal labourer at harvest-time and for eleven years as foreman. By his hard work he became an estate-owner and, through this qualification, a decurion in his home town, where he ultimately became chief magistrate of the community. But such a career was certainly not common, not least because it was hard to save the minimum property qualification required of a decurion – even in the small towns – from the wages of a landless agricultural labourer. It was easier to make money in urban occupations. But even in the cities there were limitations to upwards social mobility, not least through the many restrictions relating to personal origin and legal status, which hindered integration into the upper stratum even in the case of the economically successful, in many instances, particularly the resourceful freedmen.

Thus in the Early Empire, by contrast with modern industrial society, it was only seldom possible and in any event atypical for a man to work his way up from the very base to the very heights of the social pyramid. The lifestyle of the leading members of the *familia Caesaris* and the wealthy freedmen (which prompted Trimalchio to say that he had turned from a frog into a king: Petronius, *Sat.*,77) was no indication of unlimited social mobility, for social barriers stood in their way. Moreover, such men as these owed their careers not to personal ability, but to personal luck – rich inheritances from childless masters and membership of the *familia Caesaris* through birth or purchase. The only institutionalised path for upwards mobility from the base to the top of the social pyramid was the career of a centurion who entered the equestrian order through the primipilate. But in the mid second century AD, for example, there were only about 2,000 centurions at any one time, of whom only about a third could ever reach the primipilate with its equestrian rank and less than a tenth a high equestrian post. The career of the emperor Pertinax, as he became, is unique. He was the son of an ex-slave, who at first taught as an impoverished tutor; he gained entry to the equestrian order through patronage, distinguished himself by his brilliant military skills, gained senatorial rank, came to be reckoned among the leading consulars and, upon the demise of Commodus, was chosen as emperor. His career was only possible under the new conditions brought in by the political and military crises of the empire from the second half of the second century AD. Such an advance by a family was only conceivable before that period over several generations at best. Thus tradition had it that the Vitellii were descended from a freedman who had been a cobbler. His son acquired property by auction at the end of the Republic. From the marriage of the latter to a prostitute came a son, who was admitted to the equestrian order and gained the rank of imperial procurator under Augustus. This *eques* then produced four sons, who all became senators: one of these held the consulship three times and was one of the most eminent men in Rome. The latter's son was Aulus Vitellius, the emperor.[170]

The Roman social system offered many openings for social advancement, to which one might, at least, aspire. This elasticity was essential to its strength and stability. Moreover, social demotion, which could seriously embitter those who suffered it, was a rare occurrence under the consolidated conditions of the Early Empire. Those who suffered demotion in large numbers were principally the inhabitants of the provinces in the first generation after their conquest – their numbers were ever smaller under the Empire. Of course, there were always impoverished and indebted families, particularly in the countryside, who had to sell their children into slavery, but it seldom happened that broad strata of the population suffered social demotion at the same time. In time of natural catastrophe, for instance, as in the great earthquake in Asia Minor in AD 17, the imperial regime came to the help of the population (Tac., *Ann.*, 2.47). In particular, a person was very seldom stripped of his privileges, once given – freedom, citizenship, membership of an *ordo* – for the most part only for criminal acts. And the descendants of the privileged inherited freedom and citizenship automatically and the membership of an *ordo*, in most cases, at least in practice.

The internal constitution of Roman society explains why the social tensions and conflicts of the Early Empire hardly ever led to open revolts. In view of the social structure, class struggles were as fundamentally impossible now as they had been in the Late Republic. The particular groups of the lower population were bound to the upper strata in a variety of ways and, therefore, often pursued very different courses: nor were there any clear social divisions within the lower strata. No universal revolutionary class could thus develop. Moreover, many groups of the lower population in various parts of the empire felt solidarity not with their fellows elsewhere, but with their *domini* and *patroni*. In general, the Roman ruling system was so strong in the Early Empire and the internal conditions of the empire were consolidated to such an extent, that the social tensions that existed could break out into open conflicts hardly at all.

The Principate was the political framework best fitted to hold together Roman society with its aristocratic rule, given the conditions of a world empire. It incorporated a coherent and stable system of government, which best suited the interests of the upper strata. Through the construction of an ordered imperial administration and through the maintenance of a standing army of 350,000 to 400,000 men, a machinery of power was created, which guaranteed the permanent and coherent control of the governed and which secured political stability in place of the desolate situation of the Late Republic. At the same time, this machinery was made more tolerable than before even for the masses, since uniform standards were fixed with regard to the exercise of power and officials were under centralised control.[171] Moreover, the members of the upper strata were brought into the system of government in accordance with a well-balanced hierarchy of power. Whereas in the Late Republic various, warring oligarchical factions had held power and broad leading strata in society (for example, most of the *equites*) had had little share of power, the division of public functions now, between the *ordo senatorius, ordo equester* and *ordines decurionum*, under the centralised government of the empire by the emperor, corresponded to social realities.

At the same time, the Principate also secured the ideological and ethical norms of Roman society, which provided a coherent value system for the leading social strata in particular, but also broader groups in the population. These norms were generated by the renewal of the religious and ethical tradition of Rome, which was adjusted to the needs of the Principate in that it was entwined with ruler cult and a moral obligation of loyalty towards the emperor. The various groups in society honoured the cult of the ruler through their own particular priests. The *sodales Augustales* and the members of other sodalities were senators, the provincial high priests *equites* for the most part. In the cities there were municipal *flamines* from the decurional order, *Augustales* drawn from the leading freedmen and *magistri* and *ministri* of the emperor's *Lares* drawn from the other freedmen and slaves. Except in the eastern provinces, where the payment of religious honours to rulers had a long history, the imperial cult could not satisfy deep religious needs. But that was not the function of Roman religion even in earlier times: its most important function was always to prescribe a code of behaviour, which demanded, above all else, allegiance to the interests of the state - this was the political ethic that was its substance under the emperors too. The preferences for traditional values is apparent in inscriptions: these show how far the behavioural norms of Rome had extended over the empire. There were not really any obvious alternatives to this value system in the Early Empire: the slaves, for example, kept cults which were more or less widespread even among the upper strata. Thus the very few enemies of the Roman order known to us – mostly the representatives of a few philosophical sects and trends – met with only very limited success.[172]

Given the strength of the Principate, any rebellion against Roman rule was pointless: Flavius Josephus formulated the argument clearly enough (*BJ*, 2.345ff.). And there was far less reason for social unrest than in the last two centuries of the Republic, though social harmony, as bruited by Aelius Aristides in his speech on Rome (Chapter 29ff.), was wishful thinking. Through the re-definition of the positions of power within the framework of the Principate there were hardly any conflicts within the upper strata which could not be settled by peaceful means. The needs of the urban *plebs* were met on a fairly regular basis. The slaves were much better treated than earlier and very often received their freedom. Even the peasant masses – including the rural population of some of the areas conquered for the first time by Augustus, who were very restless at the outset, as in northern Dalmatia and southern Pannonia – could secure a few social advantages with the progress of Romanisation and urbanisation.

Nevertheless, even in the Early Empire there were occasional instances of social unrest and even open political conflicts without any social relevance: they were isolated from each other in time and space and their motivations were different. These conflicts can only be reduced to a common denominator in one respect, a common denominator which is important for an understanding of the social conflicts of the Empire: these uprisings originated for the most part among groups in the population who were, for specific reasons, under a pressure that was especially heavy and generally atypical.

The position of the slaves under the Empire gave rise to no more of the great slave revolts that had occurred under the Late Republic. But maltreatment of slaves in particular cases – particularly on the *latifundia* – could still sometimes lead to open rebellion. Thus, the senator Larcius Macedo, a contemporary of Pliny (*Ep.*, 3.14.1ff.), was fatally wounded by his slaves on account of his cruelty. Under Nero a slave killed the urban prefect Pedanius secundus, according to Tacitus, either because he had refused his manumission (which was otherwise usual) or because of jealousy (*Ann.*, 14.42). But there were only slave revolts proper, as far as we know, in AD 24 in Apulia and in neighbouring Calabria and in AD 54, again in Calabria. These were the traditional areas for slave uprisings with their many herdsmen whose situation was especially dire and who could only be controlled with difficulty. Normally, however, the opposition of a particular slave to his master was expressed, at most, in flight – particularly from the estates.[173]

Moreover, there might be uprisings among the *plebs* of some cities when the central problem of the poor urban population – the provision of food – was not solved to their satisfaction. Philostratus (*Apoll.*,1.15) describes how such an uprising broke out at Aspendus in Pamphylia at the end of the first century AD: its cause was famine, brought about when the landowners kept back grain for export. Dio of Prusa recounts how he was almost killed at about the same time, together with the landowners in his home town because the mob suspected them of forcing up the price of grain. Dio, again, tells us how it came to open conflict in Tarsus, the Cilician capital, between the members of the local *ordo* and popular masses whipped up by Cynic philosophers – particularly the 'linen-weavers', who as non-citizens of that city were especially disadvantaged. The affair of Paul the apostle and the silversmiths of Ephesus shows how easily the masses of craftsmen could be made to rise.[174]

All these uprisings were no threat to Rome: at most, they required police measures. The same cannot be said of the mass revolts of oppressed provincials against Roman rule. As with the revolt on the lower Rhine and in northern Gaul in AD 69, they posed a great threat to the Roman empire, a threat which could only be dealt with by means of a large military presence and extensive warfare. Of course, these revolts were no more social movements than had been the revolts of the Italian allies and of provincials against the Roman Republic. Their causes were principally political and military measures of Rome which had the same effect upon quite different strata in the population. In the Gallic uprising of AD 21, brought about by the violent economic exploitation of the Gallic provinces, tribal nobles, their peasant clients and even slaves took part (Tac.,'*Ann.*, 3.40ff.). In AD 69 the rebellious Treveri and Batavians were led against Rome by their nobles. Yet, even in these uprisings, social motives played a part, as they had done in the Late Republic in the revolts of the Italians and provincials. Most of those who opposed Rome were always simple members of the rural population: the burden of Roman rule fell particularly on them, for the members of the local upper strata could easily come to a compromise with Rome. Vitellius' forced levies, which sparked off revolt among the Batavians in AD 69, affected the ordinary masses in particular (Tac., *Hist.*, 4.14) and the upper stratum less. Whereas Iulius Civilis, a member of the elite of the tribal aristocracy, led the rebels, his own nephew, Iulius Briganticus, fought on the Roman side as an officer with equestrian rank (ibid.,4.70). Most obvious are the social roots of the great Jewish revolt of AD 66-70. The causes of this revolt against Rome lay in the extremely severe oppression of the Jewish population of Palestine. The bulk of the rebels were recruited from the peasants whose plight was particularly desperate. And the most important groups among them aimed not only at liberation from the Roman yoke, but also at the removal of the rule of their own landowners and high priests.[175] But even all these revolts could not shake the Roman social system: the crisis of Roman imperial society had its roots elsewhere.

6 THE CRISIS OF THE ROMAN EMPIRE AND STRUCTURAL CHANGE IN SOCIETY

The Crisis of the Roman Empire and Roman Society

When Aelius Aristides produced his speech on Rome in 143 he was convinced that the *imperium Romanum* had reached its acme in his day: men no longer believed in warfare (Chapter 70), the world was celebrating one long festival, so to speak, and the cities vied in splendour and beauty (97ff.). Some two decades later the Roman empire found itself fighting a war of defence on its northern frontier which seemed the worst war that anyone could remember (HA, *MA*, 17.2). To later generations the reign of the emperor Marcus (161–80) seemed a period in which, without that emperor, '*profecto quasi uno lapsu ruissent omnia status Romani*' (*Epit. de Caes.*, 16.2). With an eye to the political crisis of Commodus' autocracy (180–92) and the changed power structures under Septimius Severus (193–211) and his successors, Cassius Dio saw in the death of Marcus the end of a golden age and the beginning of a period of iron and rust (71.36.4). Under Philip (244–9), an observer of the Roman empire described it as a sick and wasted body and as a sinking ship, hopelessly lost. A few years later, St Cyprian thought the end of the world was nigh. Under Valerian (253–60) and the rule of Gallienus (260–268) the fate of the empire seemed sealed by barbarian invasions and internal decay. There was, one may say, a general crisis of the Roman empire: its most important constituent elements are to be seen in the following three areas – the instability of the whole system obtaining at Rome, the accelerated change of the structural foundation of this system and the realisation (or at least the feeling) of contemporaries that their period – unlike earlier periods – was marked out by instability and change. A degree of stability was only achieved by the soldier emperors after Gallienus, especially Claudius II (268–70), Aurelian (270–75), Probus (276–82) and, above all, Diocletian (284–305). But this stability no longer rested on traditional foundations.[176]

The onset of the crisis did not occur simultaneously everywhere. Further, it manifested itself in different ways in the various parts of the empire. For example, Egypt and Africa were less affected than,

157

say, Spain or Syria: Egypt and Africa had largely been spared from barbarian incursions and these were areas wherein the concentration of property and the colonate were already far advanced before the third century. In the Danubian provinces, particularly in Pannonia, Moesia and Dacia, the economy flourished under the Severans more than ever: in consequence, the decline of the decades that followed was all the sharper.[177] Nevertheless a change occurred throughout the Roman empire which affected every area of life and brought about thoroughgoing changes in the stratification of Roman society. This was more than a realignment of society: it was the evolution of a new social model. Thus this process of change can only be compared in importance with the structural change of the second century BC. Contemporaries had a limited idea of its significance as early as the Severans. The consequences of Rome's internal political crisis led Tertullian to remark that '*humiles sublimitate, sublimes humilitate mutantur*' (*Apol.*, 20.2). Similarly, Cassius Dio lived to see that, in the Roman social hierarchy, 'everything was turned on its head' (80.7.2).

The crisis was total. It is most evident in the external relations of the empire, which were in a catastrophic state. Marcus' successful counter-offensive against the Germans had won the empire a respite. But the storm broke again from Severus Alexander (222-35) and Maximinus Thrax (235–8) through the onslaughts of the Germans and their allies upon the Rhine and Danube frontiers and through the expansionist policy of the new Persian Empire at the expense of the eastern Roman provinces. The defeat of the emperor Decius (249–51) at the hands of the Goths, the capture of Valerian by the Persians nine years later, the barbarian incursions into Germany, Gaul, Spain, the Danubian lands, the Balkans, Asia Minor, Cappadocia and Syria under Gallienus, and the German advance into Italy under Aurelian were only the troughs in an unbroken line of defensive wars. The internal political situation was equally catastrophic. The emperor's claim to power was insatiable. In the new political system, the Dominate, the state became an all-powerful institution, which demanded total obedience from its subjects, whom it regimented frequently with brutality. But at the same time, the power of particular emperors became ever less stable. Between the death of Marcus on his sick-bed and the abdication of Diocletian, there were hardly any emperors who were not brought to the throne by outright force of arms, whether by military revolts or by civil wars, and who were not also removed in the same fashion. The wars between pretenders to the throne after the death of Commodus, the bloody ends of six emperors in AD 238 alone, the ongoing usurpations and the emergence of splinter empires in the Gallo-Germanic provinces, on the middle Danube and in the east under Gallienus, again only mark the troughs of the internal political crisis. The instability of the monarchy evidenced here was a direct result of the pre-eminence of the army, especially of the great provincial armies in Pannonia and Moesia, on the Rhine, and in Cappadocia and Syria. At the same time, the rule of the military meant a radical change in the earlier power structures.

The economy of the empire was also in a severe crisis. About AD 253 St Cyprian painted a grim picture: food was short, prices were rising, the mines were exhausted, craft skills were in decline. Moreover, there was a shortage of peasants in the rural economy (*Ad Demetr.*, 3f.). In agrarian production the difficulties were increasingly obvious, largely through the increasing shortage of manpower. The urban sectors of the economy were affected particularly severely. Craft production suffered a marked decline. Thus production stopped, for instance, in the *terra sigillata* concerns of the north-western provinces. Trade was repeatedly interrrupted, particularly in the war zones of the frontier provinces. Inflation could not be checked: in the mid-third century it assumed catastrophic proportions. The consequences of the continuous wars and the economic crisis were devastating for the population. There was a general decline in the numbers of the population and in their life expectancy. Dionysius of Alexandria, a contemporary of St Cyprian, was deeply affected by these developments in his own city.[178] Poverty and misery took a firm hold, sometimes made still firmer by natural disasters.

And great changes also occurred in the structure of society. The political and economic position of different privileged social strata was shaken. The previous, clear-cut hierarchy of the orders of the *honestiores* began to falter. The lower strata of the population, who had to bear most of the burdens of the crisis, bowed under increasing oppression and often found themselves in a desperate plight. The legal distinctions between particular groups in the lower population swiftly lost their social importance. Even the 'free' were treated ever more like slaves by the state and by the powerful. And moreover, once Caracalla (211–17) had granted Roman citizenship to all 'free' inhabitants of the Empire, that privilege no longer performed its previous and important role as a social division. This development set the course for the emergence of a new sort of *humiliores*, who were relatively homogeneous by comparison with the sharply differentiated lower strata of the Late Republic and Early Empire. All these economic and social changes generated new tensions and conflicts, which repeatedly erupted and undermined the old system still further. And the faster the traditional social system and its respective system of government fell into decline, the greater was the ideological and moral vacuum, into which flowed new intellectual and spiritual currents – the oriental mystery religions, Christianity and NeoPlatonism.

The crisis did not break out overnight with the wars under Marcus or the internal political conflicts under Commodus. Rather it grew to maturity somewhat earlier, behind the façade of the Antonine monarchy. Migrations and social and political changes among the Germans and their neighbours on the northern frontiers of the empire posed new threats which were partially recognised at Rome even before the outbreak of the Marcomannic Wars in AD 166 or 167. Moreover, the rise to power of the army and thus the increasing political importance of the military provinces did not begin with the civil wars fought out between Didius Iulianus, Septimius Severus, Pescennius Niger and Clodius Albinus from 193 to 197. The changes in the economic and social structure of the empire, which were very clearly and sharply accelerated from the later Antonine period and the Severans, can be traced back to processes of change which began, to a significant extent, somewhat earlier, behind the façade of the apparently healthy world of Marcus' predecessors, wherein they can only be perceived with difficulty. The economic problems – particularly in the cities – which were to lead to the stagnation of crafts and trade, to difficulties in agriculture, to heavier burdens on the decurions and thus to major changes in the social structure of the cities, did not put in their first appearance in Italy and some of the Mediterranean provinces only in the third century AD. In Spain, for example, the upper strata of the cities desplayed certain signs of exhaustion as early as the mid-second century AD. Even the economic activity of the energetic freedmen took a great step backwards in the cities in the second century AD. The reasons are visible, in particular, in the structural weaknesses of an economy based on the cities and their territories. These structural weaknesses arose in two ways: first, in that immense sums were invested, in the first two centuries of the Empire, in unprofitable building for prestige purposes, as, for instance, on fora, temples, theatres, amphitheatres, etc.; and second, in that, with the decline of slavery, the problem of finding an adequate labour force became acute. That search, like the extension of the colonate in some parts of the empire, pointed the way to structural change in the lower strata of society long before the actual onset of crisis. And the spread of new value systems, whose religious and philosophical doctrines fulfilled deep spiritual and intellectual needs, began well before the fateful blows of the third century.

Even a passing consideration of this historical process, with all its variety and scope, shows that it is impossible to reduce the causes of the crisis of the Roman empire to a simple common denominator. Any mono-causal attempt at a solution of this problem is inevitably unsatisfactory. This is the 'problem of problems' for the historian and a problem still very controversial today. It has not been solved by M. Rostovtzeff, who saw it in terms of the conflict between the urban bourgeoisie and the rural masses, nor yet by most Marxist scholars, who see it in terms of the crisis of the slave economy generated by inadequate sources for the supply of slaves – not to mention many other theories, of which some stress social and economic causes, others ideological and moral or even external causes.[179]

It is quite clear that the growing pressure of barbarians on the imperial frontiers after Marcus and especially towards the middle of the third century was a factor of crucial importance, yet only one of many causes of the crisis. Wars against the foreign foes of the empire might accelerate the crisis markedly – for example, through their economic consequences, such as the loss of manpower involved. They might also stimulate the process of change to a significant extent – by contributing to the increase in the power of the military, for example. But Rome's weaknesses, which made it possible for the barbarians to succeed, stemmed from changes within the empire, which began before the first great onslaught under Marcus or were unconnected with the barbarian attacks (as were the losses of manpower due to plague). These internal processes of change were very different: they ran parallel with each other, then entwined and had a two-way influence on each other over time, so that it is hard to know what was cause, what was symptom and what was effect. For example, the weakening of the decurional order in many cities – without doubt, one of the most important phenomena of the structural change in society – was an important cause of the decline of cities in various parts of the empire. Yet it was at the same time a symptom of the general economic crisis and, moreover, a consequence of the structural weakness of the cities, whose economic prosperity in the Early Empire – in the west at least – was mainly due to the temporary boom created when the provinces were opened up. Further, the weakening of the decurional orders must be related to the structural change in the countryside. The general growth in large estates meant dangerous competition for many owners of medium-sized estates – thus for typical decurions. At the same time, the decline of slavery and the binding of the peasant masses to large estate-owners under the colonate brought about an evident labour shortage for the average estate-owner, in particular. Moreover, the crisis of the decurional order cannot be separated from the gradual shift of the Empire from Principate into Dominate, a shift which meant that imperial regimes increasingly laid claim to the sources of the decurions' wealth. Furthermore, the destruction wreaked by the barbarian hordes in the cities and in the countryside hurt a decurional family more badly and more permanently than a great senatorial estate-owner, who often had estates in various parts of the empire.

The last example clearly illustrates the interaction of various transformational processes in the period of the great crisis. By way of assessment it may be said that, in short, the crisis of the Roman empire came about through a combination of internal and external causes: the barbarian invasions struck the Roman empire at a point in time when its internal weaknesses were becoming aggravated and they struck with a force for which Rome's internal structures were scarcely prepared. This combination can be seen in concrete terms in that, particularly in the period of continuous and dangerous barbarian onslaughts, the empire will have needed more soldiers than before, more money and goods to feed and supply them and, at the same time, a larger labour force. But it was precisely in this period that the empire could call upon less economic power and less productive capacity. The results were instability, the transformation of the former system and resignation among contemporaries.

Changes in the Upper Strata

No sector of Roman society remained undisturbed by the great change that occurred in the period of crisis – not even the senatorial order, whose members still constituted the richest and most prestigious group in Roman society in the third century AD and even later, as they had in the Early Empire. There was no radical change in the ethnic composition of the *ordo senatorius* after the mid-second century. The number of senators of provincial origin continued to rise, while that of Italian senators continued to decline: among the provincials, Africans and the aristocracy of the eastern provinces were present in greater numbers than before.[180] But even in the third century, at least a third of the senators came from Italy. And, moreover, the further advance of provincials into the highest order did not lead to any significant change in senatorial ideals and behaviour, any more than it had in the second century. It is also important that the leading figures in the military, who were often of very humble origin and who mostly came from the peripheral areas of the empire, such as Pannonia and Moesia, did not seek admission to the senatorial order, by and large. For these reasons there was no change in the composition of the Senate of a sort which would have directly reflected the shift of political power to the frontier lands.

The wealth and great social prestige of the senators also remained untouched. As before, the main source of the wealth of senatorial families was the ownership of land, as in the case of the Gordians, who are said to have had an unprecedented number of estates in the provinces (SHA,*Gord.*,2.3). Of the various sectors of production the agrarian economy was affected least by the economic crisis: the basis of the wealth of senators was therefore undisturbed by and large. Rather, they could extend their *latifundia* still further through the acquisition of medium-sized and small properties, whose owners were much more severely affected than they by wars, investment difficulties and natural disasters. And the prestige of the senators remained much the same. From the late Antonine period the members of the *ordo* had proudly used the term *clarissimus* in their inscriptions on a regular basis: now as then it indicated the highest social rank beneath that of the emperor. Cassius Dio says that the most noble, the best and the richest men, from Italy and the provinces alike, ought to belong to the senatorial order (52.19.2): senators were of the same opinion even later. It is significant that emperors who rose to the throne from a humble background now laid claim to senatorial rank as naturally as they laid claim to the most prestigious senatorial office, the consulship.

But the situation was quite different where the functions and political power of the senatorial order were concerned. While the *clarissimi* retained their prosperity and their high prestige, they lost the power they had enjoyed under the Early Empire in the most important sectors in the imperial government. The main reason was that the emperors of the Dominate had to use means quite different to those used by earlier rulers in order to hold the Roman empire together in the difficult circumstances of the great crisis. To that end a more effective organ was required than the Senate, which could no longer be 'lovingly pampered like a venerable, but paralysed grandfather' by the rulers.[181] Moreover, the emperors needed to have at hand a wider and better-qualified pool of talent than the senatorial order. Accordingly a change occurred which led to the de-politicisation of the senatorial order in two ways: first, the Senate as an institution – one which had often proved an obstacle to the realisation of various objectives of imperial policy – was largely excluded from political decisions: the imperial *consilium* and the imperial bureaucracy grew to take its place. Second, the high administrative posts and military commands which had previously been the preserve of the senators were transferred to another group of people, namely the *equites*.

The harmonious relationship between emperor and Senate, upon which Trajan, Hadrian, Antoninus Pius and Marcus had based their monarchy in the second century, was disturbed as early as Commodus. There were recurrent political clashes between Commodus and the elite of the senatorial order, clashes which cost the lives of many senators. The clearest illustration of the new attitude of the authoritarian emperors towards the leading order is Commodus' appearance in the Colosseum, as described by Dio. The young ruler, dressed as a gladiator, 'killed an ostrich, cut off its head and then came over to where we senators were sitting. In his left hand he held the head and in his right hand, his bloody sword. He said nothing all the while, but simply grinned and wagged his head to show that he had the same fate in store for us' (72.21.1f.). After the fall of Commodus and his successor Pertinax, the senatorial order splintered into separate political groupings which supported various pretenders to the throne. Septimius Severus, who by family tradition and disposition was by no means hostile to the Senate, did away with his opponents in AD 197 without mercy, as later did Caracalla with his senatorial enemies, real or imagined.[182] At the same time, the Senate was called upon less and less often to make important decisions. Maximinus Thrax was the first emperor who did not claim the sanction of his proclamation by the Senate, at least after the event. And he was the first emperor not to enter the Senate House and the city of Rome during his three-year reign. In particular cases, the Senate might still take the political initiative, as in AD 193 when Pertinax was proclaimed emperor by the Senate (a scenario which was, of course, prepared by his supporters). The Senate acted again in AD 238, when it declared war on Maximinus Thrax and put forward two of its own candidates, Pupienus and Balbinus, as emperors. And again in AD 275 when a 'senatorial emperor' was chosen once more after the sudden death of Aurelian, namely Tacitus. But these are exceptions: in such situations, the political initiative normally rested with the army.

At the same time the senators were gradually stripped of their most important offices. The ideal Roman senator was by tradition *'domi militiaeque pollens'* (SHA, *MA*, 3.3, on a leading senator of the Antonine period), both administrator and commander. But though he had a sound legal training, he was by no means a professional officer. As early as Marcus, warfare had shown that the new and difficult requirements of imperial defence could not be met by senatorial generals of the old school. In a speech which he puts in the mouth of Septimius Severus against his principal enemy Clodius Albinus, Herodian formulates with brutal frankness what many contemporaries may have thought of the military abilities of the old aristocracy: this man, from a most eminent family (2.15.1), belongs not in battle, but in a dancing troupe (3.6.7). The only solution was the appointment of *equites* to important military commands: through the equestrian military career they had more military experience than the average senator. Thus from Marcus onwards emperors increasingly resorted to the (precedented) method of admitting meritorious equestrian officers to the senatorial order and transferring to them the commands of the armed forces. The two most successful generals of Marcus were men of this sort, namely Pertinax and Valerius Maximianus, the first attested Pannonian senator. But this practice made the gulf between *viri militares* and *viri docti, diserti, litterati* in the senatorial order ever wider – all the more so, since, during their long military careers in the provinces, the former often had little opportunity to spend time at Rome, to participate in meetings of the Senate there and to imbue themselves in the traditions of the aristocracy.[183] Moreover, the growing imperial bureaucracy also needed more and more specialists for the civil administration: these too were to be found among the *equites*. It is significant that from the Antonine period it is not senators that predominate among the leading jurists, as before, but *equites*.

Gallienus, a great reformer of the Roman army, took the obvious

lesson: from AD 262 military commands and associated governorships were given – with only a few exceptions – to *equites* who did
not now enter the senatorial order.[184] There was no formal prohibition of senators from military service, as later accounts of this
reform mistakenly suggest (Aur. Victor, *Caes.*, 33.34). Nor was the
reform a stab at the senators, for the majority of senators no longer
sought after demanding military service. But in effect the senatorial
order henceforth lost the most important positions in the government of the empire. The senatorial *cursus honorsum* was reduced to
a few minor civil offices at Rome, the consulship, the governorship
of some provinces which had no armies and a few other posts. This
meant that the functions of the senators were also severely
restricted in the field of civil administration. It would be wrong to
describe this as the total political emasculation of the *ordo
senatorius*: the senators could still wield power by virtue of their
remaining posts and their wealth and influence, but the erstwhile
leading role played by the senatorial order in the empire had come
to an end.

The third century AD was the heyday of the equestrian order.
Since most officers and most imperial administrators belonged to
that order, the *equites* constituted the most active group in the military and political fields and the most important pillars of the state.
Since Macrinus (217–18) who rose to the throne from the praetorian
prefecture, the *equites* even furnished a series of emperors, including Maximinus Thrax, Philip, Claudius II, Aurelian, Probus and
Carus. This enormous growth in the power of the equestrian order
was due both to the qualities and ambitions of its members and to the
self-interest of the imperial regime. Many *equites* had a sound military training: they were often professional officers with a long military career behind them, as in the case of Traianus Mucianus from
Thrace, who worked his way up from being a simple soldier in the
latter half of the third century. Others were distinguished professional lawyers, as were Papinian, Ulpian, Paulus and Macrinus in
the Severan period. At the same time many *equites* strove after high
posts in the government of the empire with particular zeal, for these
posts brought not only social prestige and high salaries, but also ever
more power. The advancement of such persons was in the emperors'
own interests both because of the increasing burden of imperial
defence and administration and in order to provide a loyal body of
support in the political upheavals of the third century through the
creation of an elite dependent upon themselves. The rise to power

of the *equites* was thus a distinctive feature of the third century. This trend was apparent as early as Septimius Severus who put the three new legions he created under equestrian prefects, not senatorial legates: it reached its zenith with the reform of Gallienus.[185]

The number of *equites* rose with the need of the Roman state for specialised officers and administrators. From the time of Septimius Severus, centurions and even *principales* (soldiers detached from ordinary service and given special duties, usually in the administration) could obtain equestrian rank more easily and more regularly than before. Among the military, membership of the *ordo equester* was commonly hereditary in practice, for the sons of equestrian centurions were also admitted to the order. The increase in the number of procurators shows most clearly the growth of the need for personnel in the higher reaches of the administration. Under Augustus there were a little more than 20 procuratorial posts, under Trajan more than 80, under Antoninus Pius more than 100, under Marcus some 125, under Septimius Severus more than 170 and under Philip more than 180. Since the soldiers among the *equites*, in particular, very often came from the provinces, especially the militarised frontier provinces, the number of provincials in the *ordo equester* rose still more sharply than in the second century. Among these provincials there were more men from the eastern provinces, North Africa and the Danubian lands than before. The rise of many soldiers of humble origin into the equestrian order brought about a significant social realignment. And the level of education of common soldiers from the frontier provinces was often poor. Maximinus Thrax, for example, was regarded as a primitive 'semi-barbarian'. But there was by no means a 'barbarisation' of the entire equestrian order: even in the third century there were still many *equites* from the thoroughly Romanised provinces and even Italians. Moreover, many uneducated officers sought to adopt Roman ideals: they were even convinced that they were the true heirs of the once great Romans, as in the case of the Pannonians, of whom it is said, at the end of the third century, that their native land was, through its *virtus*, as much the mistress of the world as was Italy through its old reputation.[186]

The economic position of these militarily and politically active *equites* was very good, for the most part. Many of them came from landowning families and the majority invested their high salaries in land. Their prestige and self-confidence were greatly raised by the growth in their power. Their status was, as before, that of the 'second rank' among the privileged (Dio, 52.19.4). But it is significant that the highest equestrian posts, from Marcus onwards, bore titles that were almost as splendid as senatorial rank: the praetorian prefects were *eminentissimi*, the highest procurators were *perfectissimi* and the next level of procurators were *egregii*.[187] The view taken of these successful *equites* by themselves and by others is apparent from the statements of contemporaries (outside the senatorial order) on the personal abilities of lawyers and, especially, of officers. Herodian makes the emperor Macrinus state that his rise from the equestrian order to the throne was fully justified, because the best qualification for the position of emperor was neither noble birth nor wealth – which even the unworthy might possess – but personal merit (5.1.5ff.). In AD 291 Mametinus said of Diocletian and his co-ruler Maximian what many soldiers from the frontier provinces would doubtless wish to hear: 'You were not born and raised in some peaceful part of the world corrupted by pleasures, but in these provinces which, though faced by a weakened enemy, always stand ready to fight in defence of the Empire and prepared to struggle all day without tiring and to endure – here where all life is military service, where even the women are stronger than the men of other peoples'(*Paneg.*, 3.3.9).

But this development did not affect the whole equestrian order by any means. Even in the third century there were many *equites* who owed their membership of the *ordo equester* only to the property qualification in land and who belonged to the local upper strata of a city, as, for example, one Aurelius Vettianus at Aquincum, who, like several decurions, was a *possessor* in the vicinity of the city (*ILS*,7127). The social differences between ordinary *equites* and those engaged in politics or the military were much greater in the third century than in the Early Empire. In consequence a kind of bipartite equestrian order gradually developed: while one part, the numerically smaller group of *equites*, became the most powerful elite in the Roman state, the other, the ordinary *equites*, shared the fate of the decurions and sank with them to the level of a social grouping that was still privileged and relatively prosperous, but was heavily oppressed by the state.

There were wealthy and prestigious men in the *ordo decurionum* in the cities even in the third century. Such a man was Titus Sennius Sollemnis, of Gallia Lugdunensis, known from the 'Thorigny Marble': under the Severans he was chief magistrate in the community of the Viducassii four times in succession.[188] He could spend 332,000 sesterces on gladiatorial games alone: he distinguished himself by his authority among his fellow countrymen in the Gallic council and even gained the friendship of governors who counted him among the *boni viri*, who praised his *honesti mores* and who sent him valuable gifts. However, most decurions were far less prosperous – firstly, because of the general economic weakness of the cities which affected the upper strata too. Since the wealth of many decurions depended not only on the ownership of land but also on crafts and trade, it was the decline of these sectors of the economy in particular that hit them hard. Yet there were also craftsmen and traders among the decurions who were better placed, as, in particular, were those on the Danube-*limes* under the Severans: many traders from Syria and Asia Minor were to be found among them, men who had come to exploit the temporary economic prosperity of these cities – they often became members of the local *ordo*, as happened at Aquincum and Brigetio for example. But the most widespread type of decurion was, still more than in the Early Empire, a landowner on the urban territories, like the *possessores* around Aquincum (*ILS*, 7127). Many of these decurions sought to withdraw from the cities to their estates, where they often possessed villas. It is significant that many villas were built in the latter half of the second and beginning of the third centuries – in the northern provinces of the empire, for example. The shortage of manpower and devastation caused by barbarian invasions and civil wars had a serious effect on agricultural production on municipal estates, too. In Noricum, for example, a number of villas on estates were destroyed in the mid-third century and were not re-built, while in Gaul in the second half of this century extensive tracts of land remained uncultivated.[189]

The increasing burden of the state was still more serious for the decurions. The great senatorial landowners and the leading *equites* enjoyed extensive economic privileges and were treated with caution by the emperors for political reasons. At the same time, the lower population of the cities and the countryside were so poor that little could be taken from them. Thus the decurional order in the various cities was the social group whose financial might was particularly important in meeting the rapidly escalating needs of the Roman state. After the burden of civic expenditure had already become heavier in the second century, it was systematised under state control from Septimius Severus onwards. The stipulations of Septimius Severus and his immediate successors were largely the basis for the prescriptions of Roman law on the burdens (*munera*) of decurions and of the holders of magistracies (*honores*) in the Late Empire (*Dig.*, 50.4.1ff.). In this way the duties of the members of the *ordo decurionum* were precisely fixed: these duties included, among many others, the provision of food and drinking water for the city, the renovation of the roads, the heating of public baths, the presentation of public games and advocacy in the interests of the community.[190] The bearing of these burdens was no longer a matter of free choice: they were distributed in accordance with fixed regulations by the state – by the governors in the provinces. This put an end to the personal initiative that had played such a major role in the economic life of the cities in the Early Empire. These duties were not to be evaded: if, for example, a decurion left his community, the governor was required to summon him back and burden him with the appropriate *munera*.

And the decision as to who should be admitted to the *ordo* of a city and who should not was not a matter for the council of the community and the individuals concerned, as it had been. Anyone with the requisite mimimum property qualification for a decurion was compelled to become a decurion – either directly or through the tenure of a magistracy – and to bear the appropriate burdens. In consequence, the rank of decurion was still more hereditary than it had been before, since the sons of decurions had no choice but to enter the *ordo* upon their inheritance of the family property. So much is evident in the list of decurions from Canusium, dating to AD 223, for its contains many decurions from one and the same family and, as well as 100 regular members of the council, 25 sons of decurions who were minors (*ILS*,6121). Thus the once valued civic *honores* increasingly evolved into what were largely compulsory offices, which were no more than a commitment to bestow *munera*, so that unwilling decurions regarded their duties as *onera invita* (*Dig.*, 50.1.18). Of course, by virtue of their social prestige and the legal privileges brought by the tenure of office these *honores* might still be attractive for many, especially social climbers. But, on the whole, the troubles (*vexationes*) that decurions must have suffered through the bureaucratic stipulation of their duties and, still more important, the financial burdens themselves shook this once strong and confident social grouping – in some cities they completely ruined it.

Another stratum of the urban population disappeared almost without trace after the Antonine period: it, too, had been very wealthy and particularly active in the economy. This was the stratum of the rich freedmen. The likes of Trimalchio could not exist in society under the economic conditions of the great crisis. The organisations of the *Augustales*, wherein rich *liberti* had come together in the Early Empire, still existed in the colonies and municipalities of the third century, but their members were not now usually freedmen, but persons of free origin: by and large, the *Augustales* had no very great financial power. The backbone of this once wealthy group was broken. A similar fate awaited another social group that had been very influential and wealthy in the Early Empire, though for quite different reasons: that is, that of the imperial slaves and freedmen. Under Commodus and the Severans this group still occupied an important position of power – even more so than under the emperors from Trajan to Marcus, because the authoritarian emperors, like Commodus, Septimius Severus and Caracalla were particularly dependent upon the loyalty of the court personnel in their political conflicts with the elite of the empire. Under Elagabalus (218–22) the freedmen at court seem to have all but taken over the leadership of the state. But the subsequent political development of the Empire led to the destruction of the power of the *familia Caesaris*. Upon the death of Severus Alexander in AD 235 the history of the imperial dynasties came to an end for a century: through the continuity of power within certain ruling families these dynasties had provided the most necessary conditions for the evolution of a court personnel that was powerful. The ever more common changes of regime – usually carried through by the murder of an emperor – brought about a constant fluctuation in the composition of the court personnel. After the murder of an emperor his most faithful personal servants were usually the first to be done away with. Thus, Caracalla, for example, after the assassination of his brother and co-ruler Geta, immediately had Geta's slaves and freedmen killed.

To all these changes in the upper levels of the social pyramid must be added the change in the social position of the military.[191] It was not only officers and commanders with equestrian rank who enjoyed an elevated social position in the third century: the soldiers from the rank of centurion upwards formed a fairly coherent social group with political influence, prestige and privileges and with a relatively sound economic position. Their elevation is most apparent in the fact that Septimius Severus allowed centurions and *principales* to wear a gold ring – the status symbol of the *equites* (Herod., 3.8.5). This was an expression of the fact that these privileged soldiers – who had usually worked their way up from the ranks – were regarded as potential *equites*. The *esprit de corps* among the soldiers is very evident in their creation of associations (*scholae* or *collegia*),usually divided according to rank. Moreover the soldiers shared common cults and were proud of the political importance of the army, a pride reinforced by imperial propaganda, particularly by the coinage, which bore legends like *fides exercitus*. But the social stratum thus formed also comprised broader groups in the population. It was of prime importance that soldiers – who had previously only been permitted to live with women in concubinage during their military service – could legally marry from the time of Septimius Severus. An independent social stratum thereby developed in the frontier provinces, which consisted of soldiers in their encampments and their dependents who lived in the immediate neighbourhood. This stratum was further strengthened by the fact that soldiers also often settled, after their discharge, in the area in which they had served. There they became part of the upper strata in the settlements near the auxiliary camps and in the cities which had grown up even earlier beside the legionary camps. Usually, as in the cases of Aquincum and Carnuntum, there were two settlements – the erstwhile *canabae legionis* close to the camp and the 'civilian town' a little further away. The inheritance of the soldier's profession also played a part in strengthening this stratum. Since, despite its many dangers, military service brought with it social privileges, many sons of soldiers' families chose to follow their father's occupation. And their choice corresponded to the interests of the state, for the ongoing expansion of the army could best be ensured in this way.

Apart from the enormous opportunities for advancement through personal ability, these social privileges were particularly financial and fiscal privileges. Since the emperor's position now depended upon the loyalty of the army much more than in the Principate, that loyalty had to be bought at a high price. The famous last words of Septimius Severus to his sons show very clearly how important it was to secure the loyalty of the soldiers by financial means: 'Stay on good terms, enrich the soldiers and don't take much notice of anything else' (Dio,76.15.2). An ordinary legionary soldier, who was paid 225 denarii per annum under Augustus and 300 denarii per annum from Domitian onwards, drew 550 denarii under Septimius Severus and 750 denarii from the time of Caracalla, though the cost of living had not risen much over this period. Upon his discharge a soldier either received land or a sum of money, 5,000 denarii from Caracalla on. Yet donatives bestowed when emperors changed were still more important to them. As early as AD 161 the emperor Marcus had given 5,000 denarii to every soldier in the praetorian guard at Rome: in the third century – when a change of emperor was an everyday occurrence, so to speak – a soldier could easily raise a fortune from donatives. And there was also the chance of booty, especially in civil wars. Moreover, the military received regular and preferential supplies of food and clothing even at times of the highest inflation. Thus military service was a risky but profitable affair even for soldiers who did not attain the rank of centurion. A veteran might easily have property commensurate with a decurional *census*, but was not called upon by the state to make the payments of a decurion.

Changes in the Lower Strata

The lower strata of the population were also affected by the process of realignment. The true victims of the crisis were the masses of workers, both in the cities and in the countryside. However heavily the decurional order in the cities might be burdened, its members could still live a pleasant life, in many cases, in their villas and, as *honestiores*, could invoke their privileges against the excesses of the military and the state bureaucracy. By contrast, the poverty and oppression of the lower strata of the population markedly increased in the third century. Despite the frequent wars their position was rather better in the military zones, where they benefited from their close relationships with the army. In Pannonia, for example, small peasants resisted the spread of large estates more successfully than in, say, Africa. But in most parts of the empire the lot of the lower strata was very grim: place of domicile, occupation, regional affiliation and legal status made little difference. For this reason the broad mass of *humiliores* became an increasingly uniform entity.

Many sources reveal the poverty of the masses. Under Decius a prefect of Egypt refers to the impoverishment of the towns and the villages after Septimius Severus as a generally acknowledged fact (*Pap. Lond.*, 2565). But even under Severus different groups of the population – slaves and nominally free peasants for example – were afflicted to the same extent. Bulla, a leader of bandits in Italy, stated that slaves fled from their masters and joined robber bands, because their masters did not feed them: even poorly paid imperial freedmen threw in their lots with him (Dio,76.10.5). It was at this time that estate-owners wrote to the emperor from Egypt to the effect that entire villages were threatened with depopulation in the area of Oxyrhynchus, since the burden of taxation was destroying their inhabitants (*Pap.Oxy.*,705). As the economic and financial crisis grew more severe after the Severans, the situation deteriorated considerably. The figures on prices and wages given in the edict on maximum prices of AD 301 shows how the poorer strata of the population lived, even after the energetic and stabilising measures of Diocletian.[192] For example, one pound of meat cost between 6 and 20 denarii, depending on its quality; 1 sextarius (0.547 litres) of wine, between 8 and 30 denarii; 1 sextarius of oil, 8 to 40 denarii; and a pair of shoes, 50 to 120 denarii. Compare the daily wage of a simple agricultural labourer – 25 denarii plus his own subsistence. A carpenter earned 50 denarii per day. A family with children, which had to find rent, clothes and food from such wages and had in addition to pay high taxes, had no more than the bare minimum for existence.

No less grim was the crude and often brutal oppression that was necessary for the extraction of the required amounts of labour and tax: most social groups among the lower population were afflicted by it, willy-nilly. To this end the state recruited a security force and officials. City-dwellers and villagers made constant complaints against the excesses of this apparatus. Thus, for example, under Commodus, the *coloni* of the saltus Burunitanus in Africa begged the emperor to regulate once more, in accordance with an earlier imperial decree, the amount of labour required of them, which had been arbitrarily raised by the chief tenant of this imperial domain. We should note that the tenant even set soldiers upon them: they made arrests and beat up many *coloni* (ILS,6870). In the third century such events were the order of the day, as for instance in Asia Minor, where a number of petitions and complaints against the violence of officials and police forces have survived. One of these documents from Asia contains the complaint that the representatives of the state had robbed the population in one place even of their most vital possessions.[193] Of course, the measures which were entirely in line with the laws and imperial ordinances were hard enough. The power of the state was all-pervasive. Even the urban masses – especially the craftsmen and traders – were afflicted by it. Like the members of the urban upper strata in the decurional orders, they were forced to come together in *collegia*, so that their activities could be controlled and directed. A rescript of Septimius Severus, even, concerning an association of craftsmen at Solva in Noricum clearly, reveals the intentions of the state. The poor should perform work useful to the community and should be absolved from the burdens of the community to that end. However, any member of a *collegium* in a better financial position or seeking to escape craft work, should be loaded with public *munera*, like the decurions.[194]

Social positions within the lower strata were thus made level: major consequences were to follow. Freedom or unfreedom by the old rules was no longer regarded as the crucial criterion of social dependency. The great reduction of the number of slaves and thus freedmen in the third century accelerated this process still further. The reasons were twofold: on the one hand, there were great difficulties in obtaining slaves and, on the other, the exploitation of slaves and freedmen, which had always been profitable in the past, proved unprofitable under the new economic conditions. There were ever fewer people who could afford to pay for slaves or to feed and bring up *vernae* or slaves bought as children without any immediate return – the investment would only prove profitable after the passage of a great deal of time. But slavery did not disappear by any means: the traditional legal distinctions between slaves, freedmen and free persons were maintained and precisely formulated in law. Yet, at the same time, the development of the law followed in the footsteps of social change and established ever more firmly the new forms of dependency. The uniform regulations laid down for the inclusion of the urban *humiliores* in *collegia* are indicative of this change: from the *plebs* of the cities emerged a broadly uniform social stratum.

This change can be seen quite clearly in the laws and ordinances which regulated the position of the *coloni*. The decline of many small and average estates during the economic crisis of the third century led inevitably to the concentration of land in the hands of a few: the extension of *latifundia* in most parts of the Empire brought about the expansion of the colonate. Large estate-owners were reliant upon the the masses of dependent labour: since there were no longer vast numbers of slaves, the institution of the colonate seemed the most suitable form of exploitation. It is significant that a large number of the regulations of Roman law which relate to the colonate originated in the third century. The following pattern was created: A landowner and a *colonus* concluded an agreement (*locatio*, *conductio*). Under this agreement the owner let a piece of land to the *colonus* for a period of five years and the *colonus* committed himself to the annual payment of a sum of money to the owner. In addition, there was *perpetua conductio* which became common as early as the third century: under this arrangement, the *colonus* was bound to his rented plot for life. Under the pressure of taxation and devastation some were unable to meet their obligations each year. These defaulters were then kept on the estate – often by force – as cheap labour. Thus a stratum of the population emerged in the countryside which was large, generally very poor and often brutally oppressed: it was bound to the upper strata by uniform regulations and was therefore fairly homogeneous.[195]

Structural Change

The changes in the composition and the circumstances of both the higher and the lower strata of the population had very important consequences for the whole structure of Roman society. Since the crisis of the third century was a total crisis, it had an effect upon the social stratification of the Roman empire that was much deeper than that of the crisis of the Roman Republic, for instance. The traditional social system collapsed and a new system gradually took its place. As is to be expected when society develops in a period of crisis, the change was shot through with contradictions.

The first point to note is the way in which the foundations of the social stratification changed. Power, wealth and prestige were no longer as closely connected with the membership of a leading *ordo* as they had been in the Early Empire. Throughout previous Roman history it was inconceivable that a privileged aristocracy with prestige and wealth should not also be the political elite with the most important functions in the state: the history of the senatorial order in the third century showed the contrary. The metamorphosis of traditional privileges into social liabilities is no less notable. The fact that the once attractive civic *honores* became, for many, a burden was a contradiction of the earlier social system: so, too, was the tendency towards the press-ganging by the state, where necessary, of members of the once prestigious decurional order.

There was also a shift in the relative importance of origin and personal ability as criteria of position in society. Noble birth was rated high by many, as before, but political loyalty, legal training and, especially, military skills were much more valued than in the past. No longer did the parvenu strive with all his might to assimilate himself within the aristocracy of birth. Old legal criteria like citizenship and freedom were no longer of overwhelming importance. Gone, too, was the advantage that had once accrued from an origin in Italy or in one of the very urbanised provinces. It is significant that the majority of emperors came from the periphery of the empire. Macrinus came from Mauretania, Elagabalus and Severus Alexander from Syria, the Gordians from Cappadocia and Philip from Arabia. Most of the soldier-emperors came from the Danubian lands, as did Maximinus, Decius, Claudius II, Aurelian and Probus; so, too, did Diocletian and Maximian and the Caesares they appointed, Constantius and Galerius: the forces on the Danube were the most powerful and the most prestigious in the Roman army. On the last four named, Aurelius Victor rightly remarked, 'They all had their homes in Illyricum: though they only had a little education, they were knowledgeable enough about the misery of the countryside and of military service and acquitted themselves well to the benefit of the state' (*Caes.*, 39.26). All these changes led to the dismantling of the old social hierarchy. Cassius Dio was disturbed that one-time dancers might hold important commands (77.21.2) and that centurions and doctors' sons might rise to become legionary legates (80.7.1). But nothing shows the invalidity of the hierarchical rules that had once been taken for granted more clearly than the reply ascribed by Dio (76.10.7) to the bandit leader Bulla: the praetorian prefect Papinian asked Bulla why he had become a bandit – Bulla retorted, 'And why are you prefect?'

The social pyramid was divided differently than before. Under the Principate the upper strata consisted – the rich freedmen and court personnel apart – of the orders of senators, *equites* and the decurions of the cities, with more or less graduated distinctions in function, wealth and prestige. The division of the upper strata in the new social system was not uniform, but contradictory. There was a senatorial order which was very wealthy and prestigious, but largely emasculated. There was an equestrian order, in which the leading group was marked out by its enormous power, but the ordinary members were scarcely distinguishable from the decurional order in the various communities. A man who belonged to the upper strata through his property and prestige might bear the mark of an oppressed social stratum through the burdens which he now had to bear. Moreover, the soldiers and their dependents might be reckoned among the higher strata in the population, because of the powerful position of the army, in particular, but also in view of their relative prosperity and legal privileges. They even constituted a group which was something like an order, both through the uniform privileges and functions and through the corporate identity of its members. Thus despite a few shared privileges, the differences among the *honestiores* were much more marked in the third century than in the Early Empire.

By contrast with the upper strata, the differences between the positions of the various groups among the *humiliores* grew increasingly smaller. This development could not be halted on account of the growing financial burden and the mounting political oppression suffered by all the lower groups in the population. The differences that remained both between the various parts of the empire and between various occupations had little effect: the social advantages enjoyed by the urban masses under the Early Empire had largely gone.

The structural change in Roman society during the third century may therefore be best characterised in terms of the different development of the *honestiores* and *humiliores*. The dissolution of the traditional Roman social system followed a contradictory course. The more elevated section of society fell apart into strata which were structured in very different ways, while the lower strata displayed an ever more unified structure. Thus, even during the third century, the upper strata of Roman society did not evolve into a 'class' (cf. p.149). All they had in common was the ownership of land: in every other respect they were different from each other – even in respect of their relationship to productive labour, for soldiers' families usually worked their land themselves, as did the families of decurions in many cases (together with dependent labour occasionally). By contrast, the *humiliores* without doubt displayed more criteria of a 'class' than in the Early Empire. But despite their common share in productive labour and their common dependency, they were still very different in one respect. Some of them, particularly the *coloni* with tenancies and the craftsmen, still controlled the means of production, but others did not – for example, the totally impoverished peasants who had to eke out an existence as casual and seasonal labourers.

The contradictory development of Roman society during the crisis was not without its consequences: social tensions were aggravated, new conflicts arose and outright social conflicts broke out more often – conflicts which could no longer be settled by peaceful means, only by brutal violence, as in the Late Republic. These conflicts were very different, in accordance with the multi-faceted nature of the crisis and of the changes in society. They were fought out both within the upper strata and between particular groups of the lower strata and those in power. Thus the senatorial order and the decurional order in the many cities were affected as much as the oppressed masses in town and country. But these conflicts had one feature in common: for all the aforesaid groups the principal enemy was the new ruling elite, consisting of equestrian officers and administrative officials as well as the military and represented by, above all, the authoritarian emperors of the Dominate. The latter had mostly risen from this elite and owed their power to it. Herodian's account of the violent regime of Maximinus Thrax shows the degree of hatred that might be felt against an emperor in the third century by the broadest cross-section of the population, from the senators to the urban *plebs* and the simple peasantry (7.3.1ff.): that emperor oppressed not only the senators and the rich but also the citizens of the towns and the provincial masses: hatred seized the whole empire, everyone called upon the gods of vengeance, until finally an insignificant incident sparked open revolt.

The senatorial order was not complacent about its loss of power in the decades after Marcus, but it was much too weak to stage an open revolt. Its opposition to authoritarian emperors was limited principally to conspiracies which aimed at the installation of a new emperor, through which a return to the old ideal of the ruler was expected. There were repeated conspiracies of this sort under Commodus, until an emperor gained the throne who was acceptable to the senators, in the person of Pertinax. But it is significant that this ruler, who was popular with the civilian population and the provincial armies, was toppled after only three months by the praetorian guard. Nor did it help the senatorial order that its conservative sectors usually supported the weaker rulers or pretenders during internal political troubles – thus Clodius Albinus against Septimius Severus and Geta against his brother Caracalla. The revenge of the victor undermined the power of the Senate still further. Only in AD 238 did senatorial revolt and warfare meet with success (against Maximinus Thrax) and then only because the people of Rome joined with the Senate against the rule of the military (Herod.,7.7.1ff. and 7.11.1ff.) and because opposition to that emperor also flared up within the population of Italy and the provinces.[196]

Discontent with the *status quo* must have been still greater among many decurions: unlike the senatorial order they had been forced to make great financial sacrifices. Of course, in normal circumstances, the decurions could do nothing against the military and administrative machinery of the state. It is therefore all the more significant that in AD 238 decurions chose the dangerous course of revolt. Open opposition to Maximinus Thrax first broke out at Thysdrus in Africa where the civic landowners from the vicinity of Carthage, together with their peasant followers, murdered a procurator of the emperor and proclaimed Gordian, the proconsul of Africa, as emperor (Herod.,7.4.1ff.). This movement also included the lower population of the cities and the countryside in the province of Africa. But it was brutally suppressed by the army of the neighbouring province of Numidia: the subsequent repression fell principally upon the leading members of the cities, but the urban and rural lower strata did not go scot-free either (Herod., 7.9.1ff.).

The alliance against Maximinus of the decurions and the urban and rural masses in Africa shows how discontented the lower strata must have been with the system of government. From the end of the second century the urban *plebs* revolted time and again: it was forced to work within the framework of the *collegia*, to pay taxes from the most meagre resources and, when there were general economic crises, to suffer from shortage of food.[197] Under Commodus the shortage of grain at Rome led to a proper civil war between the people and the garrison.[198] Serious political demonstrations against the existing regime recurred later, as in AD 193, for example, against Didius Iulianus. In AD 238 there was an actual popular uprising against the praetorian guard. Under Aurelian riots broke out among the workers at the imperial mint, in which, according to Aurelius Victor, 7,000 men took part (*Caes.*, 35.6). The simple population of many cities felt a similar hostility towards the imperial regime and its machinery of power: they often had to suffer still more from the brutality of the military government in the provinces than did the people of Rome. The massacre instigated by Caracalla at Alexandria, for example, or the reputation of Maximinus, before whose army the population of Emona fled to the last man (Herod.,8.1.4), increased and increased these feelings of hatred. And the hostility of the army towards the *plebs* was obvious: Herodian expresses it clearly when he makes Maximinus say that the people of Rome are fit only for shouting and would panic at the sight of two or three armed men (Herod.,7.8.6).

The position of the rural strata of the population was often still worse, for they had the least protection from oppression and violence. When Maximinus Thrax moved against Italy in AD 238, the entire population in the vicinity of Aquileia fled to that city, the most important rebel stronghold, since they could expect nothing but evil from the soldiers (Herod., 8.2.4). Indebted *coloni* and slaves increasingly had recourse to flight: Roman law was obliged to grapple continually with the problem from the latter half of the second century AD. These *fugitivi* often formed up into bands of robbers, together with people in flight from the cities and deserters from the army: these *latrones* were such a danger to public safety from the end of the second century that security forces had to be mobilised against them in every province, as Tertullian says (*Apol.*, 2.8). In a few instances actual revolts grew out of these disturbances. As early as the reign of Marcus there was a revolt of herdsmen (*boukoloi*) in Egypt. Under Commodus, Rome had to fight a full-scale war in Upper Germany against the masses of deserters and rebellious peasants (*bellum desertorum*). In the latter half of the third century the Gallic provinces were engulfed in the revolt of the *Bagaudae* ('the fighters'), in which participated broad masses of the independent peasantry, fugitive *coloni* and bandits. Although Maximian was successful in his campaign against them, revolts of this type recurred in Gaul and Spain thereafter.[199]

The events of AD 238 make it particularly clear that the system of government of the third century – especially in its extreme form under the likes of Maximinus Thrax – generated alienation and opposition within the senatorial order, among the decurions and among the urban and rural masses alike. But the very composition of this 'coalition' inevitably prevented the formation of a unified revolutionary movement of the oppressed. So long as the issue was opposition to the violent rule of the military and the imperial bureaucracy, the objectives of all the groups affected were the same. But on other issues their interests were necessarily very different. This too is very clear in the events of AD 238. The urban *plebs* of Rome rose against Maximinus together with the senators, but it, at first, rejected Pupienus and Balbinus, the emperors appointed by the Senate, and proclaimed a third emperor – the grandson of Gordian and thus a popular man (Herod.,7.10.5ff.). When Pupienus and Balbinus were subsequently murdered by the rebellious praetorian guard, the people did not stir. In view of the differences in their objectives these social movements could achieve nothing against the new system of government. In any case, almost every act of opposition was pointless, for the military were the decisive factor in bids for power. The bloody suppression of the African revolt against Maximinus by a single legion is a clear indication of the might of the army. Maximinus was deposed during the siege of Aquileia because his own discontented soldiers killed him. That did not change the system of government, nor did all the other revolts of the army: it was always the person of the emperor that was removed, while the foundations of the regime were left unchanged.

Social problems were thus only to be increased, not solved, by open conflicts: they gave still further impetus to the change of the traditional social system. The tensions were not even to be relaxed by the social mobility permitted by the new system that was evolving.[200] Rather, it was one of the remarkable contradictions of the social change that occurred during the great crisis that internal mobility within Roman society, which had helped to mitigate conflicts and tensions in the Early Empire, only caused new points of friction in the third century. The population of the frontier zones of the empire, whence the Roman army was recruited for the most part, had opportunities for social advancement through military service which were scarcely conceivable in earlier times. The change is obvious in the careers of most of the soldier emperors, who often came from very humble backgrounds, as did Maximinus Thrax and Galerius, for example. And there were also vast opportunities for advancement in the imperial bureaucracy for able and ambitious men from humble origins, who had attained a certain level of education. But the broad masses of the population had less chance to exploit these opportunities than they had had in the Early Empire. The career of the agricultural labourer of Mactar who rose to become chief civic magistrate (p.151) was not typical: rather, the decurions, the members of the urban *collegia* and the *coloni*, who were bound to their prescribed roles by strict regulations, had scant chance of advancement. These strata of the population were hardly in a position to amass wealth, for any wealth acquired was immediately hived off in taxes to the state. Moreover, by contrast with the Early Empire, the chances of social demotion increased massively through wars, economic difficulties and repression. As Herodian remarked on the reign of Maximinus, one might meet poor men every day who had been rich men the day before (7.3.3).

And the development of the political and ideological forces that should have held Roman society together, was also full of contradictions. The rule of an emperor became the rule of a despot.[201] It was not simply that the machinery of power had been enlarged: the concept of the ruler also changed. Whereas Augustus had still been the 'first' among the citizens and the 'father' of the people, the Roman emperor from Septimius Severus onwards claimed the official title of *dominus* and was thus the 'master' of his subjects, like a regular master over his slaves. From the Severans on, he regularly demanded an official declaration of readiness for *devotio* from the army and from the civic communities, *devotio* being the complete surrender of body and life. From Aurelian on he demanded, openly and without any refinement, to be worshipped as a god. But at the same time the power of particular emperors was less stable than ever before: they were the footballs of their own machinery and every man who came to the throne had to prepare himself for a violent end. The Empire was therefore strong enough to suppress social movements and revolts by means of its machinery of power, but not — as in the Early Empire — to create a consolidated political framework, in which broad social groups could be won over to support the existing order.

The old value system of Roman society had failed in the great crisis: a concern for tradition, a political ethic and imperial cult could no longer provide intellectual, spiritual and moral orientation for a society that was collapsing, tortured by poverty, warfare and, not least, by its own state system. By contrast, the oriental mystery religions and Christianity not only promised consolation and redemption, but also fulfilled deep and vital theological, moral and liturgical needs. Moreover, Christianity, like pagan philosophy, was ready to offer a systematic theory in explanation of the causes of all evil. Thus, these spiritual and intellectual currents gained a greater following each day. The military attached itself, significantly, to the cult of Mithras in particular: Mithras, the invincible sun god, embodied the soldierly ideal. Broad masses of the population – particularly in the east and in Africa – declared for Christianity. The senators, an educated stratum, often gave themselves over to Neoplatonism. After the crisis had grown worse around the middle of the third century, the successful advance of Christianity was unmistakeable: its attraction for the society of the Roman empire is apparent not only in its extension throughout the whole empire, but also in its ability simultaneously to appeal to different social strata – even to members of the dominant elite in some instances. The Roman state could only react to this development. It did so by seeking to

rejuvenate the *mos maiorum*, with all its religious and ethical implications, together with the imperial cult, integrated within it. And
the attempt was not without a measure of success, especially in the
army. Those new spiritual and intellectual currents which could be
reconciled with the *mos maiorum*, as could Mithraism, were fostered, but those that seemed at odds with it, like Christianity, were
suppressed with the brutality usual under the new system of government.[202]

But this meant that during the crisis of the third century Roman
society was also divided into opposed ideological camps. Moreover,
the powerful in that society – namely the rulers, the leading administrators and the officers of the army – called, in their con-
servatism, for an old value system, which was none other than the
value system of the social and political order that they themselves
had destroyed. The contradiction was blatant, but it was not recognised. The emperors of the third century did not want to change the
Roman world. On the contrary, they were convinced that their violence was necessary for the restoration of an old, proven system and
that it would be successful. For them 'reform' meant to return the
Empire *ad antiquam firmitatem* and *ad pristinam gloriam*.[203] The
only political programme known to us from the third century – the
fictional speech which Cassius Dio, in his history, makes Maecenas
declaim before Augustus – is nothing more or less than a call for a
return to the ideals of the Antonine period. To an extent, this conservative attitude of emperors of the third century was appropriate to
the times: it could promote the realisation among the most important pillars of the regime – the soldiers, especially – that the
emperors were the potential saviours of the Roman Empire in its
crisis. But this ideology no longer had any relevance for broad strata
of the population: it was too late to find a long-term solution along
these lines.

Thus from the crisis of the third century emerged a Roman society
which was deeply disturbed and fundamentally changed. We have
seen, above all, that the divergent forces in society were no longer
to be held together within a system of government popular among
broad sectors of the population, as was the Principate. The settlement of the internal and external political crisis under the great soldier emperors of the last third of the third century was not due to any
mass movement: it was due to the increased violence of the government of a military and bureaucratic machine. And, for the time
being, the future of Roman society was only conceivable in a politi-

cal framework of this sort. The only point at issue was when this system of government would come to a compromise with the most important new intellectual and spiritual influence, Christianity. Constantine the Great took this inevitable step. But the Christian Empire also had a problem: how long could the imperial monarchy constitute a broadly adequate political framework for Late Roman society?

7 LATE ROMAN SOCIETY

Conditions and General Characteristics

The social circumstances of the Late Empire rested broadly on the structures which had been forged in the period of crisis from the latter years of the Antonines to Diocletian. And change in Roman society thereafter did not take a completely new direction: it was a direct continuation of the process of change that had begun during the crisis of the third century.[204] New forces in society first came about from the fifth century in consequence of the gradual emergence of German territorial states on Roman soil. But they could not change the foundations of the Late Roman social system in that century. The social system of late antiquity was not even replaced by a totally new social structure in the sixth century, when the Roman system of government in the west no longer existed. The transition from 'Antiquity' to 'the Middle Ages' did not happen over night. Rather, there was a 'broad strand of gradual changes': the fall of the western empire was only a decisive turning-point in so far as it meant the collapse of the political framework of Roman society in the west.[205]

This continuity in social development resulted principally from the fact that the economic conditions, formed anew during the crisis of the third century, held good and underwent no fundamental change. Under Diocletian (284–305) and Constantine the Great (306–37) the economic situation of the Roman empire was broadly stabilised by severe measures. In the following period, down to the reign of Valentinian I (364–75), it was hardly disturbed at all. Yet the consequences of the structural change that had occurred in the third century were no longer to be reversed. Many cities in the empire even experienced a final flourish, but their craft production and trade – particularly in the western half of the empire – no longer enjoyed the prosperity of the Early Empire. The importance of agriculture as the main source of wealth and income therefore rose still higher than before. Yet it suffered from persistent structural weaknesses, particularly the shortage of labour and the use of *coloni* which was often not very profitable. Economic difficulties escalated massively after the onset of a new political crisis precipitated by the migrations that began under pressure from the Huns (AD 375). In the short term there followed the devastating defeat of Rome at Adrianople at the hands of the Goths (AD 378). And the long term is not to be neglected. After the death of Theodosius I (379–95) the western half of the empire was swamped with barbarians, with the result that many cities were destroyed or largely depopulated. For craft and trade the consequences were particularly grim, though even in the Roman west the situation might be very different from one area to another. But craft production and trade persisted everywhere; nor did urban life come to a standstill anywhere in the empire. But the relationship of town and country was no longer based on the strength of the urban centres of production, as in the Early and High Empire, but on the growing importance of the rural estates. It is significant that from the fourth century on the large estates increasingly ceased trading for the craft products they needed – they now produced them themselves.[206]

In Late Roman society, in accordance with these circumstances, the owners of *latifundia* were – still more obviously than before – the dominant elite in the economy, while the unpropertied masses of the lower population were increasingly dependent upon the large landowners. That this process of social development was connected with the collapse of the Roman Empire was not simply the result of the growing pressure of barbarians: it has complex and numerous causes – the social causes are best encapsulated in the concept of alienation, the alienation of Roman society from its state system. Compulsion and centralisation were the only responses that the imperial monarchy could offer to the growing economic difficulties, the social and political problems and the ideological conflicts of Late Antiquity. But an enormous and expensive machinery of power was required to apply these responses: the state was faced with the ever more pressing problem of financing this machinery from the sparse trickle that dribbled in from economic sources in town and country. Increasingly, the Late Roman state – like the monarchy of the third century in part – could only find methods of force in order to oblige decurions, traders, craftsmen and agricultural labourers to deliver the requisite taxes and services. It perfected this method through enforcing the inheritance of occupations and through the creation of a complex revenue system involving both old and new taxes. Lack of freedom and the massive burden of taxation meant the oppression of the broadest groups of the population, who viewed the state as no more than an enemy. Yet, at the same time, the state no longer embodied the interests of the large landowners.[207]

The despotic character of the imperial monarchy was even more apparent in the Late Roman Empire than in the third century. The emperors were regarded as 'rulers of all the earth under the sun and victorious lords' (ILS, 8809) and as 'masters of all things human' (ILS, 807). An audience with them was characterised by a strict court ceremonial, heavily influenced by oriental models. Disobedience to the ruler was regarded not only as a criminal act but as sacrilege. The pagan and Christian concepts of the ruler were different: for the pagans, the emperor was a god, as before (for instance, *Paneg*. 12.4.5), whereas the Christians saw in him one ruling by the grace of God. But that did not change the sacral character of the emperor and therefore did not close the infinite gulf between ruler and subjects, for the emperor, even on the Christian view, was the chosen one to whom *summa divinitas* 'transferred the government of all things on earth'.[208] After the administrative and military reforms of Diocletian and Constantine, his position of power was secured by a massive bureaucratic machine and a reorganised army with a strength, in the fourth century, of at least 435,000 (but more probably about 560,000) men. The machinery of power comprised the private personnel of the ruler (*sacrum cubiculum*) and the personnel of the central administration (which together constituted the personnel of the court: *comitatus*), and the countless officials of the civil administration and officers of the military in the various larger areas and provinces of the empire. The main duty of this machine was to secure the coherence of the empire and the system of compulsion with regard to taxes and services. The intensified concern for law, expressed in energetic legislative activity and in the codification of laws and ordinances, was directed towards the same ends.[209] The dominance of the emperor is underlined, particularly, by the fact that, in exercising its authority, the Senate no longer constituted the still significant organ of control that it had been in the Early Empire. In the west of the empire regular consultations between emperor and Senate were a thing of the past: emperors had their seats not at Rome but at Trier, Milan, Ravenna or elsewhere.

In the fourth century this regime was strong enough to hold fast and thus to safeguard the unity of the empire. But through the violent oppression of the broadest groups in society, it increasingly cut itself off from its roots in the Roman social system. Thus the rule of the emperor and his machinery of power gradually became an end in itself, a pure burden which only oppressed society with its system of compulsion and which put a block on social development. From the beginning of the migrations the state was increasingly unable to protect its subjects from foreign enemies. At the same time, it was very much weakened by barbarian pressure which had risen to unprecedented proportions. Once the Empire had effectively been divided into two halves in AD 395, its collapse could no longer be halted. The Empire of the east, with social circumstances that were in part more favourable and with less of a threat from barbarians, could survive and gradually reform its own system of government, whereas the Empire of the west met its end. The weakness of the Empire was quite apparent in the recurrent barbarian invasions, the temporary besieging of the city of Rome, first by the western Goths (AD 410) and then by the Vandals (AD 455), and especially the creation of German territorial states within the Empire – particularly in North Africa, Spain and Gaul.[110] The end of the old political system in the west was marked by the deposition of the last emperor of the west, Romulus Augustulus, by the German mercenary leader, Odoacer, in AD 476.

Under these circumstances, the traditional foundations of the social stratification shifted still more in the Late Empire than they had in the third century. The gulf between rich and poor was made still wider by the economic difficulties of the Empire. An edict of Julian (361–3) on the regulation of privileges under the criminal law shows the importance accorded to property as a qualification (the edict laid down the confiscation of property instead of the death penalty as the punishment for concealment of the property of the condemned). In that edict the emperor drew a distinction not between *honestiores* and *humiliores*, as was usual, but between *locupletes* and those who '*per egestatem abiecti sunt in faecem vilitatemque plebeiam*' (*Cod. Theod.*, 9.42.5). The social difference between the holders of power and the powerless grew still greater than before, too, in accordance with the state's increased demand for power. An author of the fourth century saw the two main groups of Roman society as the *potentes* on the one hand and the *tenuiores* on the other, who were also poor (Anon.,*De reb.bell.*, 2.3). In accordance with the structure of power under the monarchy of the Late Empire, the actual power of particular groups in society naturally depended still more upon their relationship to the ruler than it had in the Early Empire. The personnel of the court enjoyed more influence than ordinary senators. Most power belonged to the permanent advisers of the emperor – all the more so, because a number of emperors came to the throne as children, so that they were under the direction of the machinery of power from the first. The most influential groups of persons were the members of the holy *consistorium* – which comprised the heads of the highest administrative offices and was a standing body, unlike the *consilium principis* of the Early Empire – leading generals, trusted personal servants of the emperor and prestigious churchmen. Accordingly social prestige rested, above all, on property and power, while membership of an exclusive order lost its earlier importance to an extent. The equestrian order was all but totally absorbed both upwards into the senatorial order and downwards among the decurions in the various cities (as members of civic councils (*curiae*) decurions were often described in the Late Empire as *curiales*). Yet, as before, broad sectors of the officer corps and the administrative machinery did not belong to the senatorial order: they formed their own status groups beneath the senators. But at the same time a new hierarchy emerged within the senatorial order itself.

An edict of AD 412, wherein the penalties for heresy were laid down in proportion to rank, shows how far the (in part) newly formed status groupings might replace the earlier *ordines* as social categories. The list in this edict contains the *illustres* and *spectabiles* (members of the two highest senatorial status groupings), *senatores* and *clarissimi* (members of the Senate and other persons of senatorial rank), *sacerdotales* (persons with the rank of provincial priest), *principales* and *decuriones* (eminent and ordinary *curiales*), *negotiatores*, *plebei* (ordinary 'free' persons in town and country), *circumcelliones* (independent seasonal labourers on the estates), and *servi* and *coloni*, who are listed separately (*Cod. Theod.*, 16.5.52 and 54). It should be noted that the penalties for *sacerdotales* are the same as those for *senatores*, and the penalties for the *clarissimi* are the same as those for the *principales*. And it is noteworthy that the slaves and *coloni*, obviously the members of the totally poor strata are not subject to fines, like groups on the higher rungs of the hierarchical ladder, but to flogging. Further, a law of AD 382 from Constantinople stipulated that the members of certain groups should dress every day according to their status as *senatores*, *milites*, *officiales* (members of the civil administrative machine) and *servi* (ibid., 14.10.1).

Regional and ethnic background were now of minimal importance in determining membership of a social status grouping: wealth, power and prestige did not depend on background. It is symptomatic that even from Constantine onwards the Roman army of the Late Empire recruited increasing numbers of its officers from barbarians, especially Germans.[211] Even legal status played only a secondary role. Citizenship had completely lost its importance some time before. Moreover, the distinction between free and slave now had only a theoretical importance, for the system of compulsion relating to taxes, services and the inheritance of occupations constituted a new form of unfreedom. This unfreedom afflicted most groups of the population to a similar extent and, for all practical purposes, made the old categories of freedom and slavery irrelevant.

By contrast, the importance of personal origin increased considerably in the determination of social position – an inevitable consequence, direct or indirect, of the forced inheritance of occupations among the decurions, craftsmen, traders and *coloni* and of the extension of this compulsory inheritance to the soldiers and the *officiales*. No one expressed the attitude of the aristocracy of birth more clearly than the senator Quintus Aurelius Symmachus: good blood would always out (*Or.*, 8.3). Yet, at the same time, personal ability and merit – and thus education – also played a major part. The contradiction may be explained: the barriers, whose strength increased markedly on account of the compulsory inheritance of positions in society, could only be breached, in normal circumstances, by extraordinary personal efforts. But at the same time, the governmental structure of the Late Roman Empire not only permitted the development of personal ability and individual merit, so far as they were in the interests of the state, but actually required it. The interests of the imperial government demanded the operation of the system of compulsion. Since a great machinery of power was needed for its operation, the individual could thus work his way up quickly by personal efforts within the state bureaucracy or the military. And there were opportunities for social advancement in the Church, for which it was not a lofty origin but education, ability to speak and organisational capability that was necessary, as with the imperial bureaucracy.

Given this context, the division of society in the Later Roman Empire was very different from that of the Early Empire. In its basic features the construction of the social pyramid was much the same as the model that had developed during the crisis of the third century, though it more clearly expressed the consequences of the change in the structure of the higher and lower strata of the population which had taken place in the third century. The *honestiores* consisted of very heterogeneous social groups, which were much divided according to rank: this sub-division was related to very different circumstances of landownership and power. The imperial house apart, the upper strata consisted of the senatorial order, formally including the top officials of the administration and top officers (an order which was itself divided into separate, hierarchical groups), the other status groups of the officer corps and the administrative personnel, other educated strata, together with the higher members of the Church hierarchy, and, finally, the local orders of the *curiales* – though, in view of their heavy burdens and lack of freedom of movement, they were in several respects close to the lower strata. By contrast, the *humiliores* of the cities and the rural areas constituted a relatively homogeneous stratum of the population, whose groups shared basic common features – obligations to work and pay taxes, compulsory occupations, severe social dependency, poverty and low prestige. In view of these common features this broad stratum (unlike the upper strata) displayed characteristics which are undeniably those of a 'class' as early as the third century. But the crucial criterion was still lacking, namely a uniform relationship to the means of production. As before, the lower strata comprised both direct and indirect owners of the means of production (craftsmen with their own equipment, smallholders with their own land, *coloni* with their rented plots) as well as groups with no property at all (craftsmen in state manufactories, seasonal agricultural labourers).

Thus, in the Later Empire, as in earlier periods, Roman society was divided into two basic categories, the upper strata and the lower strata, though the structure of the orders in the former was not as important as before. Nevertheless, the development of the curial orders pointed, still more than in the third century, to the creation of a new model, wherein the imperial aristocracy was ever more firmly divided from the upper strata of the cities. The *curiales* did not satisfy the criteria for a 'middle order' proper.[212] But the major social differences, which separated them not only from the lower strata but also from the owners of large estates and the representatives of the state authority, clearly distinguished Late Roman society from the society of the Early Empire, with its privileged orders on one side and the simple masses of the population on the other. It is significant that the notion that society was divided into three main groups, not two, emerged as early as Constantine: a law of AD 326 distinguishes between those with *potior dignitas*, the *decuriones* and the *plebei* (*Cod. Theod.*, 13.5.5). Ammianus Marcellinus speaks of *honorati*, *urbium primates* and *plebei* (14.7.1), while an edict of AD 409 mentions three groups – *possessores*, *curiales* and *plebei* (*Cod. Theod.*, 9.31.1).

Upper Strata

The history of the imperial Roman elite during the crisis of the third century seemed to be leading to a conclusion whereby the senatorial order totally lost its leading position to the equestrian order. Yet the result of this political process was not the demotion of the *ordo senatorius* to a second order – and certainly not its abolition. Quite the opposite: the long-term consequence of the structural change of the third century was that the leading groups of the equestrian order entered the senatorial order and that the *ordo equester* ceased to exist as an order. Given the prestige of the senatorial order – as much based on its now very old tradition as on the wealth and prestige of its members – it was natural that it should have the highest social status beneath that of the emperor in the Later Roman Empire. As in the past, it was reckoned to be *'pars melior humani generis'* (Symm., *Ep.*, 1.52) and its members were considered the *'nobilissimi humani generis'* (Symm., *Or.*, 6.1). Thus, the highest honour that could be bestowed upon the most meritorious equestrian officers and administrative officials, was not the elevation of their status outside the first order (as under Gallienus and especially under Diocletian), but admission into that order. This attitude originated with Constantine the Great, who, between AD 312 and 326, enrolled highly placed *equites* into the senatorial order and, at the same time, transformed the higher equestrian offices into senatorial offices. We know of one Gaius Caelius Saturninus, a loyal comrade of the emperor – he was a leading *eques* who was admitted to the *clarissimi* with consular rank after a long equestrian career (*ILS*, 1214). He is no exception: very many persons, from all the provinces, joined the senatorial order at that time (*Paneg.*,10.35.2). Only the *equites* who belonged to the status grouping of the *perfectissimi* and below, remained outside the senatorial order: but for the future the rank of the *perfectissimi* was undermined by its extension to lower offices of state and by the enrolment of many former *perfectissimi* into the senatorial order. This was, in practice, the end of the equestrian order, though it was not formally abolished. It was replaced in Late Roman society partly by particular groups in the senatorial order and partly by public officials and officers of lower rank. But the latter no longer constituted their own order: if they reached high offices during their careers, they too gained senatorial rank.[213]

But it should not be concluded that Constantine the Great aimed, through this policy, at the restoration of the power of the senatorial order so that his reign would mark the end, not the perfection, of the Dominate.[214] His concern was much more to bring the status of the highest state functionaries into line with that of the highest social status. And the effect of his reform was not the resurrection of the power of the Senate. In so far as senators gained new positions of power, they did so, above all, in new court offices at the head of particular administrative sections, wherein they were employed, once and for all, in the service of the imperial monarchy. Significantly, no military offices were transferred to them: in the Later Roman Empire the civil administration and the military commands were completely separate (*Cod.Iust.*,1.29.1). A senatorial career did not take in the high military posts, such as those of the *duces* (commanders of provincial forces), *comites* (commanders of mobile supraregional forces) and *magistri militum* (heads of the army). The incumbents of these posts were not from the senatorial aristocracy: they were usually professional officers, who were often of lowly origin. The *magistri militum* possessed senatorial rank and from the end of the fourth century all the other commanders were enrolled in the senatorial status groupings, but, nevertheless, the fact remained that the senatorial aristocracy was excluded from these commands. The senatorial aristocracy did not join the *viri militares* – the *viri militares* were formally accorded the rank of senator.

As a result of the reform of Constantine the senatorial order grew considerably. Whereas the number of senators in the third century was little more than 600 – thus matching the figure once set by Augustus – that number trebled at least under Constantine. And a second Senate was instituted in the newly founded imperial capital of Constantinople: according to Themistius, the number of its members rose from 300 to 2,000 in the first three decades of its existence (*Or.*, 34.13). We may therefore estimate a total of about 4,000 persons of senatorial rank in the mid-fourth century (not including women). And this number was hardly reduced in the decades that followed, as *homines novi* took the places of families which became extinct. 'New men' were brought into the senatorial order time and again after Constantine. Admission took two forms: at an early age, through entry upon an official career and the post of *praetor*, at least, or at a more advanced age – for example, after great service in a military career – through *adlectio* with high rank.[215]

But all these changes in the configuration of the leading stratum could not bring about the formation of a homogeneous order from the various groups. Those groups with senatorial rank had no more in common than the basic privileges and obligations of their members. They were exempted from the usual burdens and taxes borne by the civic landowners. Under the criminal law, they were not only spared severe treatment (torture, for instance), but were also brought before special courts appropriate to their order. On the financial side, they were subject only to an annual tax on the ownership of land (*collatio glebalis* or *follis*), to common dues on special occasions (*aurum oblaticium*) and to the presentation of public games. In accordance with the economic structure of the Late Roman Empire, they were usually large landowners and enjoyed high prestige in society. But their various sections differed in respect of wealth and of rank. And there were the other differences – regional affiliation, origin, function, education, tradition and, last but not least, belief.

Economic development in the Late Roman Empire, which brought down many small and average landowners, favoured the creation of massive senatorial estates. According to Ammianus Marcellinus, the size of incomes from estates in different provinces was a matter of prestige for senators (14.6.10). That income consisted of money and of agrarian products, especially grain and wine. The scale of incomes was very different among the various senatorial groups. At the beginning of the fifth century the richest senators might make 4,000 pounds of gold from their estates each year, the next division of the rich, 1,500 to 2,000 pounds.[216] The lands of these magnates were often distributed over quite different areas of the empire: as a result, their wealth was far less affected by barbarian invasions or natural disasters than the limited estates of the decurions. According to Ammianus, Sextus Petronius Probus, a member of the prestigious family of the Anicii and *consul* in AD 371, had lands scattered about almost the whole of the Roman world: he was distinguished as much by his wealth as by the renown of his family and his power (27.11.1). His younger contemporary, Quintus Aurelius Symmachus, *consul* in AD 391, a leading personality among the pagan senators, possessed three houses in Rome, a string of villas in the vicinity of Rome and in the most beautiful parts of

Italy and lands in Samnium, Campania, Apulia, Sicily and North Africa. The richest senatorial family at the turn of the fourth century into the fifth was reckoned to be the family of the Valerii, until Valerius Pinianus and his wife Melania became confirmed Christians and sold their property at the beginning of the fifth century. They had estates in northern Italy, Campania, Apulia, Sicily, Gaul, Spain, Africa, Numidia and Mauretania, and an annual income of, apparently, 120,000 pounds of gold (rather, 120,000 *solidi* – gold coins) and a house at Rome on the Caelian, which no senator was in a position to buy. Other senators had much more modest wealth. Decimius Magnus Ausonius, the orator and poet (*consul* AD 379), who was a *novus homo* in the Late Roman Senate, inherited from his father – a *curialis* – a stretch of land in Aquitania comprising 50 hectares of arable, 25 hectares of vineyards, 12.5 hectares of grazing land and more than twice that much woodland. The many *curiales* who rose into the senatorial order in the east and the west were scarcely richer.[217] Differences of wealth such as these led Constantine to divide the senators into three categories according to the amount they paid in tax on landed property (2, 4, or 8 *folles* = 'bags of money'). And, at the request of the Senate, Theodosius I introduced a fourth category, the lowest, for those who paid seven *solidi* as their annual tax requirement.

Other differences between the various groups of the senators resulted from their positions within the hierarchy: that position corresponded not simply to size of property, but to the estimation of particular senatorial offices and the power associated with them. The traditional hierarchy of senatorial offices no longer applied – several posts had been abolished in the middle and latter part of the third century, while new positions had been created under Diocletian. Yet there were attempts at the resurrection of the prestige of some traditional offices: thus, particularly from the reign of Constantine, the office of *consul ordinarius* was accorded much higher status on the career ladder than previously. Yet, at the same time, the consulship was degraded by the admission of barbarian generals, even, who had not passed through a senatorial *cursus honorum*. The commanding heights went to the incumbents of some older offices, now modified, and to the new officials at court: the city prefects of Rome and Constantinople, the praetorian prefects, the proconsuls (of Achaea, Asia and Africa), the principal of the court (*quaestor sacri palatii*), the head of the chancelleries and security personnel (*magister officii*), the head of personnel (*primicerius notariorum*) and the two heads of the financial sections (*comes sac-rarum largitionum, comes rei privatae*), as well as the *magistri militum*.[218] The definitive form of the new hierarchy was fixed by a law of Valentinian I (AD 372). The senatorial order was divided between the three status groupings of the *illustres, spectabiles* and *clarissimi*: the first two held the top positions. This categorization held good, though Theodosius I raised the status of particular offices and thereby changed the composition of the status groupings (and other status differences still remained, like that between members of the Senate and 'ordinary' *clarissimi*). Thus, for example, the seats of honour in the Colosseum were alloted to the senators of the city of Rome in accordance with this hierarchy as late as the fifth century.[219]

The senatorial order of the Late Roman Empire was still more heterogeneous through the regional composition of its membership. And the formation of regional groupings of senators had much more important consequences than in the Early Empire when common political interests and ideals had very much overcome the differences between particular regional groupings. First, there was a sharp division between senators from the west and senators from the east: the former belonged to the Senate at Rome, while the other belonged to that at Constantinople. Whereas the Senate at Rome could boast many prestigious families of traditional wealth – such as the Anicii, Ceionii and Valerii – parvenus predominated in the Senate at Constantinople, in the early generations at least, so that that body was regarded as a *senatus secundi ordinis* (*Exc. Val.*, 1.30). At the same time, the senators of the west were much more an aristocracy of large landowners than the senators of the east, many of whom had risen from craftsmen of Constantinople (Libanius, *Or.*, 42.11 and 22ff.). The western senators were also, by and large, much more conservative in their attitudes than the easterners, as is most apparent from the stout opposition of the former to Christianity. But even in the west there were groups that were very much regional, not least because many senators with large estates always lived in their homelands – their only contacts within their order were with their neighbours. *A priori*, in view of the barbarian invasions which presented a common danger to the senatorial domains of a particular region, special interests must have developed among these groups, which would not always correspond with the interests of the other groups, nor, very often, with the interests of the imperial authority. The most important regional groupings in the western provinces consisted of the senatorial magnates of Spain, Gaul (in particular) and North Africa, where there were very extensive senatorial estates. But there was also a very strong senatorial grouping in Rome itself. Its members lived, if not in Rome, at least in Italian villas; they participated in the Senate and were active in politics. They were proud that they represented the oldest and best traditions of Rome and laid claim to particular prestige. At the same time, they led a determined struggle against the Church, in which they saw a danger to the *mos maiorum* and thus a threat to the foundations of the Roman state. The most obvious embodiment of this group is Quintus Aurelius Symmachus and his circle in the latter half of the fourth century. Symmachus was the 'first' senator of his time (Socr., 5.14), the son of a prestigious senator, a wealthy large landowner, an author, an orator, the holder of public offices and a pagan who was as committed as he was influential. He himself gave clear expression to the ideals and interests of this senatorial group.[220]

Yet, within the senatorial order, the clearest social differences derived from the manner by which a man became a senator. On one side stood the descendants of senatorial families and the 'new men' who could join the leading order at an early age. On the other side were the administrative officials and, especially, the generals of humble origin, who only attained a senatorial position after a long career, either in the official machinery or in the army, at an advanced age. The former had, in most cases, inherited their property from their forebears; they learned from an early age how to conduct themselves in a manner befitting an eminent personage; they very often had a good grooming in the traditional areas – law, oratory, literature and history, for example; and they had cultivated senatorial virtues at an early stage in lower senatorial offices, as *quaestor* or *praetor*, for example. They thus constituted a prestigious aristocracy, conscious of its traditions. Symmachus was a very typical example of this sort of noble of the Late Roman Empire. The public officials and military commanders of humble origin were much less able to achieve assimilation to this aristocracy than had been the *equites* admitted to the senatorial order in the Early Empire. The main reason for this was the fact that the *homines novi* of this kind under the Late Roman Empire were not – like the majority of *equites* in the Early Empire – from a relatively high level in society: rather, they often rose into the senatorial order from very lowly social circumstances. Sextus Aurelius Victor, the historian, for example, came from a simple peasant family of Africa: through education he worked his way up, gained entry to the *vita honestior* and finally even became city prefect of Rome (*Caes.*, 20.5). Yet such 'new men', officials of the state bureaucracy, were connected with the members of the aristocracy through their activity in the civil administration and through the education demanded by that role. But there were scarcely any such bonds between the aristocracy and the generals. The military were very often men of barbarian or semi-barbarian origin, as was the *magister militum* Flavius Stilicho, son of a Vandal officer and a Roman woman. Their careers, like that of Stilicho ('*ab ineunte aetate per gradus clarissimae militiae ad columen regiae adfinitatis evectus*: *ILS*, 1278), proceeded within the army, which no longer had anything to do with the aristocracy. Accordingly, many higher officers could by no means live up to the educational standards of the senatorial order. A case in point is Vetranio, *magister militum* in Illyricum, who was proclaimed emperor by his troops in AD 350: he was even described as *prope ad stultitiam simplicissimus* (*Epit. de Caes.*, 41.25).

Thus there were also great differences in the attitudes and ideals of particular senatorial circles. The polarity of pagans and Christians drew further ideological divisions within the order: whereas the pagans persisted in championing all virtues *ad exemplum veterum* (*ILS*, 1243), Christian senators behaved in ways that were even 'un-Roman', as did Valerius Pinianus, who distributed the immense sums raised from the sale of his property among the poor. Under the pressure of the state, senatorial families were generally converted – formally at least – to Christianity by the beginning of the fifth century: yet, even thereafter, their circle issued powerful propaganda against the Church (in Rome at least).[221] It was only later that the senatorial aristocracy was ready for a synthesis of ancient tradition and Christian doctrine, a synthesis personified, for example, by Boethius (who died in 524).

Still more serious was the disintegration of the upper strata of the society of the Late Roman Empire because broad groups of the upper strata were not only excluded from the senatorial order, but also represented, in part, quite different interests with regard to their functions, lifestyle and ideals from those of the traditional aristocracy within the first order. These were the broad groups of the *officiales* and officers beneath the rank of *clarissimi*, together with the intellectuals, especially the representatives of the hierarchy of the Church. These groups were qualified for elevated places in society by virtue of their financial position which was usually secure through fixed salaries, their fiscal and legal privileges, their good opportunities for upwards mobility and, last but not least, their considerable political influence. The influence of Ambrose, Bishop of Milan, over Theodosius I indicates the heights that the prestige of leading churchmen might attain at the imperial court. But the different spiritual and intellectual planes and ideals of the aforementioned groups make it quite clear that they could not constitute coherent pillars of the imperial regime, as had the orders of senators, *equites* and decurions in the Early Empire. The officers of the army were very often barbarians without a Roman education; among the *officiales* there were as many educated pagans as Christians; the best representatives of the intellegentsia were in part committed pagans and in part avid Christians – and even the avid Christians were further divided into groups which supported the orthodoxy or particular heresies, groups at odds with each other.

Thus the imperial regime of the Late Roman Empire could not rely upon broadly homogeneous upper strata with uniform interests. The position of the *curiales* in Late Roman society was a major contributory factor. In several respects the *curiales* belonged to the privileged upper strata. Indeed, even in the fourth century, there were some for whom admission to the curial order of a community was a step up in society worth fighting for. The *curiales* were landowners. As stated in a rescript of AD 342, a mere 25 *iugera* of property (6.3 hectares, about a third of the size of Ausonius' property at Bordeaux) became enough to qualify a *curialis* (*Cod. Theod.*, 12.1.33). But there were also rich *curiales*, who constituted the *principales* in the various cities: Symmachus calls them the *optimates* (*Ep.*, 10.41) of the civic population, while Ausonius calls them the *proceres* (*Mosell.*, 402). And the *curiales* possessed legal privileges, prestige and even power, where their fellow townsmen were concerned. According to Salvian, the *curialis* was a tyrant in his city, who even believed he had power and honour (*De gub. Dei*, 5.18). In the *album* of the African city of Timgad (in AD 363), the 190 members of the local *ordo* are listed with their old titles and in their traditional order of rank. A century later, the *curiales* actually gained the highest imperial recognition: the seventh novella of the emperor Majorian states that '*curiales nervos esse rei publicae ac viscera civitatum nullus ignorat*'. Yet the public offices held by particular members of the *ordo* at Timgad were still no more than *munera* for most *curiales*: the functions of the *curiales* stressed by Majorian still consisted in no more than expenditures to the benefit of the state.[222]

After the legislation of Constantine the Great in particular, the members of the *curiae* were oppressed and treated little better than common people. The compulsory inheritance of curial status was not enshrined in law, but, for the most part, it was a fact of life in practice, for the sons of curial families were usually enrolled in the *curiae* by virtue of their property. And the state had recourse to other measures of compulsion in order to fill the *curiae*. Thus, under a law of AD 317, propertied persons were obliged to enter the curial order of a city even if they were only temporary residents in that city (*incolae*) or if they were foreigners in possession of land in its vicinity (*Cod. Theod.*, 12.1.5). The freedom of the *curiales* was very limited. They could only leave their community with the permission of the governor – even when they wished to visit the emperor on civic business. If they were away for more than five years their property was forfeit. They were even forbidden from permanent residence on their estates outside the city. And the permission of the governor was required even for the sale of their own lands.[223] But they suffered most from the expenditure required of them. The *curiales* were responsible for the grain supply, public order and public buildings in their city: while in office as magistrates they had to finance public games. They were also required to conduct the financial affairs of their city and to bear full liability for its debts. And, most important, they were required to collect the poll tax and land tax in their community; they were threatened with severe penalties in case of default and made personally liable for the sums raised. It was particularly because of this last obligation that they were regarded as 'tyrants' by their fellow townsmen. The imperial policy of making *curiales* tax gatherers in their own communities played a large part in aggravating the hostilities in Late Roman society. But under the economic conditions of the Late Roman Empire, it was by no means always possible to meet this obligation: in that event the *curiales* themselves fell victim to the state. The cities can no longer be said to have administered themselves, given these circumstances. The most important role in the administration of the cities was played by the *curator*, an overseer of civic finances appointed by the regime. No wonder, then, that the rank of *curialis* was regarded by many not as a privilege, but as a punishment. It is significant that in AD 375 the Arian governor of the diocese of Pontus acted against orthodox Christians in a way that would have been inconceivable at an earlier date: he had his enemies entered in the civic lists of *curiales*.[224]

202 Late Roman Society

Many *curiales* appreciated the situation and sought to escape their burdens by a variety of means. The flight of *curiales* from the cities was the subject of repeated legislation in the Late Roman Empire. Many members of the civic upper strata fled to the army, which was still a very good hiding place despite regulations demanding their return to their *curiae* (*Cod. Theod.*,12.1.22). Others tried more refined techniques: for example, they might gain the protection of a large and powerful landowner by contracting a relationship with one of his slave-women.[225] The regulation against this last trick, from AD 319, is included not only in the *Codex Theodosianus* (12.1.6), but also in the *Codex Iustinianus* (5.5.3): Evidently this form of escape, like others, was frequently practised. But repeated measures could not in fact restrict the depopulation of the *curiae*. As early as AD 339, there is evidence that a city as great as Carthage no longer had sufficient *curiales* (*Cod. Theod.*, 12.1.27). Libanius wrote in the 380s that there were now never more than 60 *curiales* in his home town of Syrian Antioch, where there had once been 600 or twice that number (*Or.*,48.4). At the same time the Cappadocian cities were so short of *curiales* that on one occasion a four-year-old boy was enrolled among the *curiales* because he had inherited property (Basil, *Ep.*, 84.2). In AD 429 it was stated that '*nullus paene curialis idoneus inordine cuiusquam urbis*' was to be found in Africa (*Cod. Theod.*,12.1.186). A regulation of AD 445 states that the *ordo* of a city should be regarded as quorate if it has as few as three *curiales* (*Nov. Val.*, 13.10). These details are of course indications of the decline of the curial order and thus the catastrophic weakening of the city in the affected areas. The general trend, as set out above, could not be stopped, even though the depopulation of the *curiae* was not always caused by the intolerable burdens placed upon them and even though circumstances might be very different in different parts of the empire.

Lower Strata

Whereas the *honestiores* of the Late Empire fragmented into numerous strata with very different positions in society, the various strata of the *humiliores* took on an ever more uniform shape. They were made level by the general poverty in town and country and by the 'unfreedom' of the urban and rural masses, founded on broadly uniform economic, social and political dependence. Slavery had already lost its importance as a social and economic institution. But the result was not that slavery gave room to free labour; rather, free labour and slavery declined together. The new situation, consolidated from the end of the third century, no longer entailed free labour: there was only forced labour in orders that had become hereditary, in the rural population, among the *coloni*, among the craftsmen, in the guilds – and, as is well known, among the councillors who had become the principal bearers of the tax burden.[226]

But slavery did not disappear in the Late Empire, either in the cities or in the countryside. According to Augustine, almost all families at Carthage had slaves: all households at Cyrene, according to Synesius. At Antioch in the time of Libanius the owner of two or three slaves was not reckoned among the rich. Around the turn of the fourth into the fifth century there were still 400 *servi agricultores* at work on the lands of the senatorial Valerii in Sicily. And at about this time, *servuli* were working on the large estates in Spain.[227] Sources of supply were available apart from the natural reproduction of slave families. Even in the Late Empire there is evidence for child exposure as a source of slaves: there were enough cases of indebted persons selling their children into slavery. Slaves could also be bought from the barbarians. Sometimes, barbarian prisoners were even enslaved, as in AD 406 when great masses of Germans who had pushed into Italy under Radagaesus were enslaved. In legal theory slaves were treated as a separate category, as before: even in the *Institutiones* of Justinian (AD 527–65), the criterion of personal freedom or unfreedom was the most important distinguishing feature under the law of persons.[228]

Yet the distinction between freedom and unfreedom in the traditional sense was only of limited importance for social circumstances. The process of levelling is evident even in the development of the law. On the one hand, the legal position of slaves was improved in the fourth century by a variety of laws: in several respects they were set on a par with the free. Thus Christian slaves were afforded protection against Jewish masters; the castration of slaves was prohibited; even the corporal punishment of slaves was only permitted as a last resort.[229] A law of Constantine (AD 325) strikes a particularly humane note: it prohibited the separation of the members of a slave family by sale to different owners (*Cod. Theod.*, 2.25.1). But, on the other hand, the 'free' masses of the population were reduced almost to the level of slaves through the prohibition of free choice of domicile and occupation and through the compulsory demand for payments of taxes and services. Gradually even legal theory came to draw virtually no distinction between 'free' and 'unfree', particularly where *coloni* were concerned.[230] Through their bondage to the soil (*adscriptio glebae*) *coloni* were regarded as 'slaves of the soil' as early as the end of the fourth century: '*et licet condicione videantur ingenui, servi tamen terrae ipsius cui nati sunt aestimentur*' *Cod.Iust.*, 11.52.1.1). But their obligations to make payments to large landowners constituted a very strong personal bond, so that, even in legal theory, they appear as almost the slaves of the estate-owners: thus, imperial legislation occasionally speaks of the *coloni* even as 'property' (*Cod.Theod.*,4.23.1). Laws on property were applied to the *coloni* as they were to slaves, who could only have a *peculium* of their own by the goodwill of their masters: *coloni* only had the right to buy, not to sell, and their purchases belonged by law not to them, but to the estate-owners (*Cod.Iust.*, 11.50.2.3). Thus Justinian could rightly state that there was really no difference between *servi* and *adscripticii* (*coloni* bound to the soil): both were under the *potestas* of their masters and while the slave could be freed with his possessions, the *colonus* could be sold with the plot of land that he worked (ibid., 11.48.21.1). There was usually hardly any difference between the everyday living conditions of slaves and 'free' men – in the cities, as well as on the estates. According to Libanius free craftsmen, so called, had to work harder than slaves, if they did not wish to starve (*Or.*, 20.37). Moreover, the powerful took much the same attitude to the nominally free as to the slave: it is significant that imperial edicts used the word *faex* ('scum') for the lower population in general as much as for the slaves in particular.[231]

Naturally there were also social differences within the broad stratum of the *humiliores* – between townsmen and countrymen, but also between particular groups in the towns or in the countryside, formed according to occupation, level of property and forms of social ties to the *honestiores*. The difference between the urban and the rural *plebs* was not simply that of domicile and occupation – it was also one of position in society. Under Diocletian the *rusticana plebs* was defined as that group of the population which lived outside the walled core areas, which made the appropriate payments in agrarian products (*annona*) and which was required to pay the poll tax (*capitatio*) (*Cod.Iust.*, 11.55.1). By contrast the *plebs urbana* received exemption from the poll tax under Diocletian and Constantine confirmed the privilege in AD 313 (*Cod.Theod.*, 13.10.2). The obligations placed on this stratum took the form of special taxes, such as the *collatio lustralis* (a property tax which merchants had to pay in gold every five years), and services. And there was another social difference: the masses of the rural population had at the same time to pay the greater part of the taxes needed for the maintenance of the state machinery and to meet the further obligations placed upon them by the estate-owners. By contrast, the urban traders and craftsmen had in theory only to meet one requirement fixed by the state. Thus the city-dwellers had some advantages when compared to the rural population: in some cases at least they could exploit that fact. In the fourth century at Antioch for example there were merchants and craftsmen whose financial position was comfortable: they could exploit the buying power of the considerable official machinery of state that was resident there. Yet it is improbable that the social gulf between the *plebs urbana* and the *plebs rustica* was as marked in the Late Roman Empire as it had been in the Early Empire. Even the burdens of the city population were heavy enough. Poverty and misery were rife in many cities too. And direct state control was often much worse than the oppression of estate-owners. Moreover, the agricultural worker could find a measure of protection with the owner of his estate against the excesses of the greatest exploiter – the state. By contrast, an urban trader or craftsman was almost totally at the mercy of corrupt public officials. We know well enough of the scale that the corruption of officials might reach – even at the highest levels – under the Late Roman structure of government (for instance, Amm.Marc., 28.6.7ff.).[232]

The *plebs urbana* included traders, craftsmen, the lower personnel of the administration of the community, the domestic personnel of the urban upper strata and totally impoverished casual labourers. Accordingly, it was composed – especially in the larger cities – not only of the nominally 'free', but also of slaves and, to a limited extent, of freedmen. Therein, the slaves mostly constituted the domestic personnel of the wealthier townsmen and were employed for the purposes of communal administration: and there were also some among the craftsmen. In the fourth century, especially, the number of craftsmen and traders was still of considerable size (particularly in the larger cities of the empire, but also in many smaller cities in the east). Libanius tells us that Antioch contained bakers, greengrocers, silversmiths, goldsmiths, inn-keepers, barbers, stonemasons, perfume-dealers, metalworkers, cobblers, weavers, grocers and cloth-merchants. At Rome alone there were 254 small bakers' businesses according to the *Notitia urbis Romae*. At Constantinople, according to John Chrysostom, one constantly came across cobblers, weavers and fullers: according to Themistius, that city was full of carpenters, builders and other craftsmen.[233] Many urban craftsmen worked in their own small concerns, yet there were also larger private businesses with a slave or free work-force. But the 'big businesses' were the state manufactories (*fabricae*). They were created in the Late Roman Empire in order to eliminate or at least reduce difficulties in supplying the needs of the state and of the army in particular with the necessary craft products. According to the *Notitia Dignitatum* there were 20 such 'factories' in the west and 15 in the east, most specialised in one product – shields at Lauriacum, Carnuntum and Aquincum, bows at Ticinum, arrows at Concordia, uniforms at Trier and elsewhere. In these manufactories worked both free-born craftsmen and slaves – the slaves including convicts.[234]

Thus, in the larger cities at least the *plebs* were divided into different strata, whose social hierarchy ranged from the most prestigious and, in part, prosperous merchants to the slave-convicts in the state manufactories. However, the factors which levelled the urban lower strata, by and large, are evident. All traders and craftsmen operated under strict state control. As before, control encouraged the formation of the craftsmen and traders into corporations, whose members were easy to oversee and supervise. The traders of Milan, for example, were formed into such a body (*corpus mercatorum Mediolanensium*): at Rome the particular occupational groupings formed similar organisations, as did, for example, the bakers (*pistores*). From the first, the work-force of the various state *fabricae* formed exclusive groups organised on the model of *collegia*. They were run with particular strictness: the usual punishments there were the same as those in the army. The dependency of the traders and craftsmen was all the greater in that they were not free to choose their occupations – in the west, at least. Shippers, for example, were expressly forbidden to change their occupation (*sint perpetuo navicularii*): its inheritance was obligatory. Such inheritance was also compulsory among the craftsmen. So much so among the bakers, for example, that even a son-in-law of a baker had to take up the burden of this occupation: his obligation to become a baker was as great as if he had been born into a baker's family.[235] And as the state's difficulties over craft production became greater, so the oppression of craftsmen in the compulsory corporations became more severe. After the death of Theodosius I, craftsmen in the western part of the empire were expressly forbidden to hold civic offices, to move to the countryside or to enter military service or the service of the Church.

And the economic position of the *plebs urbana* was poor on the whole. Given the ruthless exploitation of the traders and the oppression of the craftsmen only a few such men were any better off (mostly in the east). And they were under the constant threat of the loss of their property through compulsory entrance to the curial order. According to Libanius, even in a great city like Antioch, unusually rich by the standards of Late Antiquity, the traders of the fourth century could only pay their quinquennial tax 'in tears'. If they could not pay, their only recourse was to sell their children into slavery in order to raise the requisite sum. Most craftsmen at Antioch were poor. Their living conditions were wretched: they often lived in miserable hovels. Some were so poor that they were ruined by the cost of re-painting their own small workshops.[236] In many other cities the position of the lower strata of the population must have been still worse. By and large, sick beggars were to be seen everywhere: the Church cared for and fed them. A story told by Augustine speaks volumes on poverty in the cities of Africa. An old tailor at Hippo lost his cloak and had no money to buy himself a new one. As if by a miracle, he came across a fish, which he was able to sell, but the money he got for it was still not enough to buy a cloak – only some wool, out of which his wife managed to produce a makeshift garment for him. According to Ammianus there were many people at Rome so poor that they spent the nights not under their own roofs but in taverns and public buildings. This poverty matched the generally low social prestige of the urban lower strata: according to Ammianus, the *plebs* of the city of Rome were only interested in dice and races, so that nothing serious could be organised there any longer.[237]

The *plebs rustica*, like the urban *plebs*, included many groups of the population. Their general situation was bad. There were no longer the great social divisions among them that had existed in the first century AD, separating, for example, an independent peasant from a slave working in chains on an estate. The great majority of the rural population consisted of agricultural workers. But there were also many craftsmen, especially on the large estates: Palladius recommended the owners of such estates to acquire specialists to furnish them with the necessary craft products. In mining areas, the miners were not only slave-convicts but also nominally free contractors.[238] Even the agricultural workers came from different social strata. On the large estates most of the work-force consisted of *coloni* tied to the soil. Yet *inquilini* were also to be found on *latifundia*: they were agricultural workers resident on the estates who retained the right to leave them, until Valentinian I. And there were casual labourers who concluded a *contractum* with the estate-owner and received an agreed wage (*merces placita*) (*Cod.Iust.*,11.48.8.1). Seasonal labourers were a special group within this category: such men were the many itinerant labourers of North Africa (*circumcelliones*), who found work each summer in the harvest on the great Numidian estates. And even independent peasants with their own smallholdings had not completely vanished by the Late Empire: in Syria, for example, according to Libanius, there were not only villages with one single master (that is, with a large landowner), but also others with many small landowners. A particular group of the rural population consisted of barbarian prisoners who were distributed among various estate owners: they were *quadam servitute dediti* (Cod.Iust.,11.50.2), though their legal status was not quite that of slaves. These *tributarii* had to render their services in the labour of production. And finally, there were also slaves, at least in some parts of the western Mediterranean, such as Sicily and Spain, where they worked on the large estates. Yet in many provinces, such as Syria and Cappadocia, they are not attested as working on the land, by and large, despite the relative ease of acquiring slaves in such areas. The latter fact indicates that the varied composition of the agricultural strata was made still more varied by regional differences. The same may be said of the colonate which was not a universal and uniform phenomenon. In some areas on the fringe of the empire, where the *latifundia* economy had developed only late, the colonate did not become an institution before the latter part of the fourth century: such was the case with Illyricum (AD 371) and Palestine (AD 386).[239]

Nevertheless the *coloni* constitute the most typical and most homogeneous stratum of the rural population in the structure of the Late Roman agrarian economy. Unlike the slaves, the *coloni* had the right to own land themselves and the right to contract a legal marriage: they also had the right, originally at least, to enter military service. But in view of his obligations and social immobility the *colonus* often lived, *de facto*, in greater dependency than a slave. The binding of *coloni* to the land they rented and farmed became ever more commonplace during the crisis of the third century; Diocletian institutionalised their bondage to the soil in connection with his reorganisation of the tax system. It is significant that this system of dependency, considered fundamental, was developed ever further by new laws – a development that was all the more necessary because the opposition of the rural population to this system (especially by flight from an estate) became an ever more serious threat to its operation. According to Lactantius, Diocletian's measure, with the *enormitas* of the tax burden placed on the *coloni*, resulted in the depopulation and desertion of the land.[240] Constantine ordained in AD 332 that a person who had taken in a fugitive *colonus* must return him to the original estate-owner and pay compensation for the tax loss incurred and that, moreover, the fugitive *colonus* must be chained (*Cod. Theod.*, 5.17.1). A regulation of AD 357 states that, upon the sale of an estate, its *coloni* must not be removed, but must be left to the purchaser with the estate (ibid., 13.10.3). A string of subsequent legislation set still more strict limits upon the mobility of *coloni*. Their entry into the army or into the clergy was specifically prohibited. Under a law of AD 419, the fugitive *colonus* must be returned, even after 30 years, to the estate on which he was born, irrespective of whether the original estate-owner was alive or dead (ibid., 5.18.1). Naturally, the compulsory inheritance of occupations applied to the offspring of a family of *coloni* (a *colonus originarius*), as it did to urban traders and craftsmen: under a law of AD 380, *coloni* were even forbidden to marry outside their circle (ibid., 10.20.10).

A few dependent groups of the rural population were sometimes rather better placed in the Late Roman Empire than were the *coloni*. But social development within the *plebs rustica* (as within the *plebs urbana*) ran in the direction of a general levelling out. It is of prime importance that the dependency of the *coloni adscripticii* became ever more widespread, while there was a general decline in the numbers of country-dwellers with a different legal status. The introduction of the colonate as an institution in Illyricum and Palestine in the late fourth century is a clear expression of this trend. Further, it should be noted that social dependency assumed an increasingly uniform pattern in the various agricultural strata. This development is not only to be seen in the assimiliation of slaves and *coloni* through the allocation of certain rights to the former and mounting lack of freedom of the latter. The *inquilini*, who were at first very different from the *adscripticii* by virtue of their right to free movement, had that freedom of movement ever more restricted under Valentinian I and lost it completely immediately thereafter, so that, like ordinary *coloni*, they had to be returned to an estate even after 30 years, under a law of AD 419. Still more important was the fact that the living conditions of the various groups of the *plebs rustica* were much the same – that is, uniformly bad. The rural population bore the brunt of the tax burden: it was prey to the harassments of tax collection without distinction between smallholders and mere tenants. Accordingly, poverty was as generalised in the countryside as it was in the cities. Moreover, the working conditions of the rural labourers were especially hard in most cases. It is very significant that Constantine declared Sunday a day of rest for judges, craftsmen and all *urbanae plebes*, but at the same time prescribed that the inhabitants of rural areas, on Sundays too, 'should devote themselves freely and without restriction to agriculture' (*Cod.Iust.*, 3.12.2.).

Late Roman Society and the Fall of the Roman Empire

In all periods of Roman history, poverty, lack of freedom and oppression were the normal facts of life for broad strata of society. But in the Late Roman Empire the sufferings of the population were worse than ever before in some respects. Above all, want and misery afflicted wider sectors than previously. The many members of the upper strata of the cities, who had once been among the beneficiaries of the Roman system of government, had been in some respects reduced to the level of the lower strata – economically, socially and politically – from the third century onwards. Thus, in the Late Roman Empire, there remained only very thin strata of the population that lived in untroubled prosperity. Social tensions were therefore very fraught: contemporaries gave clear voice to the antagonisms between rich and poor. Ambrose demanded angrily, 'What wealthy man does not strive to push the poor man off his small property, to chase the needy off their inherited plot? ... The poor are done away with daily' (*De Nab.*,1). In the fifth century Salvian painted a gloomy picture of social injustice in the failing Roman Empire (*De gub. Dei*, 4.30): 'At a time when the Roman state is either already dead or lies gasping on its death-bed and, where it still seems alive, is being throttled to death by the chains of payments as if by bands of robbers – at such a time, there are so many rich men whose payments must be made by the poor, that is, there are so many rich men whose payments kill the poor ...'

The recurrent social uprisings that broke out in the city and the countryside time and again show how tension-laden was Late Roman society. The immediate causes of these uprisings covered a wide range. After the experiences of the third century it was nothing new that rural labourers – including legally dependent peasants, like the *coloni* and slaves – very often fled from the pressure of taxation and maltreatment, that they formed themselves into bands of robbers and that they forced the Roman state to take military action. The uprising of the *Bagaudae* (whose members are described by the sources as *rusticani, agrestes, rustici, agricolae, aratores, pastores,* and *latrones*) was in the old style: it recurred in Gaul and Spain down to the fifth century. But even rural opposition might be linked with issues not met before. The point is most apparent in the Agonistic movement, which seriously disturbed North Africa – especially Numidia – in the fourth century and at the beginning of the fifth. Besides the revolts in Gaul and Spain, this movement constituted the most comprehensive rural resistance in the Late Roman Empire. Its principal members were the *circumcelliones*, the seasonal labourers on the great estates of Numidia. They had no steady income and thus lived in particularly bad social circumstances, but they were not as personally dependent upon the large landowners as were the slaves and *coloni* – though fugitive *coloni* and slaves also took part in the resistance. But this was not so much a social, as a religious movement, for it arose out of the Donatist schism in the Church. It directed itself not simply against the rich, but particularly against the Catholic Church, whose *episcopi et clerici* were treated by the *circumcelliones* with special hatred, according to Augustine.[241]

In the cities the catalysts of social unrest were very varied and might even be trivial on occasion. At Rome hunger riots broke out repeatedly: corn and wine were often in short supply at Rome on account of bad harvests, difficulties of transport, political conflicts and, last but not least, because of corruption. Three such *seditiones* are attested in the 350s alone. But it is typical that the immediate cause even of a revolt such as that of AD 356 might be as insignificant as the arrest of a popular charioteer (Amm.Marc., 15.7.2): the arrest unleashed pent-up hatreds. At Thessalonica in AD 390 the arrest of a charioteer precipitated a riot against the German *magister militum* Buthericus, who, in the view of the people, represented the hated, foreign military machine. At Rome in AD 366 even a papal election was enough to cause a riot, which cost more than 100 lives (Amm.Marc., 27.3.11ff.). A few years later a revolt flared up in Caesarea in Cappadocia against the emperor Valens' plan (364–78) to depose Basilius, a bishop not acceptable to him. In AD 387 there was a great disturbance at Antioch when the population was informed of an increase in taxes. But the variety of these stimuli to unrest should not obscure the fact that the same basic causes lay at the root of these uprisings – the social tensions in the cities, caused by the poverty of broad masses of the population and by brutal state oppression.[242]

Yet all these opposition movements, revolts and disturbances could not lead the lower strata to social revolution. Neither the fall of the Roman system of government nor the passage from the 'ancient' to the 'medieval' social system were brought about by revolution. After the fall of the empire in the west, as before, the most important form of social dependency within the borders of the *imperium Romanum* was the bondage of the masses of the *coloni* to the large landowners. And from the fourth to the sixth century the structure of the strata of large landowners changed as little in its foundations as did that of the rural masses. The revolts and disturbances that broke out in the various rural areas and cities were separated from each other in space and often also in time – as most such movements of opposition had been in earlier periods of Roman history. A unified revolutionary movement was never able to develop. Such a movement was fundamentally impossible, for the conceptual horizon of the oppressed social strata stretched only as far as resistance to force and oppression (as always before in the history of the Roman state): it did not extend as far as the creation of a revolutionary ideology for the change of society. It is significant that the purpose of fugitive slaves and *coloni* was not usually to band together against the large landowners. As the legal sources reveal, they mostly fled from one estate to another, where they hoped to find better treatment from the owner. Even those who participated in open revolts – even including the paramilitary *circumcelliones* – were not in a position to develop a revolutionary ideology.[243]

Despite the levelling of the lower social strata and despite all the conflicts between rich and poor, there was no more a unified revolutionary class in the Late Roman Empire than there had been in earlier periods of Roman history. The interests of particular groups of the oppressed in society might still be different, according to their status and their degree of dependency. Such differences might be evident even in one and the same revolt. The best example is the uprising of AD 387 at Antioch. Unrest originated among the leading citizens and *curiales* of Antioch, who were the first to be informed of the increase in taxes. Thereafter, the city populace joined in, incited by the theatre claque, though their aims were not now those of the majority of the urban upper strata. At the same time, this uprising shows that it was not simply a matter of a social conflict between upper and lower strata. Hatred was, significantly, directed against the state. It was expressed most clearly in the destruction of imperial statues, something which also happened in a revolt of AD 382 in the Cappadocian city of Nazianzus. But the Roman state was strong enough to put down separate revolts like these. The military was able to suppress the riot at Antioch in no time. An indication of the terror that the Empire often launched against the rebellious is the fact that, in AD 390 at Thessalonica, Theodosius I had 3,000 slaughtered as a punishment for the murder of Buthericus. Even in the 430s the western Empire was still in a position to send the military in against rebels in Noricum.[244] Thus revolts and disturbances played only a limited role in the process that led to the disintegration of the Roman system of government. In some cases they did contribute to the weakening of the empire, as in AD 417, when the *civitas Vasatica*, a small town in Gaul, was handed to the barbarians by a *factio servilis*.[245] But the inability of the western empire to withstand the pressure of the barbarian peoples in the fifth century was not the result of a revolution: it was especially the result of the alienation of society from the state. The recurrent opposition of various social groups against the state was but one of many symptoms of this alienation. As the rebellion at Antioch showed, the main enemy of the discontented was not the large landowners but the state machinery. Resistance to imperial despotism was a course which, ultimately, accorded with the interests of the large landowners, too. The decline of the empire in the west was therefore a process in which the socio-historical aspect lay not in the resistance of the lower strata to a system of authority supported by the upper strata, but in the gradual evolution of the Roman state system into a machinery of power supported by very thin groups, yet a burden to almost the whole of society.

In the Early Empire the system of social mobility had without doubt made a major contribution to the stabilisation of the Roman system of government in its empire. In the Late Empire it became from the third century on more a force for destruction, in the west at least. In the west the imperial regime basically supported a static social system, through strict control of occupations and through their compulsory inheritance among the traders, craftsmen, *coloni* and, *de facto*, among the *curiales*. It also encouraged the inheritance of positions in society within its machinery of power, where it was possible for *officiales* to be succeeded in office by their own sons (*Cod.Theod.*, 7.22.3). Yet Late Roman society was certainly not a caste system.[246] Opportunities for social advancement were formally allocated to various groups in society. The ordinary *plebei* who acquired the property qualification of a *curialis* through ownership of land or of a sum of cash were enrolled among the *curiales* of their city (*Cod.Theod.*, 12.1.133). Rich *curiales* were made *clarissimi*. In practice, there were still many sorts of opportunity for social advancement and a change in occupation: the repeated legal restrictions upon a change of occupation by *curiales*, traders, craftsmen and *coloni* were designed to prevent this practice. Good opportunities for advancement were to be found in the service of the Church. Their possible extent – particularly in the east – is evident from the case of Eunomius of Cappadocia in the fourth century. The son of a poor peasant, he had no wish to share the poverty of his father. So he learnt to read and write, became a scribe and a pedagogue and proceeded to Constantinople where he worked as a tailor. Thence he moved to Antioch where he was ordained as a deacon. He later became Bishop of Cyzicus and spent his old age in a villa on his own estate in the neighbourhood of Calchedon.[247] Under Valentinian III (424–55), in the west, offices in the Church were forbidden to the various categories of *coloni*, to slaves, to traders and craftsmen organised into guilds and even to the *curiales* (*Nov. Val.*, 35.3). But in the administrative apparatus of the state and in the army, at least, there were always good opportunities for advancement, despite all prohibitions on the recruitment of administrative officials and soldiers from the dependent masses of the population. Noteworthy contradictions followed. While the state insisted upon the principle of compulsory occupations and of the inheritance of occupations, it incurred the odium of the groups of the population affected. But by allowing opportunities for advancement in the machinery of power, the state itself made the greatest contribution, in practice, to the recurrent transgression of the system of compulsion. And by advancing the privileged strata of officials and military men, who were often of lowly origin, the state only increased the discontent and hatred felt by the masses of the underprivileged.

There were many other facets of this alienation. The detachment of Late Roman society from the state is evident, primarily, in the development of the great estates of the west under their respective owners into entities within the state which became ever more politically and economically independent. They were largely self-sufficient: as a description of a large estate in AD 369 shows, they had vineyards, olive-yards, arable land, grazing land, woodland, settlements, town and country slaves, craftsmen, domestic servants, *coloni*, equipment, livestock and money (*Cod.Iust.*, 9.47.7.1). The estate-owner withdrew ever more to his own estate. At the end of the fourth century, Ausonius – after he had spent nearly two decades at the imperial court – lived alternately at Burdigala or on his estate in Aquitania. But as early as AD 327 and 354 laws had to be passed to compel provincial senators to attend games at Rome (*Cod.Theod.*, 6.4.2 and 4). In the fifth century many magnates settled permanently on their estates. There they exercised, *de facto*, the powers of the state. To try their *coloni* they could act as judges themselves or choose others to judge: they had the right to exact corporal punishment from *coloni* and even to execute them. From the end of the fourth century in particular they became increasingly reliant upon their own personnel to ward off barbarian attacks. Many estates were fortified, a practice officially permitted under a law of AD 420 (*Cod.Iust.*, 8.10.10). Many estate-owners armed their men to fight usurpers and barbarians, as did the brothers Didymus, Verinianus, Lagodius and Theodosiolus in Spain in AD 407, when they armed their *coloni* and slaves. Sometimes private armies such as these had more success against the enemy than even the regular forces.[248] Thus tax obligations were often almost the only bond between a great landowner and the central imperial power – a fact which in this situation only made the payment of taxes a fruitless burden.

The alienation of the population of the empire from the imperial regime was reinforced considerably by the so-called patrocinial movement, that is, a form of flight from injustice and taxation by individual independent peasants and *coloni* or by the population of entire settlements. Salvian gives us a description (*De gub.*, *Dei*, 5.38): in order to evade the violent exaction of taxes, 'they surrender themselves to more powerful persons to gain protection and security; they give themselves in bondage to the rich and put themselves, so to speak, under their power and authority'. Such men placed themselves under the protection (*patrocinium*) of an influential person in the military or in the civil administration or simply of a powerful large landowner: they repaid their patrons with agrarian products and money which were first 'gifts', but became regular payments. In the mid fourth century such patrocinial relationships are already well attested in Egypt, Syria and Illyricum.[294] Here we have a very clear community of interests between large landowners and the lower strata – interests which were very much at odds with the interests of the state. The state sought to stop the practice by the appointment (from AD 368) of *defensores plebis*, whose function was to protect communities from violence and injustice. But this attempt was as unsuccessful as the repeated regulations against *patrocinium* in AD 360, 368, 395 and 399. A law of AD 415 finally made *patrocinium* legal (*Cod. Theod.*, 11.24.6). This meant that it was no longer only the personnel of particular estates that were freed from the imperial system of government, but actually the entire population of large districts. And at the same time many civic communities sought protection by similar means. This development, together with the increasing autonomy of the large estates, makes it plain that the collapse of the Roman state system was not linked with the change or even the weakening of the existing social order. Quite the contrary, this process strengthened the strata of large landowners and extended dependency after the manner of the colonate over wider masses of the population.

The spread of *patrocinium* had crucial consequences for the imperial monarchy, graver than the various revolts and uprisings. Its sources of income were seriously threatened by the frequent avoidance of taxes required for the maintenance of the machinery of power. Almost the only course open to the state was to increase the burden of taxation in places where the system of government still operated – on the imperial domains and in the cities, among other places. Discontent with the state was thereby merely fuelled further, as is evident as early as AD 387 when the taxes were raised at Antioch. Thus the number of those still prepared to engage in the maintenance of the imperial regime became ever smaller. Indifference to the fate of the Roman system of power mounted, whereas gifted men in the Late Roman Empire served the Christian Church, as, for example, did Ambrose of Milan, Basil of Caesarea, Gregory of Nazianzus, Gregory of Nyssa and Augustine. The passivity of society in the city of Rome – under the Late Roman Empire a capital only in theory – brought swingeing criticism from Ammianus Marcellinus: he complained that there was nothing to report of in Rome save riots, goings-on in taverns and similar trivia. In the fifth century Salvian could only bear tragic witness to the indifference of Roman society: 'Despite the fear of capture, we play; as we fear for our lives, we laugh. One might think that the whole of the Roman people was glutted with Sardonian grass: it laughs as it dies.' But many took quite a different view of the obvious decline of the hated imperial monarchy. They preferred life under barbarian rule, for in the German territorial states that were developing, the system of government rested not on an oppressive machinery of power and a state taxation system, but on feudal forms of dependency. Even at the beginning of the fifth century, Orosius complains that there are Romans, '*qui malint inter barbaros pauperem libertatem, quam inter Romanos tributariam sollicitudinem sustinere*'. In the time of Salvian it was common practice for many in the population – including even highly placed and educated men – to take flight to the barbarians: 'They sought Roman humanity among the barbarians, because they could not bear barbaric inhumanity among the Romans.'[250]

Thus the forces deployed to hold back the barbarians grew ever weaker and men preferred to live under barbarian rule as the lesser evil, compared to the system of the Roman state. At the same time, it was part of the tragedy of the empire that it found itself compelled not only to tolerate the settlement of exclusive German tribal federations within its boundaries, but even occasionally to encourage their settlements in its own interests. Thus, in the west, it dug its own grave. Large areas were deserted as a result of the flight of masses of the population from the burden of taxation and the tyranny of the state to protected private estates or to the barbarians. A statement of Ambrose suggests the scale of the depopulation of extensive areas as early as the latter part of the fourth century: he states that death is a fate common not only to men, but also to cities and to rural areas: indeed, so many dead cities and plots were to be seen (*Ep.*, 39.3). The situation was still worse from the turn of the fourth into the fifth century.[251] The deserted areas had to be re-settled in the interests of the Roman economy: the settlement of barbarians in these areas was the only option. The recruitment of the army was another particularly burning issue for the empire, as entry into military service had gradually been forbidden to nearly all sectors of the population. Again, the only recourse was to barbarians, who were either admitted to the regular Roman army or – as became usual practice from the end of the fourth century – fought in their tribal federations as allies (*foederati*). The gulf was thus dug deeper between Roman society and the imperial regime, which gradually came to rely upon barbarian military assistance to maintain its position. Resentment against the barbarian military repeatedly came to a head, as in AD 390 with the murder of Buthericus and in AD 408 with the overthrow of Stilicho 'from the cowardly, greedy, treacherous and cunning tribe of the Vandals, one who thought little of the fact that he ruled under the ruler as a ruler himself' (Oros., *Hist. adv. pag.*, 7.38.1). At the same time, the admission of German tribal federations into the empire destroyed the old infrastructure of the system of government. Of course, barbarians were not only settled in thoroughly depopulated areas. Under the law on billeting of AD 398, the local population of occupied areas were obliged to hand over one-third of their house and home to the Germans – an obligation that had important consequences for administration, justice and taxation. By and large the Roman and German populations lived together in the occupied areas with less friction than might have been expected in view of their different languages and cultures. The Late Roman social system was not shaken to its foundations by the redistribution of land and wealth that was required, for the disposition of German society broadly matched that of Roman society. A few idiosyncrasies of the German social system – bands of followers for instance – were felt only gradually and even these did not clash with the structures of Late Roman society. But in the long term the central imperial authority was only weakened further by the existence of militarily powerful Germanic tribal federations within the borders of the empire. And in the Roman west where the imperial regime was completely dependent upon this machinery of force, there had to come a time when that regime was swept away by its apparatus.

The religious and ethical system common to Romans and barbarians, namely Christianity, played a crucial part in diminishing the foreignness of the Germans in the eyes of the local populations in the fifth century. It would be quite wrong to suppose that the introduction of Christianity caused the downfall of the Roman system of government – that Christian teaching undermined Roman patriotism and thus laid it open to a general resignation. By and large, the patriotism of Christian Romans was no less than that of their pagan contemporaries: '*Romanus orbis ruit, et tamen cervix nostra erecta non flectitur*', in the words of St Jerome (*Ep.*, 60.16). And the Church worked for the Christian Empire – particularly in the east –

harder than the pagan senatorial aristocracy, for example. The ideological struggles between Christians and pagans and, moreover, the quarrels between the Catholic Church and the many heresies were something of a disruptive force, but even of them it cannot be said that they weakened the Empire as a political system to a significant extent. The role of Christianity in the collapse of the Roman system of power resulted from the fact that it was taken over by the Germans and carried on. Throughout previous Roman history, the value system of Roman society had been the *mos maiorum*, which set up an insurmountable barrier between Romans and non-Romans. But Christian Romans were linked to the Christian barbarians by their common religion and morality: in the words of Orosius, a Christian Roman was '*inter Romanos Romanus, inter Christianos Christianus, inter homines homo*' (*Hist.adv.pag.*, 5.2.6): for such men Christian barbarians were no longer *hostes*, but *fratres* (ibid., 7.32.9). From Orosius' standpoint even Alaric's capture of Rome in AD 410 did not seem a really bad thing, for, after all, the western Goths were also Christians. For Salvian, the Germans embodied the Christian virtues very much more than the Romans. Orosius had a vision that Romans and Germans should live together in a Christian *Romania*. But the Christian Empire was only ever such a *Romania* in Orosius' own wishful thinking: its future lay in the evolution of territorial states ruled by Germans.

In the empire of the east social circumstances were better: there was not such a thorough alienation of society from the state as had occurred in the west. There was a close relationship between the emperor of the east and the landowning upper strata, particularly the Senate at Constantinople. The Church of the east was very much bound up with the state and supported it energetically. In general the cities of the east still possessed a fairly sound economic potential. Thus even the curial order in the various cities of the east was not only less weak, but also supported the state more than in the west. Moreover, the compulsory inheritance of urban occupations did not apply in the east, by and large. Above all, the empire of the east was much better protected against the barbarians than the western empire. Thus it was spared collapse. But in the west the collapse of the imperial system of power was inevitable. Its inhuman laws and regulations were unrealistic and impracticable: in the long term its brutal measures of compulsion met with no success. Rather, everything the western empire tried in order to maintain its own survival failed in the long run and rebounded to the detriment of its

capacity to survive. There was no fundamental change in the structure of society. Rather, that society was reinforced by the spread of
forms of dependency akin to feudalism between individual large
landowners and broad groups of the population. Yet, through this
development, the old political system became ever more anachronistic until it fell. In this respect, the crisis of the Late Roman
Empire is reminiscent of a certain stage in the crisis of the Late
Republic in the last century of its existence. Then, too, the fundamental structures of the old social system did not change: rather, an
obsolete political system fell. But, whereas a new, but ongoing
Roman state system had been erected on the ruins of the Republic,
it was now new states that took over the role of the Roman Empire
in the west.

NOTES

1. Early Roman Society

1. See E. Gabba in: *Entretiens sur l'Antiquité Classique*, vol. XIII, *Les origines de la république romaine* (Vandoeuvres-Geneve, 1966), 133ff. (henceforth, *Entretiens*, XIII); W. Pabst, *Quellenkritische Studien zur inneren römischen Geschichte der älteren Zeit bei T. Livius and Dionys von Halikarnass* (Diss., Innsbruck, 1969). Fabius Pictor: see especially A. Alföldi, *Early Rome and the Latins* (Ann Arbor, 1965) 123ff., in German: *Das frühe Rom und die Latiner* (Darmstadt, 1977), 119ff. For the work of Andreas Alföldi on early Roman history, see also id, *Römische Frühgeschichte. Kritik und Forschung seit 1964* (Heidelberg, 1976). H. P. Kohns stresses in his review of the first German edition of this book (*Viertel jahresschr.f. Soz.- u. Wirtschaftsgesch.* 64 (1977), 409ff.), quite rightly, that our sources for the social history of the early and, in part, of the Middle Republic are very defective (cf. also W. V. Harris, *AJPh*, 100 (1979), 335), and that, accordingly, I should have laid more stress on the hypothetical nature of many statements in the first chapters of this account· a point which applies not least to the chronology of social development. In the present state of the subject I see no more suitable way of presenting early Roman social history than to follow the more or less secure principal facts of the struggle of the orders.

2. On the archaeological evidence for early Rome, see in general M. Pallottino, in *Aufstieg und Niedergang der römischen Welt* (henceforth, *ANRW*), I, 1 (Berlin-New York, 1972), 22ff. with bibliography on p. 46ff. see also especially H. Müller-Karpe, *Vom Anfang Roms* (Heidelberg, 1959); id. *Zur Stadtwerdung Roms* (Heidelberg, 1962); E. Gjerstad, *Early Rome*, I-VI (Lund, 1953-73); id. *Opusc.Rom. 3* (1961), 69ff.;id., *Legends and Facts of Early Roman History* (Lund, 1962); F. E. Brown, in *Entretiens*, XIII, 45ff.

3. Institutions: U. v. Lübtow, *Das römische Volk. Sein Staat und sein Recht* (Frankfurt a. M., 1955); E. Meyer, *Römischer Staat und Staatsgedanke⁴* (Zürich, 1975); id., *Einführung in die antike Staatskunde⁴* (Darmstadt, 1980), 151ff. For the Republic, see also especially F. De Martino, *Storia della costituzione romana*, I-III (Napoli, 1951-64) and J. Bleicken, *Die Verfassung der römischen Republik²* (Paderborn, 1978), where the social strata supporting the institutions are also described in detail (cf. on this A. N. Sherwin-White, *Gnomon*, 51 (1979), 153ff.).

4. A. Alföldi, *Gymnasium*, 70 (1963), 385ff. and especially *Early Rome*, 193ff. = *Das frühe Rom*, 181ff.

5. A. Alföldi, *Atti della Accademia Nazionale dei Lincei, Classe di Scienze morali, storiche e filol., Rendiconti*, VIII, 27 (1972 (1973)), 307ff. and especially id., *Die Struktur des voretruskischen Römerstaates* (Heidelberg, 1974).

6. E. Bayer, in *ANRW*, I, 1, 305ff. On the social circumstances in the Greek cities of Italy, E. Lepore, in *Recherches sur les structures sociales dans l'antiquité classique* (Paris, 1970), 43ff. See also especially *Atti del 12. Convegno di studi sulla Magna Grecia, Economia e società nella Magna Grecia 1972* (Napoli, 1973).

7. In general, L. Banti, *Die Welt der Etrusker²* (Stuttgart, 1963); J. Heurgon, *La vie quotidienne chez les Etrusques* (Paris, 1961), in German as *Die Etrusker²* (Stuttgart, 1977); M. Pallottino, *Etruscologia⁷* (Milano, 1972), in German as *Die Etrusker* (Frankfurt, 1965).

8. In general, J. Heurgon, *Die Etrusker*, 61ff.; id., *Historia*, 6 (1957), 63ff.; id., in *Recherches sur les structures sociales dans l'antiquité classique*, 29ff.; S. Mazzarino,

Historia, 6 (1957), 98ff.; R. Lambrechts, *Essai sur les magistratures des républiques étrusques* (Bruxelles-Rome, 1959). Lower strata: Th. Frankfort, *Latomus*, 18 (1959), 3ff.; J. Heurgon, *Latomus*, 18 (1959), 713ff.

9. A. Alföldi, *Gymnasium*, 70 (1963), 389ff. and especially id., *Early Rome*, 206ff. = *Das frühe Rom*, 193ff.

10. Cf. A. Alföldi, *Early Rome*, 47ff. = *Das frühe Rom*, 44ff. R. Werner, *Der Beginn der römischen Republik* (München, 1963), dated this event to about 472-470 (cf. on this, E. Meyer, *Hist.Ztschr.*, 199 (1964), 578ff.); E. Gjerstad put it at about 450 even – see the literature cited in note 2 above and Gjerstad, in *Entretiens*, XIII, 1ff.

11. See especially A. Alföldi, in *Entretiens*, XIII, 225ff.; J. Heurgon, *Rome et la Méditerranée occidentale jusqu'aux guerres puniques* (Paris, 1969), 192ff.; R. E. A. Palmer, *The Archaic Community of the Romans* (London-Cambridge, 1970), on which see A. Alföldi, *Gnomon*, 44 (1972), 787ff. Cf. E. Gjerstad, in *ANRW*,I,1,136ff. On the social history of the Roman Republic, cf. the short account and collection of sources in L. Harmand, *Société et économie de la République romaine* (Paris, 1976), and F. De Martino, *Storia economica di Roma antica* (Firenze, 1979), I,19ff. On the importance of clientage, see A. von Premerstein, *R-E*, IV (1900), 23ff. and, now, N. Rouland, *Pouvoir politique et dépendance personnelle dans l'Antiquité romaine. Genèse et rôle des rapports de clientèle* (Coll. Latomus, 166, Bruxelles, 1979, on which, see G. Alföldy, *Gymnasium*, 88 (1981), 85ff.).

12. E. Sachers, 'Pater familias', *R-E*, XVIII (1949), 2121ff. Cf. E. Burck, 'Die altrömische Familie', in *Das neue Bild der Antike*, II, *Rom* (Leipzig, 1942), 5ff. This is not the place to consider the role of women in the Roman family in the various periods; see, in general, J. P. V. D. Balsdon, *Roman Women: Their History and Habits* (London, 1962), in German as *Die Frau in der römischen Antike* (München, 1979).

13. Liv.,2.49.3; 2.50.11; Dion.Hal.,9.15.1ff.; Plut., *Publicola*, 21.9.

14. On the institutions, see the literature cited above in note 3; on the threefold system of *curiae* and tribes, A. Alföldi, *Die Struktur des voretruskischen Römerstaates*, 42ff.

15. Dion. Hal., 5.20.1 and Plut., *Publicola*, 12.4; Plin., *NH*, 33.16. On the census figures of the Roman Republic, see A. J. Toynbee, *Hannibal's Legacy: The Hannibalic War's Effects on Roman Life* (London, 1965), I, 438ff.; P. A. Brunt, *Italian Manpower 225 BC – AD 14* (Oxford, 1971), 3ff.

16. A. Alföldi, *Hermes*, 90 (1962), 187ff.

17. A. Alföldi, *Der frührömische Reiteradel und seine Ehrenabzeichen* (Baden-Baden, 1952); id., 'Die Herrschaft der Reiterei in Griechenland und Rom nach dem Sturz der Könige', in *Gestalt und Geschichte, Festschrift f. K. Schefold* (4. Beiheft der 'Antike Kunst', 1967), 13ff.; id., *Historia*, 17 (1968), 444ff., against the contrary view of A. Momigliano, *Journ. of Rom. Stud.*, 56 (1966), 16ff., a view which Momigliano has re-stated, see *Entretiens*, XIII, 197ff. On the early patriciate, see also P. Ch. Ransuil, *Recherches sur le patriciat (509-356 av. J.-C.)* (Paris, 1975), and J.-Cl. Richard, *Rev. des Études Latines*, 54 (1976), 34ff.

18. On the magistrates, see the literature cited above in note 3, with especially J. Heurgon, in *Entretiens*, XIII, 97ff.; J. Jahn, *Interregnum und Wahldiktatur* (Kallmünz, 1970)ı F. De Martino, in *ANRW*, I,1, 217ff.

19. In general, J. Binder, *Die Plebs* (Leipzig, 1909); W. Hoffmann and H. Siber, 'Plebs', *R-E*, XXI (1951), 73ff. On the origin and structure of the early Roman *plebs*, see also I.Hahn, *Oikumene*, 1 (1976),47ff., and J.-C. Richard, *Les origines de la plèbe romaine. Essai sur la formation du dualisme patricio-plébéien* (Rome, 1978). See also the literature on clientage cited in note 11 above.

20. On slavery in early Rome, see F. De Martino, *Labeo*, (1974), 163ff. (slavery for debt) and L. A. E. Inickij, *Helikon*, 15/16 (1975/76), 575ff. (from a Marxist view

point). For a survey of research on slavery, see N. Brockmeyer, *Antike Sklaverei* (Darmstadt, 1979). On supposed early slave revolts, cf. M. Capozza, *Movimenti servili nel mondo romano in età repubblicana I*. *Dal 501 al 184 a.Chr.* (Roma, 1966), with the sources. Also on secessions, P. Frezza, *Stud. et Doc. Hist. et Iuris*, 45 (1979), 289ff.
   21. Liv.,3.15.5ff. and 3.19.6ff.; Dion. Hal., 10.14.1ff. and 10.32.2; Cato, frg., 25 (Peter). Cf. F. Münzer, 'Appius Herdonius', *R-E*, VIII (1912), 618ff.
   22. General accounts may be found in H. Bengtson, *Grundriss der römischen Geschichte mit Quellenkunde I. Republik und Kaiserzeit bis 284 n. Chr.*[2] (München, 1970), 53ff.; A. Heuss, *Römische Geschichte*[3] (Braunschweig, 1971), 16ff.; P. A. Brunt, *Social Conflicts in the Roman Republic* (London, 1971), 42ff.; J. Vogt, *Die römische Republik*[6] (Freiburg-München, 1973), 59ff.
   23. Cf. M. P. Nilsson, *Journ. of Rom. Stud.*, 19 (1929), 1ff.; A. Guarino, *La rivoluzione della plebe* (Napoli, 1975); E. Ferencz, *From the Patrician State to the Patricio-Plebeian State* (Amsterdam, 1976); J. Bleicken, *Geschichte der Römischen Republik* (München-Wien, 1980), 22ff. and 120ff. On the emancipation of the *plebs*, see also D. Kienast, *Bonner Jahrb.*, 175 (1975), 83ff.
   24. Cf. H. Siber, *Die plebejischen Magistraturen bis zur Lex Hortensia* (Leipzig, 1936); F. Altheim, *Lex sacrata. Die Anfänge der plebejischen Organisation* (Amsterdam, 1940); J. Bleicken, *Das Volkstribunat der klassichen Republik*[2] (München, 1968); R. Urban, *Historia*, 22 (1973), 761ff.
   25. But, according to A. Alföldi, *Early Rome*, 85ff. = *Das frühe Rom* 82ff., the foundation of this temple took place a century later.
   26. On the Roman tribes, see L. Ross Taylor, *The Voting Districts of the Roman Republic* (Amer. Acad. in Rome, 1960).Cf. ead, *Roman Voting Assemblies* (Ann Arbor, 1966).
   27. Text in S. Riccobono, *Fontes Iuris Romani Anteiustiniani I. Leges*[2] (Firenze, 1941); R. Düll, *Das Zwölftafelgesetz*[4] (München, 1971). See also especially F. Wieacker, in *Entretiens XIII*, 291ff.; G.Crifò, in *ANRW*, I,2,115ff.; A. Watson, *Rome of the XII Tables: Persons and Property* (Edinburgh, 1975).
   28. See Cic.,*De re p.*, 2.39ff.; Liv.,1.43.1ff.; Dion.Hal.,4.16.1ff.; *Pap. Oxy.*, 17.2088. For the different views of modern scholars, see especially H. Last,*Journ. of Rom.Stud.*,35 (1945), 30ff.; E. Stuart Staveley, *Historia*, 5 (1956), 75ff.; J. Suolahti, *The Roman Censors: A Study in Social Structure* (Helsinki, 1963); G. Pieri, *L'histoire de cens jusqu'à la fin de la république romaine* (Paris, 1968); E. Gjerstad, in *ANRW*,I,1,172ff.

2. Roman Society from the Beginning of Expansion to the Second Punic War

   29. On the rapprochement of the orders, see the literature cited in note 22; also, especially H. Siber, *Römisches Verfassungsrecht in geschichtlicher Entwicklung* (Lahr, 1952), 64ff.; J. Heurgon, *Rome et la Mediteranèe*, 303ff. On social development in the fourth century BC, see F. De Martino, *Storia economica di Roma*,I,25ff.
   30. On the much debated content of the Licinian–Sextian agrarian legislation, see, for example, G. Tibiletti, *Athenaeum*, n.s., 26 (1948), 173ff., and ibid., 28 (1950), 245ff.; A. Burdese, *Studi sull'ager publicus* (Torino, 1952), 52ff.; on its authenticity (with reference to Cato), see T. Frank, *An Economic Survey of Ancient Rome I: Rome and Italy of the Republic* (repr. Paterson, 1959), 26ff.; F. De Martino, *Storia della costituzione romana*, I, 336ff. Cf. K. Schwarze, *Beiträge zur Geschichte altrömischer Agrarprobleme* (Halle, 1912) 73ff. On its political content, see especially K. von Fritz, *Historia*, 1 (1950), 3ff.
   31. On Appius Claudius Caecus, see E. Stuart Staveley, *Historia*, 8 (1959), 410ff.

32. Cf. now R. A. Bauman, *Historia*, 22 (1973), 34ff.
33. On the problems of the higher early plebeian offices, see J. Pinsent, *Military Tribunes and Plebeian Consuls: The Fasti from 444 to 342* (Wiesbaden, 1974), according to whom the first plebeian *consul* held office in 342 BC.
34. Cf. E. T. Salmon, *Samnium and the Samnites* (Cambridge, 1967). On Roman expansion in Italy, see A. Afzelius, *Die römische Eroberung Italiens (340-264 BC)* (Aarhus, 1942).
35. A. J. Toynbee, *Hannibal's Legacy*, I, 84ff., especially 267ff. On the unification of Italy, see H. Rudolph, *Stadt und Staat in römischen Italien* (Leipzig, 1935); A. N. Sherwin-White, *The Roman Citizenship²* (Oxford, 1973); H. Galsterer, *Herrschaft und Verwaltung im republikanischen Italien. Die Beziehungen Roms zu den italischen Gemeinden vom Latinerfrieden 338 v. Chr. bis zum Bundesgenossenkrieg 91 v. Chr.* (München, 1976); M. Humbert, *Municipium et civitas sine suffragio. L'organisation de la conquête jusqu'à la guerre sociale* (Rome, 1978). On the earliest citizen colonies, see E. Kornemann, *R-E*, IV (1900), 511ff.; E. T. Salmon, *Phoenix*, 9 (1955), 63ff.; id., *Roman Colonisation under the Republic* (London, 1969). On Ostia, R. Meiggs, *Ostia²* (Oxford, 1973), 16ff.
36. On the Punic Wars and on Roman expansion, see the literature cited in J. Bleicken, *Geschichte der römischen Republik*, 220ff.
37. Coinage: A. Alföldi, *Röm. Mitt.*, 68 (1961), 64ff. Census: H. Mattingly, *Journ. of Rom. Stud.* 27 (1937), 99ff.
38. P. A. Brunt, *Italian Manpower*, 3ff. and 121ff.
39. Nobility: M. Gelzer, *Nobilität der römischen Republik* (Leipzig, 1912) = *Kleine Schriften*, I (Wiesbaden, 1962), 17ff.; J. Bleicken, *Gymnasium*, 88 (1981), 236ff. Noble families and the composition of the senatorial nobility: F. Münzer, *Römische Adelsparteien und Adelsfamilien* (Stuttgart, 1920). *Venturii*: I. Shatzman, *Class. Quart.* 23 (1973), 65ff. Admission of leading Italian families to the senatorial aristocracy: W. Schur, *Hermes*, 59 (1924), 450ff.; H. Galsterer, *Herrschaft und Verwaltung*, 142ff.
40. For the Republican list: T. R. S. Broughton, *The Magistrates of the Roman Republic I-II, Suppl.* (New York, 1951-60). On the importance of public offices, see J. Bleicken, *Chiron*, 11 (1981, 87ff. (popular tribunate); on the power of the magistrates, cf. R. Rilinger, *Chiron*, 8 (1978), 247ff.
41. E. Badian, *Foreign Clientelae (264-70 BC)* (Oxford, 1958); A. J. Toynbee, *Hannibal's Legacy*, I, 341ff.
42. See on this, F. Cassola, *I gruppi politici romani nel III. secolo a.C.* (Trieste, 1962); A. Lippold, *Consules. Untersuchungen zur Geschichte des römischen Konsulates von 264 bis 201 v. Chr.* (Bonn, 1963). A. J. Toynbee, op. cit., I. 328, stresses the role played by the institutions in integration: 'The Romans, like the Americans, believed in the value of constitutional checks and balances as a mechanism for making it difficult for any individual or group to win excessive power.'
43. Cf. H. Hill, *The Roman Middle Class in the Republican Period* (Oxford, 1952), 45ff. (the expression 'middle class' is not very happy when applied to this social stratum); see further the literature cited in note 58.
44. Cf. U. Hackl, *Chiron*, 2 (1972), 135ff.
45. On this, see G. Radke, in *Beiträge zur Alten Geschichte und deren Nachleben*, I (Berlin, 1969), 366ff.
46. Cf. On this, A. J. Toynbee, *Hannibal's Legacy*, I, 341ff.
47. On these two 'conspiracies', see M. Capozza, *Movimenti servili*, I, 75ff., with the sources.
20. On this, see J. Heurgon, *Die Etrusker*, 88ff., with the sources; cf. T. Frank, *Economic Survey*, I, 69ff.

3. The Structural Change of the Second Century BC

49. A. J. Toynbee, *Hannibal's Legacy*, II, 1ff.; cf. J. Vogt, *Historia*, 16 (1967), 119ff. In his review of the first German edition of this book (see above, note 1), H. P. Kohns questioned the 'assumption that developments unfolded, as it were, according to a regular pattern' and 'the postulate, apparently, of historical necessity' – concepts essential to my account of the history of the Republic, especially my account of the structural change of the second century BC and the crisis of the Republic. It is not my wish to support a strictly deterministic notion of history, but I remain convinced that the economic, social, political and spiritual factors of the second and first centuries BC propelled the historical development of Rome in a very clear direction – a direction which hardly admitted of an alternative solution.

50. On Roman expansionism, see especially, E. Badian, *Roman Imperialism in the Late Republic*[2] (Ithaca, 1968), in German as *Römischer Imperialismus* (Stuttgart, 1980); R. Werner, in *ANRW*, I, 1, 501ff.; P. Veyne, *Mél. École Fr. Rome*, 87 (1975), 793ff.; D. Flach, *Hist. Zeitschr.*, 222 (1978), 1ff.; W. V. Harris, *War and imperialism in Republican Rome 327-70 BC* (Oxford, 1979).

51. On Roman society in the second century BC, see in general, K. Christ, *Krise und Untergang der römischen Republik* (Darmstadt, 1979), 67ff.; see also F. De Martino, *Storia della costituzione romana*, II, 237ff., and *Storia economica di Roma*, I, 59ff.

52. Senatorial aristocracy in the second century DC. cf. especially F. Münzer, *Adelsparteien*, 98ff.; H. H. Scullard, *Roman Politics. 220-150 BC* (Oxford, 1951); U. Schlag, *Regnum in senatu. Das Wirken römischer Staatsmänner von 200 bis 191 v. Chr.* (Stuttgart, 1968). On the conduct of the Roman aristocracy (in other periods of Roman history too), cf. P. Veyne, *Le pain et le cirque. Sociologie historique d'un pluralisme politique* (Paris, 1976).

53. On this, see A. E. Astin, *Latomus*, 16 (1957), 588ff.; ibid., 17 (1958), 49ff.; G. Rögler, *Klio*, 40 (1962), 76ff. On the Senate and the senatorial offices, see U. Hackl, *Senat und Magistratur in Rom von der Mitte des 2. Jahrhunderts v. Chr. bis zur Diktatur Sullas* (Kallmünz, 1982).

54. Consuls: T. R. S. Broughton, *Magistrates*, I, 237ff. *Homines novi*: T. P. Wiseman, *New Men in the Roman Senate 139 BC-AD 14* (Oxford, 1971), 3ff.

55. On the change in the agrarian structure of Italy, see especially G. Tibiletti, in *X Congr. Int. Sc. Stor.* II (Roma, 1955), 237ff., in German under the title: 'Die Entwicklung des Latifundiums in Italien von der Zeit der Gracchen bis zum Beginn der Kaiserzeit', in H. Schneider (ed.), *Zur Sozial-und Wirtschaftsgeschichte der späten römischen Republik* (Darmstadt, 1976), 11ff.; A. J. Toynbee, op. cit. II, 155ff.; E. Gabba and M. Pasquinucci, *Strutture agrarie e allevamento transumante nell'Italia romana (III-I sec. a. C.)* (Pisa, 1979). On the ownership of land and wealth among the senatorial aristocracy in the Late Republic, see, in particular, I. Shatzman, *Senatorial Wealth and Roman Politics* (Coll. Latomus, vol. 142, Bruxelles, 1975), *inter alia* with a comprehensive 'economic prosopography' of senators and with the evidence for the concentration of many estates and great wealth into a few hands as early as the Gracchi. Cf. on this, G. Alföldy, *Gymnasium*, 84 (1977), 541ff. Estates of the Scipiones: Seneca, *Ep.*, 86.11; Plut., *C. Gracchus*, 19; Plut., *Ti. Gracchus*, 13.2. Licinius Crassus Dives: I. Shatzman, op. cit., 18, 253f.. On senatorial properties, cf. also J. H. D'Arms, *Romans on the Bay of Naples: A Social and Cultural Study of the Villas and Their Owners from 150 BC to AD 400* (Cambridge, Mass., 1970). Against the exaggeration of the size of properties, see especially K. D. White, *Bull. Inst. Class. Stud.*, 14 (1967), 62ff., in German in H. Schneider (ed.), *Zur Sozial- und Wirtschaftsgeschichte der späten römischen Republik*, 311ff. (also on the term *latifundium*, on which see also A. J. van Hooff, *Historia*, 31 (1982), 126ff.); M. W. Frederiksen, *Dialoghi di Arch.*, 4/5 (1971), 330ff.; E. Badian, in *ANRW*, I, 1, 670ff. (and see note 60). The

senatorial *census* under the Republic: C. Nicolet, *Journ. of Rom. Stud.*, 66 (1976), 20ff.

56. On the man: A. E. Astin, *Cato the Censor* (Oxford, 1978) and D. Kienast, *Cato der Censor²* (Darmstadt, 1979). On Cato's *De agricultura*: H. Gummerus, *Der römische Gutsbetrieb als wirtschaftlicher Organismus nach den Werken des Cato, Varro und Columella* (Klio-Beiheft, 5, repr. Aalen, 1963), 15ff.; N. Brockmeyer, *Arbeitsorganisation und ökonomisches Denken in der Gutswirtschaft des römischen Reiches* (Bochum, 1968), 72ff.

57. Cf. especially H. H. Scullard, *Scipio Africanus: Soldier and Politician* (Bristol, 1970); A. E. Astin, *Scipio Aemilianus* (Oxford, 1967); H. Strasburger, *Hermes*, 94 (1966), 60ff.

58. Fundamental for the equestrian order under the Republic is C. Nicolet, *L'ordre équestre à l'époque républicaine (312-43 av. J.-C.)*, I-II (Paris, 1966-74). Social typology of the *equites*: ibid., 1, 285ff. On the type of the 'new Roman businessmen', A. J. Toynbee, *Hannibal's Legacy*, II, 341ff. and, especially, E. Badian, *Publicans and Sinners: Private Enterprise in the Service of the Roman Republic* (Oxford, 1972). On the *publicani*, see also C. Nicolet, in H. van Effenterre (ed.), *Points de vue sur le fiscalité antique* (Paris, 1979), 69ff. On the origin of the equestrian order, see further, M. I. Henderson, *Journ. of Rom.Stud.*, 53 (1963), 61ff.; cf. also F. Kolb, *Chiron*, 7 (1977), 239ff. (on the importance of status symbols for the consolidation of rank groupings – including the equestrian order during the Late Republic). On the *equites* in the Late Republic, see also P. Brunt, in R. Seager (ed.), *The Crisis of the Roman Republic* (Cambridge, 1969), 83ff., in German in H. Schneider (ed.), *Zur Sozial- und Wirtschaftsgeschichte der späten römischen Republik*, 175ff. On the term *eques Romanus*, see also T.P. Wiseman, *Historia*, 19 (1970), 67ff. .

59. On the position of lower urban population of Rome during the Late Republic, cf. A. J. Toynbee, op. cit., II, 332ff., also, especially H. C. Boren, in R. Seager (ed.), *The Crisis of the Roman Republic*, 54ff., in German in H. Schneider (ed.), *Zur Sozial- und Wirtschaftsgeschichte der späten römischen Republik*, 79ff., and Z. Yavetz, in R. Seager (ed.), op.cit. 162ff., in German in H. Schneider (ed.), op.cit. 98ff. See also id., in *Recherches sur les structures sociales dans l'antiquité classique*, 133ff., and *Plebs and Princeps* (Oxford, 1969), 9ff.; also H. Bruhns, in H. Mommsen and W. Schulze (eds.), *Vom Elend der Handarbeit. Probleme historischer Unterschichtenforschung* (Stuttgart, 1981), 27ff. Cf. also note 87 below. Distributions of food and money among the poor of Rome: C. Nicolet, *Le métier de citoyen dans la Rome républicaine* (Paris, 1976, 250ff.

60. On the fate of the smallholders: A. J. Toynbee, op.cit., II 10ff., and on this, P. A. Brunt, *Italian Manpower*, 269ff.; E. Gabba, *Ktema*, 2 (1977), 269ff.; K. Hopkins, *Conquerors and Slaves: Sociological Studies in Roman History*, I (Cambridge, 1978), 1ff.; J. M. Frayn, *Subsistence Farming in Roman Italy* (London, 1979); see also note 55 above. Cf. J. K. Evans, *Amer. Journ. of Ancient History*, 5 (1980), 19ff. Paid labour beside slave labour in Italian agriculture: J. E. Skydsgaard, in P. Garnsey (ed.), *Non-Slave Labour in the Greco-Roman World* (Cambridge, 1980), 65ff.; cf. W. Backhaus, in H. Mommsen and W. Schulze (eds.), op.cit., 93ff. Archaeological evidence for the survival fo smallholdings: T. W. Potter, *The Changing Landscape of South Etruria* (London,1979); A. Carandini and A. Settis, *Schiavi e padroni nell'Etruria romana. La villa di Sette Finestre sallo scavo alla mostra* (Bari, 1979); D. W. Rathbone, *Journ. of Rom.Stud.* 71 (1981), 1ff.

61. On the position of the Italians after the Second Punic War, see A. H. McDonald, *Journ. of Rom.Stud.* 34 (1944), 11ff.; A. J. Toynbee, op cit., II,106ff.; H. Galsterer, *Herrschaft und Verwaltung*, 152ff.; V. Ilari, *Gli Italici nelle strutture militari romane* (Milano, 1974).

62. J. Deininger, *Der politische Widerstand gegen Rom in Griechenland 217-86 v.Chr.* (Berlin-New York, 1971); on the social background: 263ff. Rome and the

Greeks: T. Bernhardt, *Imperium und Eleutheria. Die römische Politik gegenüber den freien Städten des griechischen Ostens* (Hamburg, 1972). On the internal situation in the Greek world in the Late Republic, see D. Schlichting, *Cicero und die griechische Gesellschaft seiner Zeit* (Berlin, 1975).

63. On slavery in the later Republic, see in general, W.L. Westermann, *The Slave Systems of Greek and Roman Antiquity* (Philadelphia, 1955), 57ff.; E. M. Staerman, *Die Blütezeit der Sklavenwirtschaft in der römischen Republik* (Wiesbaden, 1969). See also especially W. Hofmann. *Dialoghi di Arch*.4/5 (1971), 498ff.; K. Hopkins, *Conquerors and Slaves*, 99ff.; F. De Martino, *Storia economica di Roma*, I, 69ff.

64. Full list and analysis in H. Volkmann, *Die Massenversklavungen der Einwohner eroberter Städte in der hellenistisch-römischen Zeit* (Akad.d.Wiss.u.Lit. Mainz.Abh.d.Geistes– und Soz.wiss. Kl.Jg. 1961, No.3, Wiesbaden, 1961); A. J. Toynbee, op cit. II, 171ff.; E. M. Štaerman,op.cit. 43f.

65. T. Frank, *Economic Survey*, I, 194f., 200. Slave trade: W. V. Harris, in J. H. D'Arms and E. C. Kopff (eds.), *The Seaborne Commerce of Ancient Rome* (Mem.Amer.Acad.Rome, vol.36 (1980)), 117ff. (also for the Empire).

66. Slaves in the economy: W. L. Westermann, op.cit., 69ff.; E. M. Štaerman, op.cit.,71ff. Slaves in Plautus and Terence: P.P. Spranger, *Historische Untersuchungen zu den Sklavenfiguren des Plautus und Terenz* (Akad.d.Wiss.u.Lit.Mainz, Abh.d.Geistes– u.Soz.wiss. Kl.Jg.f 1960, No. 8, Wiesbaden, 1961). On Cato: the literature in note 56; on slave barracks, R. Etienne, in *Actes du Colloque 1972 sur l'esclavage* (Besançon-Paris, 1974), 249ff.

4. The Crisis of the Republic and Roman Society

67. For Th. Mommsen, the 'Roman revolution' meant, especially, the political crisis of Rome from the Gracchi to Sulla: see *Römische Geschichte*⁵ (Berlin, 1885), vol. II. R. Syme saw the essence of the Roman revolution principally in the realignment of the leading elite under Caesar and, especially, under Augustus: *The Roman Revolution* (Oxford, 1939), in German as *Die römische Revolution* (Stuttgart, 1957). Cf. on this, G. Alföldy, *Sir Ronald Syme, 'Die römische Revolution' und die deutsche Althistorie* (Sitz.–Ber. d.Heidelberger Akad, d. Wiss., Phil–hist.Kl., Jg.1983, Heft 1, Heidelberg, 1983).

68. Cf. A. Heuss, *Hist.Ztschr.*, 182 (1956), 1ff.; also on the notion of revolution for the events of antiquity, id. ibid., 216 (1973), 1ff., but of. K. E. Petzold, *Riv.Stor.dell.Ant.*, 2 (1972), 229ff.; J. Molthagen, in I. Geiss and R. Tamchine (eds.), *Ansichten einer künftigen Geschichtswissenschaft*, (München, 1974); 34ff. On the issue of the use of the notion of revolution in German ancient history, see, too, C. Gaedeke. *Geschichte und Revolution bei Niebuhr, Droysen und Mommsen* (Diss., Berlin, 1978); E. Tornow, *Der Revolutionsbegriff und die spatere römische Republik – eine Studie zur deutschen Geschichtsschreibung im 19. und 20. Jh.* (Frankfurt am Main – Bern – Las Vegas, 1978); K. Bringmann, *Gesch. in Wiss. u. Unterricht*, 31 (1980), 357ff.; H. Castritius, *Der römische Prinzipat als Republik* (Husum, 1982), 12ff.

69. Cf. P. A. Brunt, *Social Conflicts in the Roman Republic*, 74ff. On these conflicts, see H. Schneider, *Gesch. in Wiss. u. Unterricht*, 27 (1976), 597ff., who derives the crisis of the Roman Republic from social antagonisms; see also id. *Wirtschaft und Politik. Untersuchungen zur Geschichte der späten römischen Republik* (Erlangen, 1974), on which H. Castritius, *Gymnasium*, 86 (1979), 207ff.

70. In general: J. Vogt, Zur Struktur der antiken Sklavenkriege, in *Sklaverei und Humanität. Studien zur antiken Sklaverei und ihrer Erforschung*² (Wiesbaden, 1972), 20ff.; see also P. Oliva, in *Neue Beiträge zur Geschichte der Alten Welt* II (Berlin, 1965), 75ff., also in H. Schneider (ed.), *Zur Sozial– and Wirtschaftsgeschichte der spä*

ten römischen Republik, 237ff.; E. M. Štaerman, *Die Blütezeit der Sklavenwirtschaft*, 238ff.; W. Hoben, *Terminologische Studien zu den Sklavenerhebungen der römischen Republik* (Wiesbaden, 1978); K.–W. Welwei, in H. Mommsen and W. Schulze (eds.). *Vom Elend der Handarbeit*, 50ff.
71. Principal sources for the various uprisings: Diod.,34/35.2.1ff. and 3.1ff. (Sicily); App., *BC*, 1.539ff. and Plut., *Crassus*, 8.1ff. (Spartacus). Most important literature: M. Capozza, *Atti dell'Ist. Veneto*, 133 (1974/75), 27ff. (First Sicilian Slave Revolt); V. Vavrinek, *La rēvolte d'Aristonicos* (Praha, 1957) and *Eirene*, 13 (1975),109ff.; J.–P.Brisson, *Spartacus* (Paris,1959); B. A. Marshall, *Athenaeum*, n.s.51 (1973), 109ff. (chronology of the revolt of Spartacus); A. Guarino, *Spartakus. Ende der römischen Republik* (Köln, 1980); cf. also N. Brockmeyer, *Antike Sklaverei*, 172ff. For further literature, see J. Vogt and N. Brockmeyer, *Bibliographie zur antiken Sklaverei* (Bochum, 1961), 149ff.
72. On all problems relating to religious ideas among the slaves, see now F. Bömer, *Untersuchengen über die Religion der Sklaven in Griechenland und Rom*, I-IV (Akad.d.Wiss.u.Lit.Mainz, Abh.d.Geistes–u. Soz.wiss. Kl. Jg. 1957, No.7, 1960 No.1, 1961 No.4, 1963 No.10, Wiesbaden, 1958–64, the second edition of the first part in collaboration with P. Hertz, Wiesbaden, 1981).
73. E. M. Štaerman, op.cit., 279ff.
74. Cf. E. Maróti, in *Antičnoje obščestvo* (Moskwa, 1967), 109ff.
75. On resistance among the Greeks, J. Deininger, *Widerstand gegen Rom in Griechenland*, 245ff. Roman rule in the provinces: W. Dahlheim, *Gewalt und Herrschaft. Das provinziale Herrschaftssystem der römischen Republik* (Berlin-New York, 1977).
76. E. Badian, *Foreign Clientelae*, 221ff. On the Social War and its complex social facets; H. Galsterer, *Herrschaft und Verwaltung*, 187ff.; cf. also, especially, P. A. Brunt, *Journ.of Rom.Stud.*, 55 (1965), 90ff.; E. Badian, *Dialoghi di Arch.*, 4/5 (1971), 373ff.
77. On the history of the principal conflicts of the Late Republic, see for a comprehensive treatment, K. Christ, *Krise und Untergang der römischen Republik*, 117ff. (detailed bibliography, ibid., 477ff.). Use of force: A. W. Lintott, *Violence in Republican Rome* (Oxford, 1968). Changes in the character of the state: J. Bleicken, *Staat und Recht in der römischen Republik* (Sitz.Ber.d.Wiss.Ges.Frankfurt/M., Band XV 4, Wiesbaden, 1978). Survey of the general situation at the end of the Republic: H. S. Gruen, *The Last Generation of the Roman Republic* (Berkeley, 1974). Source problems: E. Gabba, *Appiano e la storia delle guerre civili* (Firenze, 1956); I. Hahn, *Acta Ant.Hung.*, 12 (1964), 169ff.
78. Comprehensive studies of the Gracchi, see especially F. Münzer, *R-E*, IIA (1923), 1375ff.1409ff.; D. C. Earl, *Tiberius Gracchus: A Study in Politics* (Coll. Latomus, vol.66, Bruxelles, 1963); H. C. Boren, *The Gracchi* (New York, 1968); A. H. Bernstein, *Tiberius Sempronius Gracchus* (Ithaca-London, 1978); D. Stockton, *The Gracchi* (Oxford, 1979); Y. Shochat, *Recruitment and the Programme of Tiberius Gracchus* (Coll.Latomus, vol.169, Bruxelles, 1980). Bibliographical surveys: E. Badian, *Historia*, 11 (1962), 197ff., and *ANRW*,I,1,668ff. Supporters and opponents of Tiberius Sempronus Gracchus: J. Briscoe, *Journ. of Rom.Stud.*, 64 (1974), 125ff. Agrarian reform: J. Molthagen, *Historia*, 22 (1973), 423ff. Gaius Sempronius Gracchus and his reforms: K. Meister, *Chiron*, 6 (1976),113ff. (legislation on the allies); D. Flach, *Zeitschr.d.Savigny-Stiftung, Rom.Abt.* 90 (1973), 91ff. (criminal legislation). Fate of agrarian legislation: D. Flach, *Hist.Zeitschr.* 217 (1973), 265ff.; K. Meister, *Historia*, 23 (1974), 86ff.; K. Johannsen, *Die lex argraria des Jahres 111 v.Chr.* (Diss., München, 1971).
79. On the period of Marius and Sulla, see for comprehensive treatments, W. Schur, *Das Zeitalter des Marius und Sulla* (Leipzig, 1942); T. F. Carney, *A Biography of C. Marius*² (Chicago, 1970); E. Badian, *Sulla: The Deadly Reformer* (Sydney, 1970). Bibliographical survey: E. Gabba, in *ANRW*,I,1,764ff. Emergency legisla-

tion: J. Ungern-Sternberg von Pürkel, *Untersuchungen zum spätrepublikanischen Notstandsrecht*. *Senatusconsultum ultimum und hostis-Erklärung* (München, 1970).
80. On the role of the army and the soldiers in the Late Republic, see R. E. Smith, *Service in the Post-Marian Roman Army* (Manchester, 1958); P. A. Brunt, *Journ. of Rom.Stud.*, 52 (1962), 69ff., in German in H. Schneider (ed.), *Zur Sozial– und Wirtschafsgeschichte der späten römischen Republik* 124ff.; J. Harmand, *L'armée et le soldat à Rome de 107 à 50 avant notre ère* (Paris, 1967); H. Botermann, *Die Soldaten und die römische Politik in der Zeit von Caesars Tod bis zur Begründung des Zweiten Triumvirates* (München, 1968); E. H. Erdmann, *Die Rolle des Heeres in der Zeit von Marius bes Caesar. Militärische und politische Probleme einer Berufsarmee* (Neustadt, 1972); E. Gabba, *Esercito e società nella tarda repubblica romana* (Firenze, 1973), 47ff.; cf. also J. Suolahti, *The Junior Officers of the Roman Army in the Republican Period* (Helsinki, 1955).
81. On this, E. Gabba, *Athenaeum* n.s., 32 (1954), 41ff., 293ff.; Chr. Meier, *Res Publica Amissa*. *Eine Studie zur Verfassung und Geschichte der späten römischen Republik* (Wiesbaden, 1966), 208ff.
82. On this, see note 79. On the effects of the civil wars upon the social development of southern Etruria, see G.D.B. Jones, in *War and Society: Historical Essays in Honour and Memory of J. R. Westerd* (London, 1973), 277ff.
83. Unsurpassed account in R. Syme, *Roman Revolution*, 28ff. Bibliography in K. Christ, *Römische Geschichte*, 134ff., and in J. Bleicken, *Geschichte der Römischen Republik*, 234ff. A structural analysis of the situation in Rome in the 'last generation' of the Republic is given by E. S. Gruen, *The Last Generation of the Roman Republic* (Berkeley-Los Angeles – London, 1974). Cf. E. Wistrand, *Caesar and Contemporary Roman Society* (Göteborg, 1978).
84. Optimates: H. Strasburger, *R–E*, XVIII (1939), 773ff.; populares: Chr. Meier, *R–E Suppl.*, X (1965), 549ff. See further, especially id. *Res Publica Amissa*, 7ff.
85. On the senatorial aristocracy of the Late Republic, see R. Syme, *Roman Revolution*, 10ff.; bibliographical survey: T. R. S. Broughton, in *ANRW*, I, 1, 250ff. On the nobility, cf. A. Afzelius, *Class. et Med.*, 7 (1945), 150ff.; on 'new men': T. P. Wiseman, *New Men in the Roman Senate 139 BC–AD 14* (Oxford, 1971). On the division of the senators during the civil wars fought by Caesar, see. H. Bruhns, *Caesar und die römische Oberschicht in den Jahren 49–44 v. Chr. Untersuchungen zur Herrschaftsetablierung im Bürgerkrieg* (Göttingen, 1978); cf. D. R. Shackleton Bailey, *Class. Quart.*, n.s., 10 (1960), 253ff. On the economic circumstances of the senators, see M. Jaczynowska, *Historia*, 11 (1962), 486ff., in German in H. Schneider (ed.), *Zur Sozial–und Wirtschaftsgeschichte der späten römischen Republik*, 214ff. But on this topic, see now in particular the work of I. Shatzman (see above, note 55); also, E. Rawson, in M. I. Finley (ed.), *Studies in Roman Property* (Cambridge, 1976), 85ff.
86. *Att.*, 1.17.8. On the equestrian order in the Late Republic, see the literature cited above in note 58.
87. On the *plebs urbana* in the Late Republic, see the literature cited in note 59 above. On their part in the disputes that occurred during the crisis of the Republic, see P.A. Brunt, *Past and Present*, 35 (1966), 3ff., in German in H. Schneider (ed.), *Zur Sozial– und Wirtschaftsgeschichte der späten römischen Republik*, 271ff.; I. Hahn, in J. Herrmann and I. Sellnow (eds.), *Die Rolle der Volksmassen in der Geschichte der vorkapitalistischen Gesellschaftsformen* (Berlin, 1975), 121ff.; W. Nippel, in H. Mommsen and W. Schulze (eds.), *Vom Elend der Handarbeit*, 70ff.
88. On the role of the veterans in the Late Republic, see now especially H.–Chr. Schneider, *Das Problem der Veteranenversorgung in der späteren römischen Republik* (Bonn, 1977) and the literature cited in notes 80 and 94.
89. On the *coniuratio Catilinae*, see especially e.G. Hardy, *The Catilinarian Conspiracy in its Context* (Oxford, 1924); M.Gelzer, *R–E*, IIA, 2 (1923), 1693ff.;

W.Hoffmann, *Gymnasium*, 66 (1959), 459ff.; Z.Yavetz, *Historia*, 12 (1963), 485ff.; H. Drexler, *Die Catiliniarische Verschwörung. Ein Quellenheft* (Darmstadt, 1976). Social groups involved: cf. especially Cicero, *Catil.* 2. 18ff. Partication of slaves in the political conflicts and civil wars of the Late Republic: J.Annequin and M. Létroublon, in *Actes du* Colloque 1972 sur l'esclavage (Besançon-Paris, 1974), 211ff.; N. Rouland, *Les esclaves romaines en temps de guerre* (Coll. Latomus, vol. 151, Bruxelles, 1977), 77ff.

90. On the social system of the Late Republic, see in general W. Warde Fowler, *Social Life at Rome in the Age of Cicero* (London, 1907, repr. 1964); M. Gelzer, *Kleine Schriften*, I, 154ff.; F. De Martino, *Storia della costituzione romana*, III, 102ff.; H. H. Scullard, *From the Gracchi to Nero. A History of Rome from 133 BC to AD 68*[2] (London, 1963), 178ff. Economy: T. Frank, *Economic Survey*, I, 215ff.

91. On *homines novi* among the consuls, see T. P. Wiseman, *New Men in the Roman Senate*, 164ff., 203.

92. On Cicero, see the literature cited by K. Christ, *Römische Geschichte*, 136f., and J. Bleicken, *Geschichte der Römischen Republik*, 235f.

93. Diod., 36.3.1. On slaves and freedmen under the Late Republic, see W. L. Westermann, *Slave Systems*, 63ff.; E.M.Staerman, *Die Blütezert der Sklavenwirtshaft*, 36ff.; S.Treggiari, *Roman Freedmen during the Late Republic* (Oxford, 1969); G. Fabre, *Libertus. Recherches sur les rapports patron-affranchi à la fin de la république romaine* (Rome, 1981). Economic basis of the rise of freedmen in the Late Republic: St. Mrozek, *Chiron*, 5 (1975), 311ff.

94. Colonisation, citizenship: F. Vittinghoff, *Römische Kolonisation und Bürgerrechtspolitik unter Caesar und Augustus* (Akad.d.Wiss.u.Lit. Mainz, Abh.d.Geistesu. Soz. wiss.Kl. Jg.1951 Nr.14 Wiesbaden,1952), 7ff.; L. Teutsch, *Das römische Städtewesen in Nordafrika in der Zeit von C. Gracchus bis zum Tod des Kaisers Augustus* (Berlin,1962); A.J.N. Wilson, *Emigration from Italy in the Republican Age of Rome* (New York,1966); P.A. Brunt, *Italian Manpower*, 159ff.; A. N. Sherwin-White, in *ANRW*, I, 2, 23ff., and *The Roman Citizenship*[2] (Oxford,1973).

95. On the rise of particular provincials into the Senate, see T. P. Wiseman, *New Men in the Roman Senate*, 19ff.; on Balbus of Gades: J. F. Rodríguez Neila, *Los Balbos de Cádiz. Dos españoles en la Roma de César y Augusto* (Sevilla,1973).

96. On the term *ordo* in Cicero, see J. Béranger, in *Recherches sur les structures sociales dans l'antiquité classique*, 225ff.; now also in J. Béranger, *Principatus* (Genève, 1973), 77ff.; on *ordo* as a Roman term, see now in detail, B. Cohen, *Bull.de l'Ass.de G. Budé* (1975), 259ff.

97. Liv., *Praef.*,9. On the impotence of the Late Republic: Chr. Meier, *Res Publica Amissa*, 301ff.

98. On Varro and his views on slavery, see the literature cited in note 56; further, R. Martin, *Recherches sur les agronomes latins et leurs conceptions économiques et sociales* (Paris, 1971), 211ff.; id., in *Actes du Colloque 1972 sur l'esclavage*, 267ff.

5: The Social System of the Early Empire

99. The supreme general account (despite its exaggeration of the opposition between town and country and the consequences thereof) remains M. Rostovtzeff, *Gesellschaft und Wirtschaft im römischen Kaiserreich*, I-II (Leipzig, 1929). Useful are: J. Gagé, *Les classes sociales dans l'Empire romain* (Paris, 1964) and especially R. MacMullen, *Roman Social Relations 50 BC to AD 284* (New Haven-London, 1974). The most recent comprehensive account in German is J. Bleicken, *Verfassungsund Sozialgeschichte des Römischen Kaiserreiches* 1-2[2] (Paderborn-München-Wien-Zürich, 1981). Cf. also S. Dill, *Roman Society from Nero to Marcus Aurelius*[2] (London, 1905). A good collection of sources on many issues is to be found in L.

Friedländer and G. Wissowa, *Darstellungen aus der Sittengeschichte Roms*, I-IV[III] (Leipzig, 1920-22). R. Duncan-Jones, *The Economy of the Roman Empire: Quantitative Studies* (Cambridge, 1974), contains important studies on particular topics. This is the place to mention new studies of ancient views on the Roman social system: H. Braunert, in *Monumentum Chiloniense. Studien zur augusteischen Zeit. Festschr. f. E. Burck* (Amsterdam, 1975), 9ff., also in H. Braunert, *Politik, Recht und Gesellschaft in der griechisch-römischen Antike. Gesammelte Aufsätze und Reden* (Stuttgart, 1980), 255ff. (Augustus' judgement of Roman society according to the *Res Gestae Divi Augusti*); G. Alföldy, *Ancient Society*, 11/12 (1980/81), 349ff. (Suetonius); id., in *Bonner Historia-Augusta-Colloquium 1975/76* (Bonn, 1978), 1ff. (*Historia Augusta*); cf. M. Giacchero, in *Misc. di studi classici in onore di E. Manni*, III (Roma), 1087ff. (Seneca).

100. On the economy of the Empire see M. Rostovizeff, op. cit.; T. Frank (ed.), *An Economic Survey of Ancient Rome*, II-VI (Baltimore, 1936-40), and F. Heichelheim, *Wirtschaftsgeschichte des Altertums* (Leiden, 1938), 677ff. Technology: F. Kiechle, *Sklavenarbeit und technischer Fortschritt im römischen Reich* (Wiesbaden, 1969); see now also the works of M. Torelli, L. Cracco Ruggini *inter alia.*, in *Tecnologia. economia e società nel mondo romano. Atti del Colloquio di Como 1979* (Como, 1980).

101. On the size of urban populations, see R. Duncan-Jones, *Historia* 13 (1964), 199ff. and *The Economy of the Roman Empire*, 259ff. On the difficulties presented by the estimation of the population of Rome, see F. G. Maler, *Historia*, 2 (1953/4), 318ff.; Pergamum,p. 140.

102. Cf. especially R. MacMullen, *Social Relations*, 48ff. Limits of the monetary economy: Th. Pekáry, in *Les 'devaluations' à Rome. Époque républicaine et impériale* (Rome, 1980), 103ff.

103. Trimalchio's economic activity: Petronius, *Sat.*, 75ff., on which see especially P. Veyne, *Annales E.S.C.* (1961), 213ff.

104. Social foundations of the Principate: A.von Premerstein, *Vom Werden und Wesen des Prinzipates* (München, 1937); cf. P. Grenade, *Essai sur les origines du principat* (Paris, 1961). Position of the *princeps:* J. Béranger, *Recherches sur l'aspect idologique du principat* (Basel, 1953); L. Wickert, *R-E*, XXII (1954), 1998ff. and in *ANRW*, II,1 (Berlin-New York, 1974), 3ff. *Auctoritas*: A. Magdelain *Auctoritas Principis* (Paris, 1947). Imperial cult, insignia, ceremony: F. Taeger, *Charisma. Studien zur Geschichte des antiken Herrscherkultes* II (Stuttgart, 1960); A. Alföldi, *Die monarchische Repräsentation im römischen Kaiserreiche* (Darmstadt, 1970); bibliography: P. Herz, in *ANRW*, II, 16.2 (Berlin-New York, 1978), 833ff. *Patrimonium, res privata*: O. Hirschfeld, *Kleine Schriften* (Berlin, 1913), 516ff.; H. Nesselhauf, in *Hist-Aug.-Coll. Bonn 1963* (Bonn, 1964), 73ff.; H. Bellen, in *ANRW*, II,1, 91ff.; cf. on this, for example, G. Alföldy, *Bonner Jahrb.*, 170 (1970), 163ff. (patrimonial property in Noricum). Imperial estates: D. J. Crawford, in M. I. Finley (ed.), *Studies in Roman Property* (Cambridge, 1976), 35ff. Property and finances of Augustus: I. Shatzman, *Senatorial Wealth and Roman Politics*, 357ff. (he estimates the wealth of Augustus at more than one billion sesterces). Emperor and society: vast amount of material in F. Millar, *The Emperor in the Roman World (31 BC- AD 337)* (London, 1977), on which cf. K. Hopkins, *Journ. of Rom.Stud.*, 68 (1978), 178ff.; H. Galsterer, *Gött.Gel.Anz.*, 232 (1980), 72ff.; J. Bleicken, *Zum Regierungsstil des römischen Kaisers. Eine Autwort auf Ferpus Millar* (Wiesbaden, 1982).

105. Augustus and the upper strata: R. Syme, *Roman Revolution*, 276ff. Imperial council: J. Crook, *Consilium Principis. Imperial Councils and Counsellors from Augustus to Diocletian* (Cambridge, 1955).

106. Emperor and *plebs*: D. van Berchem, *Les distributions de blé et d'argent à la plèbe romaine sous l'Empire* (Genève, 1939); G. E. F. Chilver, *Amer. Journ. of Philol.*, 70 (1949), 7ff.; Z. Yavetz, *Plebs and Princeps*, 103ff.; R. Gilbert,

Beziehungen zwischen Princeps und stadtrömischer Plebs im frühen Prinzipat (Bochum, 1976). Early imperial social policy: H. Kloft, *Jahrb.d.Wittheit zu Bremen,* 24 (1980), 153ff. Oath to the emperor: P. Herrmann, *Der römische Kaisereid. Untersuchungen zu seiner Herkunft und Entwicklung* (Göttingen, 1968).

107. Rise of the provincials: R. Syme, *Tacitus,* II (Oxford, 1958), 585ff. and *Colonial Elites* (Oxford, 1958), 1ff.; G. Alföldy, *Konsulat und Senatorenstand unter den Antoninen. Prosopographische Untersuchungen zur senatorischen Führungsschicht* (Bonn, 1977). Cornelius Nigrinus: G. Alföldy and H. Halfmann, *Chiron,* 3 (1973), 331ff.

108. *RG,* 8. In AD 14 there were 836,100 provincial inhabitants within the citizen body, H. Volkmann, *Res Gestae Divi Augusti. Das Monumentum Ancyranum[3]* (Berlin, 1969), 21. Extension of citizenship under the empire: F. Vittinghoff, *Römische Kolonisation und Bürgerrechtspolitik,* 96ff.; A. N. Sherwin-White, *The Roman Citizenship[2],* 221ff.; H. Wolff, *Die Constitutio Antoniniana und Papyrus Gissensis 40 I* (Köln, 1976).

109. Ael. Aristid. *Or.* 26.93f.; Tert. *De anima,* 30. On the importance of the cities the fundamental work is M. Rostovtzeff, op.cit., I, 90ff.; cf. A. H. M. Jones, *The Roman Economy: Studies in Ancient Economic and Administrative History* (Oxford, 1974), 1ff. and 35ff.; M. I. Finley, *The Ancient Economy* (Berkeley-Los Angeles, 1973), 123ff.; R. Chevallier, in *ANRW,* II,1, 649ff.; G. Alföldy, in *Stadt-Land-Beziehungen und Zentralität als Problem der historischen Raumforschung* (Akad.f. Raumforschung u. Landesplanung, Forschungs- u. Sitzungsberichte Bd. 88, Historische Raumforschung, 11, Hannover, 1974), 49ff.; F. Vittinghoff, *Hist. Zeitschr.* 226 (1978), 547ff.; Th.Pekáry, in H. Stoob (ed.), *Die Stadt. Gestalt und Wandel bis zum industriellen Zeitalter* (Köln-Wien, 1979), 83ff.; W. Dahlheim, in F. Vittinghoff (ed.), *Stadt und Herrschaft. Römische Kaiserzeit und Hohes Mittelalter* (Hist. Zeitschr. Beiheft N. F. 7, München, 1982), 13ff.; H. Galsterer, ibid., 75ff.

110. On the social ciercumstances in the various provinces, cf., for example, G. Charles-Picard, *Nordafrika und die Römer* (Stuttgart, 1962); J.-M. Lassère, *Ubique populus. Peuplement et mouvements de population dans l'Afrique romaine de la chute de Carthage à la fin de la dynastie des Sévères (146 a.C. – 235 p.C.)* (Paris, 1977); V. Vázquez de Prada (ed.), *Historia económica y social de España I. La Antigüedad* (Madrid, 1973); J. J. Hatt, *Histoire de la Gaule romaine* (Paris, 1970); S. S. Frere, *Britannia: A History of Roman Britain* (London, 1978); H. v. Petrikovits, in F. Petrie and G. Droege (eds.), *Rheinische Geschichte,* I, 1 (Düsseldorf, 1978), 46ff.; G. Alföldy, *Noricum* (London, 1974); A. Mócsy, *Die Bevölkerung von Panonnien bis zu den Markomannenkriegen* (Budapest, 1959); id., *Gesellschaft und Romanisation in der römischen Provinz Moesia superior* (Budapest, 1970); id. *Pannonia and Upper Moesia: A History of the Middle Danube Provinces of the Roman Empire* (London-Boston, 1974); G. Alföldy, *Bevölkerung und Gesellschaft der römischen Provinz Dalmatien* (Budapest, 1965); J. J. Wilkes, *Dalmatia* (London, 1969); U. Kahrstedt, *Das wirtschaftliche Gesicht Griechenlands in der Kaiserzeit* (Bern, 1954); D. Magie, *Roman Rule in Asia Minor* (Princeton, 1950); B. Levick, *Roman Colonies in Southern Asia Minor* (Oxford, 1967); A.H.M.Jones, *The Cities of the eastern Roman Provinces* (Oxford, 1971); H. Braunert, *Die Binnenwanderung. Studien zur Sozialgeschichte Ägyptens in der Ptolemäer- und Kaiserzeit* (Bonn, 1964). The distinction between 'developed' and 'underdeveloped' provinces drawn by A. Deman, in *ANRW,* II, 3 (Berlin-New York, 1975), 3ff., with reference to the examples of Gaul and North Africa, does not correspond to historical reality. On the integration of the various provincial social systems into the Roman empire through the Romanisation of the local 'ruling classes', see P. A. Brunt, in *Assimilation et résistance à la culture grécoromaine dans le monde ancien. Travaux du VIe Congr. Internat. de la F.I.A.E.C.* (Bucureşti, 1976), 161ff. Gallic aristocracy in the Early Empire: J. F. Drinkwater, *Latomus,* 37 (1978), 817ff.; cf. R. Syme, *Mus. Helv.,* 34 (1977), 129ff. On social prob-

lems and Greek views on them, see H. Grassl, *Sozialökonomische Vorstellungen in der kaiserzeitlichen griechischen Literatur (1. – 3. Jhdt. n. Chr.)* (Historia Einzelschriften 41, Wiesbaden, 1982).
111. Ael. Aristid. *Or.*, 26. 39 and 26. 59. Legal sources (principally from the Later Empire): P. Garnsey, *Social Status and Legal Privilege in the Roman Empire* (Oxford, 1970), 221ff.; cf. id.² *Past and Present*, 41 (1968), 3ff.
112. On social strata in the Empire, cf. especially H. W. Pleket, *Tijdschr. voor Geschiedenis*, 84 (1971), 215ff.; R. MacMullen, *Social Relations*, 88ff.; cf. also M. I. Finley, *The Ancient Economy*, 35ff. Upper strata: see now M. -Th.Raepsaet-Charlier, *L'Égalité*, 8 (1982), 452ff. On social stratification in imperial literature, see below, note 168. On rank titulature, see H. -G.Pflaum, in *Recherches sur les structures sociales dans l'antiquité classique*, 159ff.
113. *ILS*, 6675 and 6509, Cf. especially R. Duncan-Jones, *Papers of the British School at Rome*, 32 (1964), 123ff. and *The Economy of the Roman Empire*, 288ff.; R. MacMullen, op.cit., 5 and 96.
114. Evidence for Egypt: R. MacMullen, op.cit., 13 with note 48. On poverty under the Empire, cf. A. R. Hands, *Charities and Social Aid in Greece and Rome* (London, 1968), 72ff.
115. On which, especially P. Garnsey, *Social Status and Legal Privilege*, 234ff.; see also D. Daube, *The Defence of Superior Orders in Roman Law* (Oxford, 1976).
116. G. Alföldy, *Konsulat und Senatorenstand unter den Antoninen*, 84ff.
117. A. N. Sherwin-White, *Racial Prejudice in Imperial Rome* (Cambridge, 1967), J. P. V. D. Balsdon, *Romans and Aliens* (London, 1979); M. Sordi (ed.), *Conoscenze etniche e rapporti di convivenze nell'antichità* (Milano, 1979). On the conduct of peoples suffering discrimination *vis-à-vis* Rome, cf., for example, N. R. M. de Lange, in P. D. A. Garnsey and C. R. Whittaker, *Imperialism in the Ancient World* (Cambridge, 1978), 255ff. (Jews).
118. On the importance of education, see especially H. -I. Marrou, *Histoire de l'éducation dans l'antiquité* (Paris, 1948, reprinted 1965); G. W. Bowersock, *Greek Sophists in the Roman Empire* (Oxford, 1969); J. Christes, *Bildung und Gesellschaft. Die Einschätzung der Bildung und ihrer Vermittler in der griechisch-römischen Antike* (Darmstadt, 1975); id., *Sklaven und Freigelassene als Grammatiker und Philologen im antiken Rom* (Wiesbaden, 1979); S. F. Bonner, *Education in Ancient Rome: From the Elder Cato to the Younger Pliny* (Berkeley-Los Angeles, 1977).
119. Rufus: Plin., *NH*, 18.37; on which, G. Alföldy, *Epigr.Studien*, 5 (1968), 100ff. Adlections under Vespasian: W. Eck, *Senatoren von Vespasian bis Hadrian* (München, 1970), 103ff.
120. Suet., *Aug.* 35.1; Dio, 52.42.1ff. and 54.14.1.
121. On what follows, see A. Chastagnol, *Mél. de L'École Française de Rome, Antiquité*, 85 (1973), 583ff., according to whom one can only speak of a senatorial order in the strict sense from the time of Augustus and Caligula.
122. Census of senators under Augustus: C. Nicolet, *Journ.of Rom.Stud.*, 66 (1976), 30ff. Pliny's finances and lifestyle: see especially Plin. *Ep.*, 2.17.1ff.; 3.19.1ff.; 5.6.1ff.; 8.2.1ff.; 9.36.1ff.; *ILS*, 2927, on which, see R. Duncan-Jones, *Papers of the British School at Rome*, 33 (1965), 177ff. and *The Economy of the Roman Empire*, 17ff.; cf. R. Martin, *Rev. d'Études Anc.*, 69 (1967), 62ff. Herodes Atticus: Philostr. *Vitae Soph.*,2.1. (546ff.), on which, see P. Graindor *Un milliardaire antique. Hérode Atticus et sa famille* (Cairo, 1930); W. Ameling, *Herodes Atticus*, I-II (Hildesheim – Zürich-New York, 1983).
123. *ILS*, 1104. Family relationships: cf. for example the – partly hypothetical – family tree of Lucius Munatius Plancus Paulinus (*consul*, AD 13) in J. Morris, *Bonner Jahrb.* 165 (1965), 88ff. (with appendix). Pliny's letters: A. N. Sherwin-White, *The Letters of Pliny: A Historical and Social Commentary* (Oxford, 1966); friends of Fronto: H. -G.Pflaum, in *Hommages à J. Bayet* (Coll.Latomus, vol. 70, Bruxelles,

1964), 544ff. Importance of personal connections for senators: cf. R. P. Saller, *Personal Patronage under the Early Empire* (Cambridge, 1982).

124. On the training of a young senator, see, for instance, Tac. *Agr.*, 4. 1ff. on Gnaeus Iulius Agricola. Law: W. Kunkel, *Herkunft und soziale Stellung der römischen Juristen*[2] (Graz-Wien-Köln, 1967).

125. Childlessness: J. P. V. D. Balsdon, *Roman Women*, 194ff.; G. Alföldy, *Konsulat und Senatorenstand unter den Antoninen*, 85f.

126. On the concept of *nobilitas* under the Empire, cf. M. Gelzer, *Kleine Schriften*, I (Wiesbaden, 1962), 136ff.; K. Schneider, *Zusammensetzung des römischen Senats von Tiberius bis Nero* (Zürich, 1942); H. Hill, *Historia*, 18 (1969), 230ff. (as he shows, the *nobilitas* included some families of particular merit, who had first achieved senatorial rank under the Empire).

127. *Homines novi*: R. Syme, *Tacitus*, II, 566ff.; under Augustus, T. P. Wiseman, *New Men in the Roman Senate*, 10f.; arrangements for entry into the senatorial order: D. McAlindon, *Journ. of Rom. Stud.*, 47 (1957), 191ff.; A. Chastagnol, *Bull. de la Soc. Nat. des Ant. de France* (1971), 282ff.; id., *Rev. Hist. de Droit Fr. et Étr.*, 55 (1975), 375ff.; cf. also id., *Historia*, 25 (1976), 253ff.

128. Tac, *Ann.*, 11.23ff. and *ILS*, 212, on which see A. Chastagnol, art.cit.; cf. also U. Schillinger-Häfele, *Historia*, 14 (1965), 443ff. Northern Italy, see G. E. F. Chilver, *Cisalpine Gaul. Social and Economic History from 49 BC to the Death of Trajan* (Oxford, 1941).

129. On the composition of the senatorial order see now *Epigrafia e ordine senatorio, Atti del Colloquio Internazionale Roma 1981*, Tituli 4-5 (Roma, 1982). On particular aspects, cf. also especially A. Chastagnol, *Mél. de philos., de litt. et d'hist. anc. offerts à P. Boyancé* (Roma, 1974), 163ff. (under Augustus); S. J. De Laet, *De sammenstelling van den romeinschen senaat gedurende de eerste eeuw van het Principat (28 v. Chr. – 68 n. Chr.)* (Antwerpen, 1941); A. Bergener, *Die Führende Senatorenschicht im frühen Prinzipat (14-68 n. Chr.)* (Bonn, 1965); P. Lambrechts, *La composition du sénat romain de l'accession au trône d'Hadrien à la mort de Commode (117-192)* (Antwerpen, 1936); G. Alföldy, *Konsulat und Senatorenstand unter den Antoninen*, 61ff.; Comprehensive: M. Hammond, *Journ. of Rom. Stud.*, 47 (1957), 74ff. Regional groups of senators: A. Pelletier, *Latomus*, 23 (1964), 511ff. (Africans); R. Etienne, in *Les empereurs romains d'Espagne* (Paris, 1965), 54ff. (Spaniards); G. Alföldy, *Epigr. Stud.*, 5 (1968), 99ff. (Dalmatians); H. Halfmann, *Die Senatoren aus dem östlichen Teil des Imperium Romanum bis zum Ende des 2. Jahrhunderts n. Chr.* (Göttingen, 1979) (easterners). Cf. also especially L. Schumacher, *Prosopographische Untersuchungen zur Besetzung der vier hohen römischen Priesterkollegien im Zeitalter der Antonine und der Severer (96–235 n. Chr.)* (Mainz, 1973), 190ff. On methodological questions, cf. W. Eck, *Chiron*, 3 (1973), 375ff. On particular senatorial families, cf., for example, G. Alföldy, *Chiron*, 9 (1979), 507ff. (the Gavii from Verona).

130. On senatorial careers and the dominant senatorial elite under the Empire, see especially, E. Birley, *Proc. of the British Academy*, 39 (1954), 197ff.; id., *Carnuntum-Jahrb.* (1957), 3ff. (also on equestrian careers); J. Morris, *Listy Filologické, 87 (1964), 316ff. and 88 (1965), 22ff.* (age regulations); G. Alföldy, *Die Legionslegaten der römischen Rheinarmeen*, (Epigr. Studien 3, Köln-Graz, 1967); id., *Fasti Hispanienses. Senatorische Reichsbeamte und Offiziere in den spanischen Provinzen des römischen Reiches von Augustus bis Diokletian* (Wiesbaden, 1969); id., *Konsulat und Senatorienstand unter den Antoninen*, 33ff.; id., *Ancient Society*, 7 (1976) 263ff.; id., *Jahrb. d. hist. Forschung* (1975 (1976)), 26ff.; W. Eck, in *ANRW*, II, 1, 158ff.; A. R. Birley, *The Fasti of Roman Britain* (Oxford, 1981), 4ff.

131. Cf. especially G. Alföldy, *Bonner Jahrb.*, 169 (1969), 233ff. (on the generalships of the Roman army).

132. On the *ordo equester* A. Stein, *Der römische Ritterstand* (München, 1927) is

comprehensive. On the symbols of the equestrian order, cf. H. Gabelmann, *Jahrb. d. Deutschen Arch. Inst.*, 92 (1977), 322ff.; see also above, *note* 58.
133. Vell., 2.118.2; see H. v. Petrikovits, *Bonner Jahrb.*, 166 (1966), 175ff.; D. Timpe, *Arminius-Studien* (Heidelberg, 1970).
134. On the careers of these *primipilares*, see B. Dobson, in *ANRW*, II,1, 392ff.; id.` in *Recherches sur les structures sociales dans l'antiquité classique*, 99ff.; id.` *Die Primipilares. Entwicklung und Bedeutung, Laufbahnen und Persönlichkeiten eines römischen Offiziersranges* (Köln-Bonn, 1978); cf. B. Dobson and D. J. Breeze, *Epigr.Studien*, 8 (1969), 100ff.
135. Dalmatia: J. Wilkes, in *Adriatica praehistorica et antiqua. Misc. G. Novak dicata* (Zagreb, 1970), 529ff. Noricum: G. Alföldy, *Noricum*, 124f., 274ff. Spain: G. Alföldy, *Flamines provinciae Hispaniae Citerioris* (Madrid, 1973).
136. Composition of the equestrian order: E. Birley, *Roman Britain and the Roman Army²* (Kendal, 1961), 154ff.; cf. id.' Epigr. Studien, 8 (1969), 70ff. Military tribunes: data from the still unpublished work of H. Devijver, *Het militaire tribunaat der angusticlavii in het Vroegromeinse Keizerrijk* (Leuven, 1966). *Equites* from Africa: M. G. Jarrett, *Historia*, 12 (1963), 209ff. and *Epigr. Studien*, 9 (1972), 146ff.; R. Duncan-Jones, *Papers of the British School at Rome*, 35 (1967), 147ff. Dalmatians, Noricans and Spaniards, see note 135; on the Spanish equites, see also especially H.–G. Pflaum, in *Les empereurs romains d'Espagne*, 87ff.; Pannonians: A. Mócsy, *R–E Suppl.* IX (1962), 713. *Equites* from the German provinces: G. Alföldy, *Corsi di cultura sull'arte Ravennate e Biz.*, 24 (1977), 7ff. From Dacia: L. Balla, *Acta Class. Univ. Scient. Debrecen.*, 13 (1977), 51ff.
137. Equestrian officers: E. Birley, *Roman Britain and the Roman Army²*, 133ff.; id.' *Carnuntum-Jahrb.* (1957), 13ff.; id. in *Corolla memoriae E. Swoboda dedicata* (Graz-Köln, 1966), 54ff.; G. Alföldy, *Die Hilfstruppen der römischen Provinz Germania Inferior* (Epigr.Studien 6, Düsseldorf, 1968), 111ff. Prosopographical collective work on equestrian officers: H. Devijver, *Prosopographia militiarum equestrium quae fuerunt ab Augusto ad Gallienum*, I-III (Leuven, 1976–80).
138. Comprehensive: H. -G.Pflaum, *Les procurateurs lequestres sous le Haut-Empire romain* (Paris, 1950) and *Les carrières procuratoriennes équestres sous le Haut-Empire romain*, I-IV (Paris, 1960-61), *Supplément* (Paris, 1982). On theposition of the *equites* in the leading grouping of the Roman Empire: G. Alföldy, *Chiron*, 11 (1981), 169ff.
139. Cf. P. Garnsey, in , II, 1, 241ff. Brief summary in J. Gagé, *Les classes sociales dans l'Empire romain*, 153ff. Legal matters: W. Langhammer, *Die rechtliche und soziale Stellung der Magistratus Municipales und der Decuriones* (Wiesbaden, 1973). On particular *ordines*, see, for example, P. Castrén, *Ordo populusque Pompeianus. Polity and Society in Roman Pompeii* (Roma, 1975), cf. also M. L. Gordon, *Journ. of Rom. Stud.*, 17 (1927), 165ff. (Pompeii); J. H. D'Arms, *Amer.Journ.of Philol.*, 97 (1976), 387ff. (Ostia). On the upper strata in the Italian cities, see also S. Demougin, *Ancient Society*, 6 (1975), 143ff. (*iudices* of the panels at Rome from the cities of Italy). On the upper strata in the cities of the north-western provinces, cf. G. Rupprecht, *Untersuchungen zum Dekurionenstand in den nordwestlichen Provinzen des Römischen Reiches* (Kallmünz, 1975).
140. R. Duncan-Jones, *Papers of the British School at Rome*, 31 (1963), 159ff.; cf. id., *The Economy of the Roman Empire*, 283ff.
141. Decurions inTarraco: G. Alföldy, *R–E Suppl.* XV (1978), 620ff.; in Spain: id., *Flamines provinciae Hispaniae citerioris*, 20ff.; in Noricum: id. *Noricum*, 117ff. (list: 264ff.); size of properties see the literature cited in ibid., 321, n.113.
142. Salona: G. Alföldy, *Bevölkerung und Gesellschaft der römischen Provinz Dalmatien*, 108ff.; Dalmatia in general: J. J. Wilkes, *Dalmatia*, 297ff. Aquincum: A. Mócsy, *Die Bevölkerung von Pannonien bis zu den Markomannenkriegen*, 70f. Sons of freedmen in civic *ordines*: cf. M. L. Gordon, *Journ. of Rom.Stud.* 21 (1931), 65ff.;

236 *Notes*

P. Garnsey, in *Essays in Honour of C. E. Stevens* (Farnborough, 1975), 167ff.
143. P. Garnsey, in *ANRW*, II, 1, 229ff.
144. G. Alföldy, *Arh. Vestnik*, 15/16 (1964/65), 137ff. On pre-eminent families of this sort in a city, see also id. *Los Baebii de Saguntum* (Valencia, 1977).
145. Cf. especially W. Liebenam, *Städteverwaltung in römischen Kaiserreiche* (Leipzig, 1900); F. F. Abbott and A. C. Johnson, *Municipal Administration in the Roman Empire* (Princeton, 1926), and A. K. Bowman, *The Town Councils of Roman Egypt* (Toronto, 1971).
146. Mustis: *AE* (1968), nos. 586, 588, 591, 595 and 599. On this system, see R. Duncan-Jones, *Papers of the British School at Rome*, 30 (1962), 65ff. and *The Economy of the Roman Empire*, 82ff.; M. Leglay, in *Akte des 4. Internat. Kongresses für griechische und lateinische Epigraphik 1962* (Wien, 1964), 224ff.; P. Garnsey, *Journ. of Rom. Stud.* 61 (1971), 116ff. and *Historia*, 20 (1971), 309ff. On the *flamines* of Africa, M. S. Bassignano, *Il flaminato nelle province romane dell'Africa* (Roma,1974).
147. On the system, B. Laum, *Stiftungen in der griechischen und römischen Antike*, I-II (Berlin, 1914); F. Oertel, *Die Liturgie* (Leipzig, 1917); N. Lewis, *Leitourgia Papyri: Documents on Compulsory Public Service in Egypt under Roman Rule* (Philadelphia, 1963). On the services of the urban upper strata in Italy, cf. J. Andreau, *Ktema* 2 (1977), 157ff. On the activity of senators in the cities, W. Eck, in W. Eck, H. Galsterer and H. Wolff, *Studien zur antiken Sozialgeschichte. Festschrift F. Vittinghoff* (Köln-Wien, 1980), 283ff.
148. Cf. especially A. M. Duff, *Freedmen in the Roman Empire*² (Cambridge, 1958), 69ff. and 124ff.; also now the work of G. Fabre on the freedmen of the Late Republic (above, note 93). Cf. also id., in *Actes du Colloque 1973 sur l'esclavage* (Paris, 1976), 417ff. (*liberti* in the cities of the Iberian peninsula). Self-confidence of freedmen as reflected in their tombstones: P. Zanker, *Jahrb.d. Deutschen Arch.Inst.*, 80 (1975 (1976)), 267ff.
149. On the *Augustales*, see now in detail R. Duthoy, *Epigraphica*, 36 (1974 (1975)), 134ff. (social importance); *Epigr.Studien*, 11 (1976), 1432ff. (distribution); *ANRW*, II, 16.2 (Berlin-New York, 1978), 1254ff. (general survey). Cf. P. Kneissl, *Chiron*, 10 (1980), 291ff. (on their origin); G. Alföldy, *Homenaje Garcia y Bellido IV* Rev. de la Univ. Complutense, 18, 1979 (1981)), 195ff. (erection of divine statues by *seviri Augustales*).
150. For comprehensive discussion, see G. Boulvert, *Esclaves et affranchis impériaux sous le Haut-Empire romain* (Napoli, 1970); id., *Domestique et fonctionnaire sous le Haut-Empire romain. La condition de l'esclave et de l'affranchi du prince* (Paris, 1974); P. R. C. Weaver, *Familia Caesaris: A Social Study of the Emperor's Freedmen and Slaves* (Cambridge, 1972); imperial slaves in Egypt: I. Blezuńska-Malowist, in M. Capozza (ed.), *Schiavitù, manomissione e classi dipendenti nel mondo antico* (Roma, 1979), 175ff.
151. Cf. especially R. MacMullen, *Social Relations*, 30ff.
152. J. P. Waltzing, *Etude historique sur les corporations professionelles chez les romains*, I-IV (Louvain, 1895-1900); E. Kornemann, *R–E*, IV (1900), 380ff.; F. M. De Robertis, *Storia delle corporazioni e del regime associativo nel mondo romano*, I-II (Bari, 1974). Emperor and *plebs*: see note 106.
153. On which, see Z. Yavetz, *Athenaeum*, n.s., 43 (1965), 295ff.
154. See for example Martial, 2.53.1ff.; 11.56.1ff.; 12.32.1ff. On the position of the *plebs* in the cities, cf. F. F. Abbott, *The Common People of Ancient Rome* (New York, 1911); R. MacMullen, *Social Relations*, 63ff. On the lower population of Rome, cf. P. Huttunen, *The Social Strata in the Imperial City of Rome: A Quantitative Study of the Social Representation in the Epitaphs Studied in the CIL VI* (Oulu, 1974). Living conditions: J. E. Packer, *Journ. of Rom. Stud.*, 57 (1967), 80ff.
155. Dio, 54.23.1ff. Much material is collected in J. Carcopino, *La vie quotidienne*

à Rome à l'apogée de l'Empire (Paris, 1939), in German as *So lebten die Römer der Kaiserzeit* (Stuttgart, 1959).

156. Urban occupations: E. H. Brewster, *Roman Craftsmen and Tradesmen of the Early Roman Empire* (Philadelphia, 1917); H. J. Loane, *Industry and Commerce of the City of Rome 50 BC-200 AD* (Baltimore, 1938); I. Calabi Limentani, *Studi sulla società romana. Il lavoro artistico* (Milano, 1958); F. M. De Robertis, *Lavoro e lavoratori nel mondo romano* (Bari, 1963); A. Burford, *Craftsmen in Greek and Roman Society* (Ithaca, 1972); S. M. Treggiari, in P. Garnsey (ed.), *Non-Slave Labour in the Greco-Roman World* (Cambridge, 1980), 48ff.; H.v. Petrikovits, in H. Jankuhn *et al.* (eds.), *Das Handwerk in vor- und frühgeschichtlicher Zeit* I (Göttingen, 1981), 63ff. (designations of craftsmen). On traders, see also J. Rougé *Recherches sur l'organisation du commerce maritime en Méditerranée sous l'Empire romain* (Paris, 1966), 269ff.; O. Schlippschuh, *Die Händler im römischen Kaiserreich in Gallien, Germanien und den Donauprovinzen Rätien, Noricum und Pannonien* (Amsterdam, 1974); J. Du Plat and H. Cleere (eds.), *Roman Shipping and Trade: Britain and the Rhine Provinces* (CBA Research Report, No. 24, London, 1978). Work of urban *liberti* and *servi*: A. M. Duff, *Freedmen in the Roman Empire*², 89ff.; W. L. Westermann, *Slave Systems*, 90ff.; id., *Journ. of Econ. Hist.*,2 (1942), 149ff., *Barbii:* J. Šašel, *Eirene*, 5 (1966) 117ff.

157. Slaves and freedmen under the Empire: R. H. Barrow, *Slavery in the Early Roman Empire* (London, 1928); A. M. Duff, op.cit.; W. L. Westermann, op.cit. 84ff.; cf. also E. M. Schtajerman, *Die Krise der Sklavenhalterordnung im Westen des römischen Reiches* (Berlin, 1964), giving an all too negative picture. Economic importance of slavery, cf. M. Corbier, *Opus*, 1 (1982), 109ff. Origin of slaves: M. Bang, *Röm.Mitt.*, 25 (1910), 223ff., and 27 (1912), 189ff.; M. L. Gordon, *Journ.of Rom.Stud.*, 14 (1924), 93ff. The distribution of slavery within the empire: J. Česka, *Die Differenzierung der Sklaven in Italien in den ersten zwei Jahrhunderten des Prinzipats* (in Czech with German summary) (Praha-Brno, 1959); E. M. Štaerman and M. K. Trophimova, *La schiavitù nell' Italia imperiale, I-III secolo* (Roma, 1975); S. Treggiari, *Trans.Amer.Philol.Ass.*, 105 (1975), 393ff. (slaves of the senatorial family of the Volusii); G. Prachner, *Die Sklaven und Freigelasseren im arretinischen Sigillatagewerbe* (Wiesbaden, 1980); J. Mangas Manjarrez, *Esclavos y libertos en la España romana* (Salamanca, 1971); A. Daubigney and F. Favory, in *Actes du Colloque 1972 sur l'esclavage* (Besançon-Paris, 1974), 315ff. (Narbonensis, Lugdunensis); L. Vidman, *Listy Filologické*, 82 (1959), 207ff., ibid., 83 (1960), 64ff. and 229ff. *Acta Ant. Hung.*, 9 (1961), 153ff. (Noricum); A. Mócsy, *Acta Ant.Hung.*, 4 (1956), 221ff. (Pannonia); G. Alföldy, *Acta Ant.Hung.* 9 (1961), 121ff. (Dalmatia); I. Biezuńska-Malowist, *Studii Clasice*, 3 (1961), 147ff. and in I. Biezuńska-Malowist (ed.), *Storia sociale ed economica dell'età classica negli studi polacchi contemporanee* (Milano, 1975), 111ff. (*vernae* in Egypt); ead., in *Atti dell'XI Congr. Internaz. di Papirol, 1965* (Milano, 1966), 433ff. (freedmen in Egypt), ead., *L'esclavage dans l'Égypte gréco-romaine*, II, *Période romaine* (Wroclaw, 1977). Slave-women: S. Treggiari, *Amer. Journ. of Ancient History*, 1 (1976), 76ff. and in M. Capozza (ed.), *Schiavità, manomissione e classi dipendenti* 185ff. Further bibliography in J. Vogt and N. Brockmeyer, *Bibliographie zur antiken Sklaverei*, 37ff.

158. P. A. Brunt, *Italian Manpower*, 124.

159. Cf. W. L. Westermann, op.cit., 100f.; Merula: *ILS*, 7812.

160. Legal status of slaves: W. W. Buckland, *The Roman Law of Slavery: The Condition of the Slave in Private Law from Augustus to Justinian* (Cambridge, 1908).

161. Cf. W. Richter, *Gymnasium*, 65 (1958), 196ff.

162. G. Alföldy, *Riv.Stor. dell'Ant.*, 2 (1972), 97ff., and in H. Schneider (ed.), *Sozial – und Wirtschaftsgeschichte der römischen Kaiserzeit* (Darmstadt, 1981), 336ff. On the frequency of manumission: cf. K. Hopkins, *Conquerors and Slaves*, 99ff. On legislation and the legal status of *liberti*, see W. W. Buckland, op.cit., 449f.;

238   *Notes*

A. M. Duff, op.cit., 12ff. The reference to Artemidorus I owe to I. Hahn.
   163. H. Lemonnier, *Étude historique sur la condition privée des affranchis aux trois premiers siècles de l'Empire romain* (Paris, 1887); J. Lambert, *Les operae liberti. Contributions à l'histoire des droits de patronat* (Paris, 1934); G. Fabre, *Libertus*, 267ff.
   164. On the Roman peasantry under the Empire, see R. MacMullen, in *ANRW*, II, 1, 253ff.; id., *Social Relations*, 1ff.; M. I. Finley, in id. (ed.), *Studies in Roman Property*, 103ff. (Italy); G. Ch. Picard, in *ANRW*, II, 3 (Berlin-New York, 1975), 98ff. (Gaul and North Africa); C. R. Whittaker, in P. Garnsey (ed.), *Non-Slave Labour in the Greco-Roman World* (Cambridge, 1980), 73ff. On agriculture: W. E. Heitland, *Agricola: A Study of Agriculture and Rustic Life in the Greco-Roman World* (Cambridge, 1921); K. D. White, *Roman Farming* (London, 1970); cf. id., *Country Life in Classical Times* (London, 1977) (source collection). *Latifundia:* see note 55 above; ibid. and note 60 for bibliography on the Empire.
   165. On which, H. Gummerus, *Der römische Gutsbetrieb*, 73ff.; N. Brockmeyer, *Arbeitsorganisation und ökonimisches Denken*, 137ff.; see also the bibliography in note 98.
   166. Fundamental is M. Rostovtzeff, *Studien zur Geschichte des römischen Kolonates* (Leipzig, 1910); see also R. Clausing, *The Roman Colonate* (New York, 1925); P. Collinet, *Le colonat dans l'Empire romain* (Bruxelles, 1937); further bibliography in J. Vogt and N. Brockmeyer, *Bibliographie zur antiken Sklaverei*, 45ff. Beginnings of the colonate in Italy, discussion of it among the jurists: N. Brockmeyer, *Historia*, 20 (1971), 732ff.
   167. *CIL*, VIII, 25902; cf. also *CIL*, VIII, 25943. On the colonate in North Africa, and on the relevant epigraphical sources, see especially J. Kolendo, *Le colonat en Afrique sous le Haut-Empire* (Paris, 1976); id., in *Terres et paysans dépendents dans les sociétés antiques. Coll. Besançon, 1974* (Paris, 1979), 391ff.; C. R. Whittaker, *Kilio*, 60 (1978), 331ff.; D. Flach, *Chiron*, 8 (1978), 441ff. (with detailed treatment of the epigraphical sources); id., *ANRWF*, II, 10.2 (Berlin-New York, 1982), 427ff.
   168. On the model of stratification here advanced and the principal characteristics of the Roman social system, cf. also G. Alföldy, *Gymnasium*, 83 (1976), 1ff. Criticism of this model: F. Vittinghoff, *Hist.Zeitschr.*, 230 (1980), 31ff.; K. Christ, in W. Eck, H. Galsterer and H. Wolff (eds.), *Studien zur antiken Sozialgeschichte* 197ff.; F. Klob, in *Bericht über die 33. Versammlung deutscher Historiker in Würzburg 1980* (Beih.zu Gesch.in Wiss. U. Unterricht., Stuttgart, 1982), 131f. In general on this: G. Alföldy, *Chiron*, 11 (1981), 207ff. Cf. id., in *Homenaje García y Bellido, IV* (Rev.de la Univ.Complutense 18, 1979 (1981)), 177ff., especially 209ff. (social stratification as reflected in the dedication of statues). On the social connections between members of different strata, W. Eck, in *Colonato y otras formas de dependencia no esclavistas. Actas del Coloquio, 1978* (Memorias de Historia Antigua, Oviedo, 2, 1978), 41ff. On Marxist theory, dissociated from the theory of 'a society of slave owners' (for example, E. M. Staerman, *VDI* (1969), 4., 37ff.), but which largely retains the definition of ancient society as a class society, see, for example, H. Kreissig, *Ethn.-Arch. Zeitschr.*, 10 (1969), 361ff.
   169. Social mobility in the Empire: K. Hopkins, *Past and Present*, 32 (1965), 12ff.; P. R. C. Weaver, ibid., 37 (1967), 3ff. (imperial freedmen and slaves); H. W. Pleket, *Tijdschr. voor Geschiedenis*, 84 (1971), 215ff.; H. Castritius, *Mitt.d.Techn.Univ. Braunschweig*, 8 (1973), 38ff.; R. MacMullen, *Social Relations*, 97ff.; B. Dobson, in *Recherches sur les structures sociales dans l'antiquité classique*, 99ff. (centurions).
   170. Suet., *Vit.*, 2.1ff. *Primipili*, see note 134. Pertinax: SHA, *P*, 1.1ff. and *AE* (1963), 52; on this, H. -G. Kolbe, *Bonner Jahrb.*, 162 (1962), 407ff.; G. Alföldy, *Situla*, 14/15 (1974), 199ff.
   171. Administrative system: see for example F. Millar, *Journ.of Rom.Stud.*, 56 (1966), 156ff.; W. Eck, *Die staatliche Organisation Italiens in der hohen Kaiserzeit*

(München, 1979). Army: A. v. Domaszewski and B. Dobson, *Die Rangordnung des römischen Heeres²* (Köln-Graz, 1967); G. Webster, *The Roman Imperial Army of the First and Second Centuries AD* (London, 1969); M. Grant, *The Army of the Caesars* (London, 1974); Social and ethnic composition: G. Forni, in *ANRW*, II, 1, 339ff., with bibliography.

172. Ruler cult: see note 104. Cults of particular social strata: J. Beaujeu, in *Hommages à J. Bayet* (Coll.Latomus, vol.70, Bruxelles, 1964), 54ff. (senatorial order); F. Bömer, *Untersuchungen über die Religion der Sklaven in Griechenland und Rom*, I (see note 72). Spread of Roman ethics within the empire: G. Alföldy, *Die Rolle des Einzelnen in der Gesellschaft des Römischen Kaiserreiches. Erwartungen und Wertmassstäbe* (Sitz.-Ber.d.Heidelberger Akad.d.Wiss., Phil.-hist.Klasse Jg. 1980, 8.Abh., Heidelberg, 1980). Anti-Roman propaganda: R. MacMullen, *Enemies of the Roman Order: Treason, Unrest, and Alienation in the Empire* (Cambridge, Mass., 1966), 46ff. On social conflicts in the Roman Empire, G. Alföldy, *Heidelberger Jahrb.*, 20 (1976), lllff. and in H. Schneider (ed.), *Sozial- und Wirtschaftsgeschichte der römischen Kaiserzeit*, 372ff. On social conflicts in the Greek world, also under the Empire, see G. E. M. de Ste Croix, *The Class Struggle in the Ancient Greek World from the Archaic Age to the Arab Conquests* (London, 1981).

173. Uprising of AD 24: Tac., *Ann.*, 4.27 and *ILS*, 961 (on the date, G. Alföldy, *Fasti Hispanienses*, 149ff.). Uprising of AD 54: Tac., *Ann.*, 12.65. Flight of slaves: H. Bellen, *Studien zur Sklavenflucht im römischen Kaiserreich* (Wiesbaden, 1971).

174 Unrest at Prusa: Dion Chrys., *Disc.*, 46.7ff.; at Tarsus. ibid., 34.1ff., on which D. Kienast and H. Castritius, *Historia*, 20 (1971), 62ff. Ephesus: *Acta App.*, 19.24ff.; on this, A. N. Sherwin-White, *Roman Society and Roman Law in the New Testament* (Oxford, 1963), 83ff. Cf. also, especially R. F. Newbold, *Athenaeum* n.s., 52 (1974), 110ff: on unrest at Rome under Tiberius.

175. H. Kreissig, *Die sozialen Zusammenhänge des judäischen Krieges* (Berlin, 1970), 127ff. On revolts of the oppressed local populations of the provinces: see S. L. Dyson, *ANRW*, II, 3 (Berlin-New York, 1975), 138ff. Batavian revolt: L. Bessone, *La rivolta batavica e la crisi del 69 d.C.* (Mem.Accad.d.Sc.di Torino, Cl.di Sc.mor.,stor.e filol., ser.4ª, vol. 24, Torino, 1972). Active and passive resistance against Roman rule in North Africa: M. Benabou, *La résistance africaine à la romanisation* (Paris, 1976).

6: The Crisis of the Roman Empire and Structural Change in Society

176. On the crisis of the Roman Empire, see now R. MacMullen, *Roman Government's Response to Crisis, AD 235-337* (New Haven, 1976); cf. on this G. Alföldy, *Hispania Antiqua*, 6 (1976 (1978)), 341ff. Bibliography in G. Walser and Th. Pekáry, *Die Krise des römischen Reiches. Bericht über die Forschungen zur Geschichte des 3. Jahrhunderts* (Berlin, 1972). Detailed studies of particular importance also on questions of social history: A. Alföldi, *Studien zur Geschichte der Weltkrise des 3. Jahrhunderts nach Christus* (Darmstadt, 1967). Social development: see especially M. Rostovtzeff, *Gesellschaft und Wirtschaft*, II, 106ff.; J. Gagé, *Les classes sociales*, 249ff. Useful survey in P. Petit, *Histoire générale de l'Empire romain* (Paris, 1974), 507ff. Awareness of the crisis: G. Alföldy, *Hermes*, 99 (1971), 429ff., *Historia*, 22 (1973), 479ff. and especially *Greek, Roman and Byzantine Studies*, 15 (1974), 89ff., in German in G. Alföldy *et al.* (ed.), *Krisen in der Antike. Bewusstsein und Bewältigung* (Düsseldorf, 1975), 112ff.

177. Egypt: A. C. Johnson, *Journ.of Juristic Papyrol.*, 4 (1950), 151ff.; Pannonia: P. Oliva, *Pannonia and the Onset of Crisis in the Roman Empire* (Praha, 1962); cf. also the similar development in Noricum, G. Alföldy, *Noricum*, 159ff.

178. In Eus. *Hist.eccl.*, 7.21.9f. On the manpower shortage and the depopulation

of the land, cf. P. Salmon, *Population et dépopulation dans l'Empire romain* (Coll.Latomus, vol.137, Bruxelles, 1974); C. R. Whittaker, in M. I. Finley (ed.), *Studies in Roman Property*, 137ff. Economy: bibliography in G. Walser and Th. Pekáry, op.cit., 81ff.

179. On the range of views on the causes of the crisis and decline of the Roman world, see K. Christ (ed.), *Der Untergang des römischen Reiches* (Darmstadt, 1970); for the Marxist view, see E. M. Schtajerman, *Die Krise der Sklavenhalterordnung*, 1ff.

180. Cf. G. Barbieri, *L'albo senatorio da Settimio Severo a Carino (193-285)* (Roma, 1952); cf. also note 129.

181. A. Alföldi, in *Historia Mundi IV. Römisches Weltreich und Christentum* (München, 1956), 211. On the senatorial order in the third century, see especially A. Chastagnol, *Rev.Hist.* 496 (1970), 305ff.

182. Conflicts under Commodus: F. Grosso, *La lotta politica al tempo di Commodo* (Torino, 1964), 125ff.; under Severus: G. Alföldy, *Bonner Jahrb.*, 168 (1968), 112ff. and A. R. Birley, *Septimius Severus, the African Emperor* (London, 1971); cf. also id., *Bonner Jahrb.*, 69 (1969), 247ff. on the events of AD 193.

183. On this, G. Alföldy, *Die Legionslegaten der römischen Rheinarmeen*, 110ff. and *Bonner Jahrb.*, 169 (1969), 242ff. Pertinax, Valerius Maximianus, see id.,*Situla*, 14/15 (1974), 199ff.

184. On Gallienus' reform, see H. -G. Pflaum, *Historia*, 25 (1976), 109ff., stressing the part played by equestrian career officers, who rose to high commands after lengthy careers as soldiers and centurions; cf. also especially B. Malcus, *Opusc.Rom.*, 7 (1969), 213ff.; on individuals, see G. Alföldy, *Byzantinoslavica*, 34 (1973), 236ff.

185. On this development, see especially C. W. Keyes, *The Rise of the Equites in the Third Century of the Roman Empire* (Princeton, 1915); G. Lopuszanaki, *Mél.d'Arch.et D'Hist.*, 55 (1938), 131ff.; H. - G. Pflaum, *Les procurateurs équestres*, 82ff.; E. Osier, *Latomus*, 36 (1977), 674ff.; Mucianus: *IGBulg.*, III², 1570, on which see M. Christol, *Chiron*, 7 (1977), 393ff.

186. *Paneg.*, 2.2.2; on this, A. Alföldi, *Studien zur Geschichte der Weltkrise*, 228ff. Composition of the equestrian order in the third century: H. - G. Pflaum, op.cit., 186ff.; E. Birley, *Epigr.Studien*, 8 (1969), 70ff. Dominant elite of the equestrian order: G. Alföldy, *Chiron*, 11 (1981), 169ff. Number of procurators: see especially H. -G. Pflaum, *Abrégé des procurateurs équestres* (Paris, 1974), 43.

187. On this, H. - G. Pflaum, in *Recherches sur les structures sociales dans l'antiquité classique*, 177ff.; G. Alföldy, *Chiron*, 11 (1981), 190ff.

188. H. - G. Pflaum, *Le Marbre de Thorigny* (Paris, 1948), on *CIL*, XIII, 3162.

189. Pannonia: cf. A. Mócsy, *R-E Suppl.*, IX (1962), 714. Noricum: G. Alföldy, *Noricum*, 171ff.

190. Bibliography in note 139.

191. On the social history of the army, see especially R. MacMullen, *Soldier and Civilian in the later Roman Empire* (Cambridge, Mass., 1963); recruitment and rank: see note 171. Cf. also H. Zwicky, *Zur Verwendung des Militärs in der Verwaltung des römischen Kaiserzeit* (Zürich, 1944).

192. S. Lauffer, *Diokletians Preisedikt* (Berlin, 1971); M. Giacchero, *Edictum Diocletiani et collegarum de pretiis rerum venalium* (Genova, 1974).

193. The inscription is J. Keil and A. v. Premerstein, *Bericht über eine dritte Reise in Lydien und den angrenzenden Gebieten Ioniens* (Wien, 1914), No.9.

194. G. Alföldy, *Historia* 15 (1966), 433ff. On the *collegia* in general, see the bibliography in note 152; on their position in the third century, see E. Groag, *Viertel jahresschr.f.Sozial-u.Wirtschaftsgesch*, 2 (1904), 481ff.

195. On the colonate in the third century, see the literature cited in notes 166 and 167; see also N. Brockmeyer, *Arbeitsorganisation und ökonomisches Denken*, 254ff.;

cf.also W. Held, *Klio*, 53 (1971), 239ff.

196. On what follows, see M. Rostovtzeff, *Gesellschaft und Wirtschaft*, II, 163ff.; on the events of AD 238, especially H. G. Mullens, *Greece and Rome*, 17 (1948), 65ff.; P. W. Townsend, *Yale Class. Stud.*, 14 (1955), 49ff.; T. Kotula, *Eos*, 51 (1959/60), 197ff.; X. Loriot, in *ANRW*, II, 2 (Berlin-New York, 1975), 688ff. Fundamental for an assessment of events in Africa is F. Kolb, *Historia*, 24 (1977), 440ff. On Maximinus Thrax and the Senate, see K. Dietz, *Senatus contra principem*. *Untersuchungen zur senatorischen Opposition gegen Kaiser Maximinus Thrax* (München, 1980), on which see G. Alföldy, *Gnomon*, 54 (1982), 478ff. For an estimation of the social conflicts of the third century, see F. Kolb, in *Bonner Festgabe J.Straub* (Bonn, 1977), 277ff. Cf. G. Alföldy, *Heidelberger Jahrb.*, 20 (1976), 111ff. and in H. Schneider (ed.), *Sozial- und Wirtschaftsgeschichte der römischen Kaiserzeit*, 372ff.; cf. also M. Mazza, *Lotte sociale e restaurazione autoritaria nel III secolo d.C.* (Catania, 1973).

197. I. Hahn, in V. Beševliev and W. Seyfarth (eds.), *Die Rolle der plebs im spätrömischen Reich* (Berlin, 1969), 39ff.

198. On this, see C. R. Whittaker, *Historia*, 13 (1964), 348ff.

199. *Fugitivi*: H. Bellen, *Sklavenflucht*, 118ff.; bondage: R. MacMullen, *Enemies of the Roman order*, 255ff.; *Boukoloi*: Dio, 71.4.1f., on which, J. Schwartz, *Anc.Soc.*, 4 (1973), 193ff.; A. Baldini, *Latomus*, 37 (1978), 634ff. *Bellum desertorum*: G. Alföldy, *Bonner Jahrb.*, 171 (1971), 367ff.; A. Baldini, *Corsi di Cultura sull'Arte Ravennate e Biz.*, 24 (1977), 43ff. (with an unwarranted exaggeration of the value of the sources, especially the Rottweiler tablets, which do not contain the text accepted by R. Egger and subsequently Baldini). *Bagaudae*: E. A. Thompson, *Past and Present*, 2 (1952), 11ff. and in M. I. Finley (ed.), *Studies in Ancient Society* (London, 1974), 304ff., in German in H. Schneider (ed.), *Sozial- und Wirtschaftsgeschichte der römischen Kaiserzeit*, 29ff.; B. Cúth, *Die Quellen der Geschichte der Bagauden* (Acta Univ. A. Józzef, Acta Arch. et Ant. 9, Szeged, 1965).

200. On the controversial problem of social mobility in the Later Empire, see the literature cited in note 246; cf. also note 169.

201. Cf. the literature cited in note 104. Obviously the development was a continuous one and the notions of Principate and Dominate cannot be applied to sharply distinguished historical periods: see J. Bleicken, *Prinzipat und Dominat: Gedanken zur Periodisierung der römischen Kaiserzeit* (Frankfurter Historische Vorträge 6, Wiesbaden, 1978).

202. Pagan religion in the Empire and its role in the third century: J. H. W. G. Liebeschuetz, *Continuity and Change in Roman Religion* (Oxford, 1979); R. MacMullen, *Paganism in the Roman Empire* (New Haven-London, 1981). Oriental cults: M. J. Vermaseren, *Die orientalischen Religionen im Römerreich* (Leiden, 1981). Religious policy: cf. J. Vogt, *Zur Religiosität der Christenverfolger im Römischen Reich* (Sitz.-Ber.d.Heidelberger Akad.d.Wiss., Phil.-hist. Kl. Jg.1962, 1. Abh., Heidelberg, 1962). On the social structure of Christianity before Constantine, see now Th.Schleich, *Geschichte in Wiss.u.Unterricht.*, 33 (1982), 269ff., with bibliography; penetration of Christianity into the senatorial order: W. Eck, *Chiron*, 1 (1971), 381ff. On the social history of the earliest phase of Christianity, which cannot be treated in the context of this book, see G. Theissen, *Studien zur Soziologie des Urchristentums*[2] (Tübingen, 1983).

203. *Paneg.*, 5.8.3 and 5.14.4; cf. G. Alföldy, *Greek, Roman and Byzantine Studies*, 15 (1974), 109f.

7: Late Roman Society

204. Social circumstances in the Late Empire: A. H. M. Jones, *The Later Roman Empire 284-602: A Social, Economic and Administrative Survey*, I-III (Oxford, 1964),

is fundamental. Social circumstances in the eastern portion of the empire: F. Tinnefeld, *Die frühbyzantinische Gesellschaft. Struktur – Gegensätze – Spannungen* (München, 1977), Social stratification: A. Chastagnol, in *Colloque d'histoire sociale, Saint-Cloud 1967* (Paris, 1973), 49ff. Useful surveys: S. Dill, *Roman Society in the Last Century of the Western Empire*[2] (London, 1905); J. Gagé, *Les classes sociales*, 335ff.; A. Chastagnol, *Le Bas-Empire* (Paris, 1969), 53ff.; A. Piganiol-A. Chastagnol, *L'Empire chrétien (325-395)*[2](Paris, 1972), 381ff.; now especially A. Chastagnol, *L'evolution politique, sociale et économique du monde romain de Dioclétien à Julien. La Mise en place du régime du Bas-Empire (284-363)*, (Paris, 1982), 265ff. Inadequate and erroneous is W. Held, *Die Vertiefung der allgemeinen Krise im Westen des römischen Reiches. Studien über die sozialökonomischen Verhältnisse am Ende des 3. und in der ersten Hälfte des 4. Jahrhunderts* (Berlin, 1974). Very useful on many particular issues is S. Mazzarino, *Aspetti sociali del quarto secolo. Ricerche di storia tardo-romana* (Roma, 1951); W. Seyfarth, *Soziale Fragen der spätrömischen Kaiserzeit im Spiegel des Theodosianus* (Berlin, 1963). On particular problems in Late Roman social history there is a wealth of material in A. Chastagnol *et al., Transformations et Conflicts au IV*[e] *siècle ap. J.-C.* (Bonn, 1978). On particular areas and provinces, see especially L. Ruggini, *Economia e società nell' 'Italia annonaria'. Rapporti fra agricoltura e commercio del IV al VI secolo d.C..* (Milano, 1961); B. H. Warmington, *The North African Provinces from Diocletian to the Vandal Conquest* (Cambridge, 1954); H. - J. Diesner, *Der Untergang der römischen Herrschaft in Nordafrika* (Wiemar, 1964); J. M. Blázquez, *Estructura económica y social de Hispania durante la Anarquia militar y el Bajo Imperio* (Madrid, 1964); R. Teja, *Organisación económica y social de Capadocia en el siglo IV, segun los padres capadocios* (Salamanca, 1974). An outstanding account of economic and social conditions in one province in the fifth century: Eugippius, *Vita Sancti Severini* (on Noricum), on which, especially R. Noll, *Eugippius. Das Leben des heiligen Severin* (Berlin, 1963).

205. On which, cf. F. Vittinghoff, in *Zur Frage der Periodengrenze zwischen Altertum und Mittelalter* (ed. P. E. Hübinger, Darmstadt, 1969), 298ff.; on the characterisation of the period of transition as one of 'broad strands', see H. Aubin, ibid., 93ff. (especially 97, with reference to id., *Antike und Abendland*, 3 (1948), 88f.); on the estimation of the period of transition from antiquity to the Middle Ages in recent scholarship, see P. E. Hübinger, ibid., 145ff. and especially K. F. Stroheker, ibid., 206ff. On theories of the causes of the decline of the ancient world, see the literature cited in note 179.

206. Economy in the Late Empire: A. H. M. Jones, *The Later Roman Empire*, 411ff. and 712ff.; see also the literature cited above in note 204, on which see especially G. Mickwitz, *Geld und Wirtschaft im römischen Reich des IV. Jahrhunderts n.Chr.* (Helsingfors, 1932); F. W. Walbank, *The Decline of the Roman Empire in the West* (London, 1946); K. Hannestad, *L'evolution des ressources agricoles de l'Italie du 4ème au 6ème siècle de notre ère* (København, 1962); T. Précheur-Canonge, *La vie rurale en Afrique romaine d'après les mosaiques* (Paris, 1962). On the importance of the city, cf., for example, F. Vittinghoff, in *Vor- und Frühformen der europäischen Stadt im Mittelalter* (eds. H. Jankuhn, W. Schlesinger and H. Steuer, Göttingen, 1973) 9?ff. See also id., note 222.

207. On which, especially A. Déléage, *La capitation de Bas-Empire* (Mâcon, 1945); A. H. M. Jones, *Journ.of Rom.Stud.*, 47 (1957), 88ff.; J. Karayanopulos, *Das Finanzwesen des frühbyzantinischen Staates* (München, 1958); E. Faure, *Étude de la capitation de Dioclétien d'après le Panégyrique VIII* (Paris, 1961); I. Hahn, *Acta Ant.Hung.*, 10 (1962), 123ff.; W. Goffart, *Caput and Colonate: Towards a History of Late Roman Taxation* (Toronto-Buffalo, 1974); A. Cerati, *Caractère annonaire et assiette de l'impôt foncier au Bas-Empire* (Paris, 1975). On the importance of the tax burden for the alienation of society from the state, A. H. M. Jones, *Antiquity*, 33 (1959), 39ff. = id., *The Roman Economy*, 82ff., in German in H. Schneider (ed.),

Sozial – und Wirtschaftsgeschichte der römischen Kaiserzeit, 100ff.
208. *Opt.Milev. App.*, 3. The concept of the emperor in Late Antiquity: W. Ensslin, *Gottkaiser und Kaiser von Gottes Gnaden* (Sitz.-Ber.d.Bayer. Akad.d.Wiss. 1943, Heft 6, München, 1943); J. Straub, *Vom Herrscherideal in der Spätantike*[2] (Stuttgart, 1964); A. Alföldi, *Die monarchische Repräsentation im römischen Kaiserreiche* (Darmstadt, 1970); cf. also A. Lippold, *Historia*, 17 (1968), 228ff. and J. Béranger, *Mus.Helv.*, 27 (1970), 242ff. Emperor and society: R. Laqueur, in *Probleme der Spätantike, Vorträge. . . von R. Laqueur, H. Koch, W. Weber* (Stuttgart, 1930), 1ff. On the history of the Late Roman imperial regime, E. Stein, *Histoire du Bas-Empire*, I-II (Paris, 1959), is fundamental.
209. Army: see especially D. van Berchem, *L'armée de Dioclétien et la réforme Constantinienne* (Paris, 1952); R. I. Frank, *Scholae Palatinae* (Amer.Acad.in Rome, 1969); D. Hoffmann, *Das spätrömische Bewegungsheer*, I-II (Epigr.Studien, Bd.7, Düsseldorf, 1969-70. Numbers of soldiers: see especially A. H. M. Jones, *The Later Roman Empire*, 679ff. Machinery of state: see especially J.B. Bury, *History of the Later Roman Empire* (repr. New York, 1958), 1ff.; A. H. M. Jones, op.cit., 321ff. and 336ff.; A. Chastagnol, *La préfecture urbain à Rome sous le Bas-Empire* (Paris, 1960); W. Sinnigen, *The Officium of the Urban Prefecture during the Later Roman Empire* (Amer.Acad. in Rome, 1957); J. - R. Palanque, *Essai sur la préfecture du prétoire du Bas-Empire* (Paris, 1933); E. Stein, *Untersuchungen über das Officium der Prätorianerpräfekten seit Diokletian* (Wien, 1922); A. E. R. Boak, *Univ. of Michigan Studies*, Human. Ser. 14 (1924), 1ff. and M. Clauss, *Der magister officiorum in der Spätantike (4.-6.Jahrhundert). Das Amt und sein Einfluss auf die kaiserliche Politik* (München, 1980) (*magister officii*); J. A. Dunlap, *Univ. of Michigan Studies.*, Human.Ser., 14 (1924), 161ff. (*praepositus sacri cubiculi*); A. Demandt, *R-E Suppl.*, XII (1970), 533ff. (*magister militum*); P. Weiss, *Consistorium und Comites Consistoriani. Untersuchungen zur Hofbeamtenschaft des 4. Jahrhunderts n.Chr. auf prosopographischer Grundlage* (Würzburg, 1975). On the machinery of state in the Late Roman Empire, see also A. Giardino, *Aspetti della burocrazia nel Basso Impero* (Roma, 1977). Development of the law: F. Wieacker, *Recht und Gesellschaft der Spätantike* (Stuttgart, 1964). Characteristic of the structure of government in the Late Roman Empire is the frequent use of eunuchs in the imperial service. The emperors could use them as the top element of official control: influential eunuchs could not be integrated into the rest of the dominant elite and could not generate a nobility of birth: see especially P. Guyot, *Eunuchen als Sklaven und Freigelassene in der griechisch-römischen Antike* (Stuttgart, 1980).
210. On which, see for example, F. Lot, *Les invasions germaniques et la pénétration mutuelle du monde barbare et du monde romain*[2] (Paris, 1945).
211. M. Waas, *Germanen im römischen Dienst (im 4. Jh. n.Chr.)*[2] (Bonn, 1972); cf. K. F. Stroheker, *Germanentum und Spätantike* (Zürich-Stuttgart, 1965), 9ff.
212. S. Dill, op.cit., 245ff., labels it as the 'middle class', while A. Chastagnol, *Le Bas-Empire*, 58, as 'la classe moyenne'.
213. On the senatorial order in the Late Empire, A. Chastagnol, *Rev.Hist.*,244 (1970), 305ff., in German in H. Schneider (ed.), *Sozial - und Wirtschaftsgeschichte der römischen Kaiserzeit*, 293ff., is fundamental; see also A. Piganiol and A. Chastagnol, *L'Empire Chrétien*, 381ff. See now especially J. Matthews, *Western Aristocracies and Imperial Court, AD 364-425* (Oxford, 1975). Cf. also P. Arsac, *Rev.Hist.de Droit Fr.et Etr.*, 47 (1969), 198ff. On the end of the equestrian order, cf. A. Stein, *Der römische Ritterstand*, 455ff. Late Roman military aristocracy: A. Demandt, *Chiron*, 10 (1980), 609ff. is fundamental.
214. Thus, M. T. W. Arnheim, *The Senatorial Aristocracy in the Later Roman Empire* (Oxford, 1972); cf. *contra* W. Eck, *Gnomon*, 46 (1974), 673ff.
215. On which, A. Chastagnol, in *Recherches sur les structures sociales dans l'antiquité classique*, 187ff.

216. Olympiodorus, frg., 43f. (=Migne, *PG* 103.280).
217. Valerii: Gerontius, *Vita Melaniae*, 1ff.; Symmachus: J. A. MacGeachy, *Quintus Aurelius Symmachus and the Senatorial Aristocracy of the West* (Chicago, 1942) and R. Klein, *Symmachus* (Darmstadt, 1971); Property of Ausonius: R. Etienne, *Bordeaux Antique* (Bordeaux, 1962), 351ff. Cf. also especially S. Dill, *Roman Society*, 143ff. and 167ff.
218. Consulate: A. Chastagnol, *Rev.Hist.*, 219 (1958), 221ff. New offices: bibliography in note 209 above.
219. A. Chastagnol, *Le senat romain, sous le règne d'Odoacre. Recherches sur l'épigraphie du Colisée au Vᵉ siècle* (Bonn, 1966).
220. Senate of Constantinople: P. Petit, *L'Ant.Class.*, 26 (1957), 347ff.; A. Chastagnol, *Acta Ant.Hung.*, 24 (1976), 341ff.; F. Tinnefeld, *Die frühbyzantinische Gesellschaft*, 59ff. Spaniards: K. F. Stroheker, *Germanentum und Spätantike*, 54ff.; Gauls: id., *Der senatorische Adel im spätantiken Gallien* (Tübingen, 1948); cf. W. Held, *Klio*, 58 (1976), 121ff.; Africans: M. Overbeck, *Untersuchungen zum afrikanischen Senatsadel in der Spätantike* (Frankfurt, 1973); Senators of the city of Rome: see notes 217 and 219. On social stratification within the senatorial order, cf. T. D. Barnes, *Phoenix*, 28 (1974), 444ff. (nobility in the Late Empire).
221. Conversion: see especially A. Chastagnol, *Rev.d.Études Anc.*, 58 (1956), 241ff.; P. R. L. Brown, *Journ.of Rom.Stud.*, 51 (1961), 1ff. On the Christianisation of the aristocracy of the Empire, see R. v. Haehling, *Die Religionszugehörigkeit der hohen Amtsträger des Römischen Reiches seit Constantins I. Alleinherrscaft bis zum Ende der Theodosianische Dynastie* (Bonn, 1978). Pagan propaganda: see especially A. Alföldi, *Die Kontorniaten. Ein verkanntes Propagandamittel der stadtrömischen Aristokratie in ihrem Kampf gegen das christliche Kaisertum* (Budapest, 1943); see now A. Alföldi and E. Alföldi, *Die Kontorniat-Medaillons. Teil 1 : Katalog* (Berlin, 1976).
222. A comprehensive discussion is A. Piganiol and A. Chastagnol, *L'Empire chrétien*, 392ff.; cf. F. Tinnefeld, *Die frühbyzantinische Gesellschaft*, 100ff. Cf. F. Vittinghoff, in F. Vittinghoff (ed.), *Stadt und Herrschaft*, 107ff., who rightly warns against generalisation on the adverse position of the *curiales* in the Late Empire, but paints a picture that is, on the whole, far too positive. On the *album* of Timgad, see A. Chastagnol, *L'album municipal de Timgad* (Bonn, 1978). On the municipal elite in Africa in Late Antiquity, see T. Kotula, *Les principales d'Afrique. Étude sur l'élite municipale nord-africaine au Bas-Empire romain* (Wroclaw) 1982). Private *munificentia* in the towns of Italy, during the Late Empire: S. Mrozek, *Historia*, 27 (1978), 355ff.
233. Regulations mentioned: *Cod.Theod.*, 12.1.9; 12.1.143; 12.8.1f.; 12.3.1f. Inheritance: Th. Mommsen, *Gesammelte Schriften*, III (Berlin, 1907). 43ff., cf., however, A. H. M. Jones, *Eirene*, 8 (1970), 79ff. = id., *The Roman Economy*, 396ff. Legislation of Diocletian, Constantine and their successors on *curiales*: see C. E. Van Sickle, *Journ.of Rom.Stud.*, 28 (1938), 9ff. (Diocletian); J. Gaudemet, *Iura*, 2 (1951), 44ff. (Constantine); M. Nuyens, *Le statut obligatoire des décurions dans le droit constantinien* (Louvain, 1964); W. Schubart, *Zeitschr.Sav-Stift., Rom.Abt.*, 86 (1969), 287ff. (fourth to sixth centuries); cf. also W. Langhammer, op.cit. (above note 139).
224. Basilius, *Ep.*, 237.2; on which, R. Teja, *Capadocia*, 181f.
225. On which, W. Seyfarth, *Soziale Fragen*, 82f. On the flight of decurions in Cappadocia: Th. A. Kopeček, *Historia*, 23 (1974), 319ff. and R. Teja, op.cit., 181ff. On Antioch: P. Petit, *Libanius et la vie municipale à Antioche au IVᵉ siècle après J.-C.* (Paris, 1955); and especially J. H. W. G. Liebeschuetz, *Antioch: City and Imperial Administration in the Later Roman Empire* (Oxford, 1972); on the flight of the *curiales*, 174ff.
226. Eduard Meyer, *Kleine Schriften*, I (Halle, 1924), 212.

227. Carthage: Augustine *Enarr. in Psalm.* 124.; Cyrene: Synesius *De regno,* 15; Antioch: Libanius, *Or.,* 31.11; Sicily: Gerontius, *Vita Melaniae,* 18; Spain: Oros., *Hist.adv.pag.,* 7.40.6. Urban slavery in the Late Roman Empire: I. Hahn, *Annales Univ.Sc.Budapestinensis, Sectio Hist.,* 3 (1961), 23ff., also in H. Schneider (ed.). *Sozial – und Wirtschaftsgeschichte der römischen Kaiserzeit,* 128ff. (on free and slave labour in the city in Late Antiquity; also fundamental for the craftsmen); on the land, W. L. Westermann, *Slave Systems,* 128ff.
228. Just., *Inst.,* 1.3.7. Slavery and legal theory: W. Seyfarth, *Soziale Fragen,* 127ff. Enslavement of barbarians in AD 406: Oros., *Hist.adv.pag.,* 7.37.16. On the treatment of slavery in political thought in the Late Empire, see I. Hahn, *Klio,* 58 (1976), 459ff.
229. *Cod.Theod.,* 16.9.1; *Cod.Iust.,* 4.42.1; *Cod.Theod.* 12.1.39. Christian slaves: P. Allard, *Les esclaves chrétiens depuis les premiers temps de l'église jusqu'a la fin de la domination remaine en Occident* (Paris, 1914).
230. Colonate: see the literature cited in notes 166 and 195; for the Late Empire also especially M. Pallasse, *Orient et Occident, à propos du colonat romain a Bas-Empire* (Lyon, 1950); A. H. M. Jones, *Past and Present,* 13 (1958), 1ff. = id., *The Roman Economy,* 1ff., in German in H. Schneider (ed.), *Sozial – und Wirtschaftsges-chichte der römischen Kaiserzeit,* 81ff.; id., *The Later Roman Empire,* 795ff.; D. Eibach, *Untersuchungen zum spätantiken Kolonat in der kaiserlichen Gesetzgebung unter Berücksichtigung der Terminologie* (Bonn, 1977).
231. *Iust. . . plebeia: Cod.Theod.,* 9.42.5; cf. also *vulgaris faex* at Amm.Marc., 26.7.7; *servilis faex: Cod.Theod.,* 16.5.21 and 6.27.18.
232. Traders and craftsmen at Antioch: J. H. W. G. Liebeschuetz, *Antioch,* 59ff. Corruption in Late Antiquity: K. L. Noethlichs, *Beamtentum und Dienstvergehen. Zur Staatsverwaltung in der Spätantike* (Wiesbaden, 1981); W. Schuller (ed.), *Korruption im Altertum. Konstanzer Symposium Oktober 1979* (München-Wein, 1982).
233. Antioch: all data in J. H. W. G. Liebeschuetz, op.cit., 52ff.; Constantinople: Migne, *PG,* 47.508f. (John); Themist.,*Or.,*18.223. On this, see I. Hahn, op.cit. (see note 227 above). On the urban plebs in the Late Empire a comprehensive account is W. Seyfarth, *Soziale Fragen* 104ff.; in *Die Rolle der Plebs im spätrömischen Reich* (eds. V. Beševliev and W. Seyfarth, Berlin, 1969) 7ff.; now also A. Kneppe, *Unter-suchungen zur städtischen Plebs des 4. Jahrhunderts n.Chr.* (Bonn, 1979). Traders and craftsmen: see also especially A. H. M. Jones, *The Later Roman Empire,* 824ff.; A. Piganiol and A. Chastagnol, *L'Empire chrétien,* 314ff.; on the specialisation of craftsmanship, H. von Petrikovits, *Zeitschr.f.Pap.und Epigr.,* 43 (1981), 285ff. On particular strata and groups, cf. A. F. Norman, *Journ.of Rom.Stud.,* 48 (1958), 79ff.
234. On this, A. Persson, *Staat und Manufaktur im römischen Reiche* (Lund, 1923); On the social status of workers in the *fabricae,* N. Charbonnel, in *Aspects de l'Empire romain* (eds. F. Burdeau, N. Charbonnel and M. Humbert, Paris, 1964), 61ff.
235. Traders at Milan: L. Ruggini, *Economia e società dell' 'Italia annonaria',* 84ff. *Pistores, navicularii:* A. Piganiol and A. Chastagnol, *L'Empire chrétien,* 315f., 319f. Laws on *navicularii* mentioned: *Cod. Theod.,* 13.5.19 and 13.5.12, on *pistores:* ibid., 14.3.2. and 14.3.14. Imposed corporations: bibliography in note 152.
236. Traders: Libanius, *Or.,* 26.23 and 46.23; craftsmen: ibid., 20.36f.; 29.27; 33.32. On this, I. Hahn, op.cit. (see note 227), 25f.;J. H. W. G. Liebeschuetz, *Antioch,* 52ff.
237. Beggars: Palladius Monachus, *Hist. Lausiaca,* 68; poverty at Hippo: Augus-tine, *De civ.Dei,* 22.8; poverty in Late Roman society in general: E. Patlagean, *Pauv-reté économique et pauvreté sociale à Byzance, 4ᵉ-7ᵉ siècles* (Mouton-Paris-La Haye, 1977). Plebs at Rome: Amm.Marc., 14.6.25f.; cf.14.6.2.
238. Crafts on the estates: Palladius, *Agr.,* 1.6 and 7.8. Miners in the Late Empire: S. Mrozek, in *Die Rolle der Plebs im spätrömischen Reich,* 61ff.

239. *Cod.Iust.*, 11. 53.1ff. and 11.51.1. On the various categories of the rural population, A. H. M. Jones, *The Later Roman Empire*, 773ff.; A. Piganiol and A. Chastagnol, *L'Empire chrétien*, 303ff.; cf. F. Tinnefeld, *Die frühbyzantinische Gesellschaft*, 33ff.; on wage labour, especially W. Seyfarth, *Soziale Fragen*, 95ff. For Syria, all data in J. H. W. G. Liebeschuetz, *Antioch*, 61ff. For Cappadocia, cf. R. Teja, *Capadocia*, 67f., who, however, supposes extensive agrarian slavery, as in the Early Empire.

240. *De mort.pers.*, 7.3. On the flight of the rural population, cf., for example, A. E. R. Boak and H. C. Youtie, in *Studi in onore di A. Calderini* (Milano, 1957), 325ff. (Egypt); H. Bellen, *Sklavenflucht*, 122ff.

241. Augustine, *Ep.*, 185.7.30; *Coloni* (*rusticana ... audacia contra possessores suos*) and *fugitivi servi:* ibid., 108.6.18. On the Agonistic movement, see especially W. H. C. Frend, *The Donatist Church: A Movement of Protest in Roman North Africa*[2] (Oxford, 1971); H.-J. Diesner, in *Aus der byzantinischen Arbeit der DDR* I (Berlin, 1957), 106ff.; id., *Der Untergang der römischen Herrschaft in Nordafrika*, 99ff.; Th. Büttnerand E. Werner, *Circumcellionen und Adamiten* (Berlin, 1959); B. Baldwin, *Nottingham Mediaeval Studies*, 6 (1962), 3ff.; E. Tengström, *Donatisten und Katholiken. Soziale, wirtschaftliche und politische Aspekte einer nordafrikanischen Kirchenspaltung* (Göteborg, 1964); R. MacMullen, *Enemies of the Roman Order*, 200ff. *Bagaudae*: bibliography in note 199.

242. Rome: H. P. Kohns, *Versorgungskrisen und Hungerrevolten im spätantiken Rom* (Bonn, 1961). Thessalonica: sources in A. Piganiol and A. Chastagnol, *L'Empire chrétien*, 283f. Caesarea: Migne, *PG*, 36.569, on which R. Teja, *Capadocia*, 201f. Antioch: R. Browning, *Journ of Rom Stud.* 42 (1952), 13ff.; G. Downey, *A History of Antioch in Syria* (Princeton, 1961), 428ff.; J. H. W. G. Liebeschuetz, *Antioch*, 104f., 164; on the uprisings of the Late Roman *plebs urbana* in general, A. Kneppe, *Untersuchungen zur städtischen Plebs des e. Jahrhunderts n.Chr.*, 20ff.

243. Cf. especially F. Vittinghoff, in *Zur Frage der Periodengrenze zwischen Altertum und Mittelalter*, 298ff., further, ibid., 358ff. (=*Hist.Zeitschr.*, 192 (1961), 265ff.), with criticism of Marxist theories of revolution. On the Marxist view of events in the Late Empire, see now R. Günther, *Klio*, 60 (1978), 235ff. (assuming a 'political revolution in the period of transition to feudalism' in tandem with 'social revolution' in the transition from antiquity to the Middle Ages). The flight of slaves and *coloni*: see note 240.

244. G. Alföldy, *Noricum*, 214. Nazianzus: Greg. Naz. *Ep.*, 141, on which R. Teja, *Capadocia*, 202f.

245. Paulinus of Pella, *Euchar.*, 328ff. (= *CSEL*, 16.304).

246. Cf. on this R. MacMullen, *Journ. of Rom.Stud.*, 54 (1964), 49ff., in German H. Schneider (ed.), *Sozial- und Wirtschaftsgeschichte der römischen Kaiserzeit*, 155ff.; and especially A. H. M. Jones, *Eirene*, 8 (1970), 79ff. =id., *The Roman Economy*, 396ff., with a high estimation of the possibilities for social advancement in the Late Roman Empire, *contra* earlier scholars, like P. Charanis, *Byzantion*, 17 (1944/5), 39ff. (but Jones's thesis that Late Roman society allowed more mobility than that of the Early Empire cannot be followed). Social mobility in Egypt in the Late Empire: J. G. Keenan, *Zeitschr. f. Pap.und Epigr.*,17 (1975), 237ff. On the purpose of imperial legislation in fixing privileges and the membership of orders on the example of Constantine's legislation, see D. Liebs, *Rev. Internat.des Droits de l'Ant.*, 24 (1977), 297ff.

247. Migne, *PG*, 35.264, on which R. Teja, *Capadocia*, 77. On the upper groups of the Church, cf. W. Eck, *Chiron*, 8 (1978), 561ff.

248. Synesius, *Ep.*, 130. Spain: see K. F. Stroheker, *Arch.Esp.Arq.*, 45/47 (1972/74), 595.

249. Egypt: *Cod.Theod.*, 11.24.1, on which, for example, G. Diósdi, *Journ. of Jurist. Papyrol.*, 14 (1962), 57ff. Syria: Libanius, *Or.*, 47.1ff.; on this, L. Harmand,

Libanius: Discours sur les patronages (Paris, 1955). Illyricum: Amm. Marc., 19.11.3. Comprehensively, especially I. Hahn, *Klio*, 50 (1968), 261ff. see also in H. Schneider (ed.), *Sozial- und Wirschaftsgeschichte der römischen Kaiserzeit*, 234ff. On similar relationships between urban communities and powerful persons, L. Harmand, *Un aspect social et politique du monde romain. Le patronat sur les collectivités publiques des origines au Bas-Empire* (Paris, 1957).

250. Ammianus: 14.6.2ff.; Salvian: *De gub.Dei*, 7.6 and 5.21; Orosius: *Hist.adv.pag.*, 7.41.7. On Salvian's critique of society, see J. Badewien, *Geschichtstheologie und Sozialkritik im Werk Salvians von Marseille* (Göttingen, 1980).

251. Claudian *In Ruf.*, 2.38ff., on the problem, especially A. E. R. Boak, *Manpower Shortage and the Fall of the Roman Empire* (Ann Arbor, 1955); further bibliography in note 178 above.

INDEX

NB: Commonly used names are entered in their familiar forms – Crassus, Pompey, etc.